"WE WILL A   to
freedom of speech   on
to worship God in ᴴis own way, _____ ᴬnd
freedom from terror."-FDR, May 27, 1941, Radio Address

"WE GUARD AGAINST the forces of anti-Christian aggression, which may attack us from without, and the forces of ignorance and fear which may corrupt us from within."-FDR, Oct. 28, 1940, Madison Square Garden, NY

"THE WHOLE WORLD is divided between...pagan brutality and the Christian ideal. We choose human freedom-which is the Christian ideal."-FDR, May 27, 1941, Address Announcing an Unlimited National Emergency

"THERE HAS BEEN definite progress towards a spiritual reawakening...I receive evidences of this from all our Protestant Churches; I get it from Catholic priests and from Jewish rabbis as well."-FDR, Jan. 31, 1938, Ministerial Union

"CHURCHES AND GOVERNMENT...can work hand in hand...Government can ask the churches to stress...social justice, while at the same time government guarantees to the churches-Gentile and Jewish-the right to worship God in their own way...State and Church are rightly united in a common aim."-FDR, Dec. 6, 1933, Fed.Council of Churches

"THE WORLD IS too small...for both Hitler and God...Nazis have now announced their plan for enforcing their...pagan religion all over the world...by which the Holy Bible and the Cross of Mercy would be displaced by Mein Kampf and the swastika."-FDR, Jan. 6, 1942, State of Union

"THOSE FORCES HATE democracy and Christianity... They oppose democracy because it is Christian. They oppose Christianity because it preaches democracy."-FDR, Nov. 1, 1940, Brooklyn, NY

"I SAW Sevastopol and Yalta! And I know that there is not room enough on earth for both German militarism and Christian decency."-FDR, March 1, 1945,on Yalta Conferece

"WE AS A Nation and as individuals will please God best by showing regard for the laws of God. There is no better way of fostering good will toward man than by first fostering good will toward God. If we love Him we will keep His Commandments."-FDR, Dec. 24, 1942, Christmas

"I HOPE you have re-read the Constitution...Like the Bible, it ought to be read again and again."-FDR, Mar. 9, 1937

"THIS GREAT WAR effort...shall not be imperiled by the handful of noisy traitors-betrayers of America, betrayers of Christianity itself."-FDR,April 28, 1942, Fireside Chat

"I KNEW THAT some day Russia would return to religion for the simple reason that four or five thousand years of recorded history have proven that mankind has always believed in God in spite of the many abortive attempts to exile God."-FDR, Feb. 10, 1940, American Youth Congress

"YOUR GOVERNMENT IS working...with representatives of Catholic, Protestant, and Jewish faiths. Without these three, all three of them...things would not be as..easy."-FDR, Oct. 28, 1940, Madison Square Garden

The
Faith
of
FDR

-From President
Franklin Delano Roosevelt's
Public Papers 1933-1945

William J. Federer

The Faith of FDR
-From President Franklin Delano Roosevelt's Public Papers 1933-1945
by **William J. Federer**

For permission to duplicate over 5,000 words, please contact:
William J. Federer
P.O. Box 4363, St. Louis, MO 63123
314-487-4395 tel., 314-487-4489 fax
wjfederer@aol.com

Library of Congress

HISTORY / BIOGRAPHY

ISBN 0-9778085-0-5
ISBN 13 978-0-9778085-0-2
paperback $29.99

CREDITS
Cover portrait c. 1933. Silver print. 13 x 8.5 in. by artist, Harris & Ewing.
James T. Patterson, Brown University, Author of Congressional Conservatism and
the New Deal, http://www.grolier.com/wwii/wwii_roosevelt.html
http://www.fdrlibrary.marist.edu/
http://www.moreorless.au.com/heroes/roosevelt.html
http://en.wikipedia.org/wiki/Franklin_Delano_Roosevelt
http://inaugural.senate.gov/history/daysevents/morningworshipservice.htm

Amerisearch, Inc., P.O. Box 20163, St. Louis, MO 63123,
1-888-USA-WORD, 314-487-4395 voice/fax
www.amerisearch.net

Dedicated

to

My Mother's only brother,

Billy Epperson

who served on a B-17

and was shot down over the English Channel

July 9, 1944

and never found

AND

My Father's only brother,

William Joseph Federer

Who fought in Okinawa

1945

"I DOUBT IF there is any problem in the world...that would not find happy solution if approached in the spirit of the Sermon on the Mount...in conformity with the teaching of Him Who is the Way, the Light and the Truth."-FDR, Oct. 1, 1938, New Orleans.Eucharistic Congress

"THE AMERICAN PEOPLE...have watched with sympathetic interest the effort of the Jews to renew in Palestine the ties of their ancient homeland and to reestablish Jewish culture in the place where for centuries it flourished...It gives me great pleasure to send my warmest personal greetings"- FDR, Feb. 6, 1937, United Palestine Appeal, Stephen Wise

"WE WILL CELEBRATE this Christmas Day in our traditional American way...because the teachings of Christ are fundamental in our lives; and because we want our youngest generation...knowing...the story of the coming of the immortal Prince of Peace."-FDR, Dec. 24, 1944

"AN ORDERING OF society which relegates religion…to the background can find no place within it for the ideals of the Prince of Peace. The United States rejects such an ordering, and retains its ancient faith."–FDR, Jan. 4, 1939

"PRESERVATION OF THESE rights is vitally important now, not only to us who enjoy them-but to the whole future of Christian civilization."-FDR, Sept.1,1941, Labor Day

"I CAN'T TALK about my opponent the way I would like to, because I try to think that I am a Christian. I try to think that some day I will go to Heaven, and I don't believe there is anything to be gained in saying dreadful things about other people."-FDR, Nov. 4, 1944, Bridgeport, CT

CONTENTS

WILLIAM J. FEDERER

THE FAITH OF FDR

INTRODUCTION

FRANKLIN D. ROOSEVELT served as President of the United States for over twelve years, longer than any other President. He won four Presidential Elections, 1932, 1936, 1940 and 1944. He was America's leader during the Great Depression and World War II.

Regardless if one agrees with his political views, the fact remains he exerted a significant influence on United States history. It is inevitable, therefore, that a serious student of history would want to examine the faith of Franklin D. Roosevelt.

In addition, since political rhetoric is usually the lowest common denominator, appealing to the largest number of voters, FDR's statements reflect a public that had generally accepted views on faith.

The statements in this book are exclusively from nearly 4,000 pages of President Franklin Delano Roosevelt's Public Papers 1933-1945, printed by the U.S. Government Printing Office, with the exception of the foreword President Roosevelt wrote for a 1941 edition New Testament distributed by The Gideons to millions of military personnel, of which this author owns an original.

BIOGRAPHY

FRANKLIN DELANO ROOSEVELT descended from Claes Martenssen Van Roosevelt, who emigrated from Holland to New Amsterdam in the 1640's. Franklin's great-great-grandfather, Isaac Roosevelt, was a member of the New York State Convention that ratified the United States Constitution.

Franklin's father, James Roosevelt, was a Harvard Law School graduate with substantial holdings in coal and transportation. In 1880, James married his sixth cousin, Sara Delano, whose father had made and lost fortunes in China trade. An aristocratic Hudson River family, James and Sara's son, Franklin Delano Roosevelt, was born January 30, 1882, in Hyde Park, New York.

Franklin was homeschooled till age fourteen, when he was enrolled in Groton, the elite Episcopal boarding school near Boston, graduating in 1900, the year his father died. He attended Harvard and earned a B.A. in history in only three years. During his fourth year he was editor of the college newspaper Crimson. After graduation in 1904, he studied law at Columbia University, New York, though not taking a degree.

Franklin married Anna Eleanor Roosevelt, his fifth cousin once removed, on St. Patrick's Day, March 17, 1905. Eleanor, who had both parents die by the time she was ten, was given away at the wedding by her uncle, President Theodore Roosevelt. Together they had six children: Anna (1906), James (1907), Franklin, Jr. (1909 - died the same year) Elliott (1910), Franklin, Jr. (1914) and John (1916). Eleanor was to be a profound influence on her husband's views for social reform.

Franklin Roosevelt passed the bar exam in 1907, and practiced law with the Wall Street law firm of Carter, Ledyard, and Milburn. In 1910, he was elected to the New York State Senate from Duchess County. He was reelected in 1912, though contracting typhoid fever during the campaign.

As a reward for supporting Woodrow Wilson for President at the Democrat National Convention, Wilson appointed him Assistant Secretary of the Navy in 1913, the same position Theodore Roosevelt held 15 years earlier. Franklin held that position until 1920.

In 1914, he ran for U. S. Senator, but lost in the primary. He founded the United States Navy Reserve and when Wilson sent the Navy and Marines to intervene in Central American and Caribbean countries in 1915, Roosevelt personally wrote the constitution which the U.S. imposed on Haiti.

As Assistant Secretary of the Navy, Franklin was an energetic and efficient administrator, concentrating on the business side of naval administration. In 1918, during World War I, he visited the American troops and naval facilities in Britain and on the front in Europe. During this visit he met Winston Churchill for the first time.

Upon his return to the United States, his wife Eleanor made the heartbreaking discovery of an affair he had with her social secretary, Lucy Mercer. Though Franklin immediately cut off the affair, it took a toll on their marriage.

Roosevelt's able handling of War Department employees, admirals, labor unions in naval yards, and his opposition to price-fixing by defense contractors, gave him administrative experience and many contacts in Washington.

In 1920, he was nominated for vice-president on the Democrat Party ticket headed by Ohio Governor James M. Cox. The public's rejection of Woodrow Wilson's League of Nations, however, resulted in Republican Warren G. Harding being elected as the 29th U.S. President.

Franklin formed a law firm in New York City and became vice president of Fidelity and Deposit Company of Maryland.

In the summer of 1921, while vacationing at Campobello Island, New Brunswick, Franklin contracted poliomyelitis (infantile paralysis) and was almost completely paralyzed.

Though he partially recovered, he never regained the use of his legs, requiring him to used a wheelchair, crutches and leg braces. During this time, Eleanor became his public voice. He eventually established a foundation at Warm Springs, Georgia, to help polio victims and directed the March of Dimes program which eventually funded a polio vaccine.

With the help of his wife, Eleanor, and political confidant, Louis Howe, Roosevelt resumed his political career. In 1924, he gave a speech at the Democratic National Convention nominating New York Governor Alfred E. Smith for President, but Smith lost the nomination to John W. Davis.

In 1928, Franklin Roosevelt again support Alfred E. Smith as the Democrat President candidate, who reciprocated by arranging for Roosevelt to succeed him as

Governor of New York. Smith lost to Herbert Hoover, but Roosevelt was elected Governor, and reelected in 1930.

When the Stock Market crashed, just eight months after Hoover took office, Roosevelt began campaigning for the Presidency, calling for Government intervention in the economy. In November of 1932, he was elected the 32nd President.

On March 4, 1933, at 10:15 a.m., prior to his swearing-in ceremony, President-elect Franklin D. Roosevelt and his wife Eleanor attended a church service at St. John's Episcopal Church, next to the White House.

Fifty-one years old at the time of his Inauguration, Roosevelt faced factory closings, farm foreclosures, bank failures and 13 million unemployed, nearly 30 percent of the nation's workforce.

Exercising broad executive power, Roosevelt closed all banks, declaring a "bank holiday" and called Congress into special session. He secured passage of an emergency banking bill, which, instead of nationalizing banks offered aid to private bankers.

He forced through an Economy Act that cut $400 million from government payments to veterans and $100 million from the salaries of federal employees. This deflationary measure hurt purchasing power.

He legalized beer of 3.2% alcoholic content by weight, and in December 1933 ended prohibition of alcohol with the ratification of the 21st Amendment to the U. S. Constitution.

Roosevelt used his radio speeches, known as Fireside Chats, to present his proposals to the public.

In his first two terms, he passed alphabet agency legislation, such as: AAA (Agricultural Adjustment Administration) to support farm prices; CCC (Civilian Conservation Corps) which employed 2.5 million men;

NIRA (National Industrial Recovery Act); CWA (Civil Works Administration) funding work relief; PWA (Public Works Administration) funding construction of large-scale projects; TVA (Tennessee Valley Administration) which built multipurpose dams to control floods and generate cheap hydroelectric power; WPA (Works Projects Administration) which provided jobs not only for laborers but also artists, writers, musicians, and authors; FERA (Federal Emergency Relief Administration) providing federal relief grants; HOLC (Home Owners Loan Corporation) providing assistance to mortgagors and homeowners; USHA (United States Housing Authority); FDIC (Federal Deposit Insurance Corporation) insuring bank deposits; SEC (Securities and Exchange Commission) regulating stock exchanges; NRA (National Recovery Administration) and NLRB (National Labor Relations Board) establishing management and labor codes in each industry, collective bargaining, minimum wages, maximum hours, outlining pricing and production policies; and the Social Security Act which provided unemployment compensation and old-age/survivors' benefits.

Though debate exists whether these programs shortened or prolonged recovery, the economy eventually grew and banks reopened. New Deal measures greatly increased federal spending and created unbalanced budgets.

Complaints were made that bureaucracies were slow and inconsistent, favoring some at the expense of others, and that enforcement was evaded. Roosevelt took the country off the gold standard, instituted higher taxes, increased government regulation of the economy and created a partial welfare state.

Roosevelt defeated Kansas Governor Alfred M. Landon in 1936 to serve a second Presidential term.

Before his Inauguration, Wednesday, January 20, 1937, Franklin and Eleanor Roosevelt attended a 10:00 a.m service at St. John's Episcopal Church.

The Supreme Court declared various items of Roosevelt's legislation unconstitutional, so in 1937 he proposed "packing" the Court by adding additional Justices. This proposal was defeated as it would undermine the separation of powers.

After deaths and retirements of several Justices from 1937 to 1943, Roosevelt was able to appoint nine new Justices to the Supreme Court, including Justices Felix Frankfurter, Hugo Black and William O. Douglas, resulting in decisions favoring his legislation.

His presidential career hit a low point when there was an addition recession in 1938, and many of the Congressional candidates he campaigned against won reelection.

In 1939, with the outbreak of war in Europe, Roosevelt concentrated on foreign affairs. New Deal reform legislation diminished and the Depression began to lift as the nation began mobilizing for war.

Though originally neutral, Hitler's attack on Poland in September 1939 made Roosevelt wary of Nazi aggression. He instituted a "good neighbor" policy to unite Latin American nations in mutual action against aggressors, and began building up the U.S. armed forces in the face of isolationist opposition.

When France fell in May 1940, American support for Roosevelt's policy increased. He made American non-military aid available to Britain, France, and China. Congress enacted the military draft and Roosevelt signed a "Lend-Lease" bill to supply aid to nations at war with Germany and Italy. Though still officially neutral, America was becoming the "arsenal of democracy."

On July 17, 1940, Eleanor Roosevelt made an impromptu speech at the Democrat National Convention which helped Franklin Roosevelt win his third Democrat Presidential nomination. In November 1940, by a narrower margin, he defeated Wendell Willkie to win an unprecedented third Presidential term.

He is the only President in United States history to serve more than two terms. In 1951, the 22nd Amendment was ratified limiting future Presidents to two terms.

Before his Inauguration, Monday, January 20, 1941, Franklin and Eleanor Roosevelt attended a 10:30 a.m. service at St. John's Episcopal Church.

On December 7, 1941, the Japanese executed a well-planned attack on Pearl Harbor, followed four days later by Germany's and Italy's declarations of war against the United States. This brought the nation into the war. Critics blamed Roosevelt's administration for leaving Pearl Harbor unprepared, thereby inviting a Japanese attack as a pretext for entering the war.

All four of Franklin Roosevelt's sons were officers in World War II and were decorated, on merit, for bravery.

As Commander-in-Chief of the Armed Forces, Roosevelt worked through his military advisers, Army Chief of Staff General George Marshall and later Supreme Commander in Europe General Dwight Eisenhower. In the Pacific there was General Douglas MacArthur and Admiral Chester Nimitz.

Roosevelt moved to unite "Allied" countries against the Axis powers through "The Declaration of the United Nations," January 1, 1942, in which all nations fighting the Axis agreed not to make a separate peace and pledged to form a peacekeeping organization upon victory.

He gave priority to the western European front, with a holding operation in the Pacific. The United States and its allies invaded North Africa in November 1942 and Sicily and Italy in 1943. The D-Day landings on the Normandy beaches in France, June 6, 1944, were followed by the allied invasion of Germany six months later.

Following the outbreak of the Pacific War, pressure came from the Democrat Governor of California, Culbert Olson, to intern the estimated 120,000 people of Japanese descent living there on the grounds they were a threat to security. FBI Director J. Edgar Hoover opposed this saying there was no evidence against Japanese-Americans, but Secretary of War Henry Stimson prevailed with the evacuation.

Anxious to secure Russian assistance against Japan, Roosevelt acquiesced at the 1943 Teheran Summit Conference and later at the 1945 Yalta Summit Conference to some of Russia's aims in Asia and eastern Europe.

The strain of war took its toll on Roosevelt's health and a 1944 medical examination revealed serious heart and circulatory problems.

In November 1944, Roosevelt defeated Thomas E. Dewey by a narrow popular vote to win a fourth Presidential term.

On the morning of his Inauguration, Saturday, January 20, 1945, Franklin and Eleanor Roosevelt had a private worship service held in the East Room of the White House.

During a vacation at Warm Springs, Georgia, on April 12, 1945, he suffered a stroke and died two and a half hours later without regaining consciousness. He was 63 years old. Less than a month later, May 7, 1945, the Nazi's surrendered, followed by Japan's surrender August 14, 1945.

President Roosevelt was buried in the Rose Garden of his estate at Hyde Park, New York.

THE GREAT TEACHER said: "I come that ye may have life and that ye may have it more abundantly"...To build character is our great task. Without it the abundant life cannot be realized."-FDR, Feb. 13, 1934

"I AM HAPPY, at this festival season of Rosh Hashanah, to renew my good wishes to my fellow citizens of Jewish faith."-FDR, Aug. 13, 1934

"IN FAMILY LIFE the child should first learn confidence in his own powers, respect for the feelings and the rights of others, the feeling of security and mutual good will and faith in God."-FDR, Jan. 19, 1940

"WITH CONFIDENCE IN our armed forces-with the unbounding determination of our people-we will gain the inevitable triumph-so help us God."-FDR, Dec. 8, 1941

"CHRISTMAS DAY OUR factories will be stilled. That is not true of other holidays...All other holidays work goes on–gladly-for winning the war. So Christmas becomes the only holiday in all the year."-FDR, Dec. 24, 1942

"ONE OF THE blackest crimes of all history...the Nazis...wholesale systematic murder of the Jews of Europe goes on unabated... thousands of Jews...are threatened with annihilation as Hitler's forces descend."-FDR, Mar. 24, 1944

"THIS NATION IS appalled by the systematic persecution of helpless minority groups by the Nazis...Their insane desire to wipe out the Jewish race in Europe continues undiminished...Christian groups also are being murdered...Nazis are determined to complete their program of mass extermination."-FDR, June 12, 1944

"WE SHALL CARRY the attack against the enemy...We must keep him far from our shores...We intend to bring this battle to him on his own home grounds."-FDR, Oct. 27, 1944

FIRST TERM
MARCH 4, 1933 - JANUARY 19, 1937

INAUGURAL ADDRESS
MARCH 4, 1933

THIS GREAT NATION will endure as it has endured, will revive and will prosper. So, first of all, let me assert my firm belief that the only thing we have to fear is fear itself - nameless, unreasoning, unjustified terror which paralyzes needed efforts to convert retreat into advance...

In such a spirit on my part and on yours we face our common difficulties. They concern, thank God, only material things...

We are stricken by no plague of locusts. Compared with the perils which our forefathers conquered because they believed and were not afraid, we have still much to be thankful for...

Unscrupulous money changers stand indicted in the court of public opinion, rejected by the hearts and minds of men...They have no vision, and when there is no vision the people perish.

The money changers have fled from their high seats in the temple of our civilization. We may now restore that temple to the ancient truths. The measure of the restoration lies in the extent to which we apply social values more noble than mere monetary profit.

Happiness lies not in the mere possession of money; it lies in the joy of achievement, in the thrill of creative effort. The joy and moral stimulation of work no longer must be forgotten in the mad chase of evanescent profits.

These dark days will be worth all they cost us if they teach us that our true destiny is not to be ministered unto but to minister to ourselves and to our fellow men...

In this dedication of a Nation we humbly ask the blessing of God. May He protect each and every one of us. May He guide me in the days to come.

MESSAGE TO CONGRESS ON UNEMPLOYMENT RELIEF
MARCH 21, 1933

MORE IMPORTANT, HOWEVER, than the material gains will be the moral and spiritual value of such work. The overwhelming majority of unemployed Americans, who are now walking the streets and receiving private or public relief, would infinitely prefer to work. We can take a vast army of these unemployed out into healthful surroundings. We can eliminate to some extent at least the threat that enforced idleness brings to spiritual and moral stability.

PRESS CONFERENCE
MARCH 29, 1933

THE THIRD PHASE relates to the fiduciary position of directors and officers of corporations and their subsidiaries. That would be just to restore the old - I was going to say the old Biblical rule, but I don't think they had corporations in those days.

ADDRESS ON THE CELEBRATION OF PAN-AMERICAN DAY, WASHINGTON APRIL 12, 1933

THE CELEBRATION OF "Pan-American Day" in this building, dedicated to international good-will and cooperation, exemplifies a unity of thought and purpose among the peoples of this hemisphere. It is a manifestation of the common ideal of mutual helpfulness, sympathetic understanding and spiritual solidarity...

Never before has the significance of the words "good neighbor" been so manifest in international relations...

I look upon the Union as the outward expression of the spiritual unity of the Americas.

FIRESIDE CHAT MAY 7, 1933

IT INVOLVED NOT only a further loss of homes, farms, savings and wages, but also a loss of spiritual values - the loss of that sense of security for the present and the future so necessary to the peace and contentment of the individual and of his family.

REMARKS TO RELIEF ADMINISTRATORS JUNE 14, 1933

I KNOW THAT I can count on your full and complete cooperation with the Federal Emergency Relief Administrator and I can assure you on his behalf of a sympathetic understanding of your problems and of decisive action when that is necessary. And so all I can tell you now is, "Go to it, and God bless you."

GREETING TO THE
CIVILIAN CONSERVATION CORPS
JULY 8, 1933

IT IS MY belief that what is being accomplished will conserve our natural resources, create future national wealth and prove of moral and spiritual value not only to those of you who are taking part, but to the rest of the country as well.

STATEMENT ON THE
GOOD NEIGHBOR POLICY IN CUBA
AUGUST 13, 1933

THE AMERICAN PEOPLE deeply sympathize with the people of Cuba in their economic distress, and are praying that quiet and strict order may soon prevail in every part of Cuba.

ADDRESS AT THE 1933 CONFERENCE ON
MOBILIZATION FOR HUMAN NEEDS
SEPTEMBER 8, 1933

WHEN WE CAME to the problem of meeting the emergency of human needs, we did not rush blindly in and say, "The Government will take care of it." We approached it from the other angle first.

We said to the people of this country, "When you come to the problem of relief, you face the individual family, the individual man, woman and child who lives in a particular locality and the first objective and the first necessity are that the citizens of that community, through the churches, the community chest, the social and charitable organizations of the community, are going to be expected to do their share to their utmost extent first."

ADDRESS AT HYDE PARK
METHODIST EPISCOPAL CHURCH
SEPTEMBER 29, 1933

IT IS TRUE that I am here tonight as your friend and neighbor, but I have never thought of myself as a preacher. Perhaps the real cause of my presence is that once upon a time I was designated as the Official Historian of the Town of Hyde Park and, as such, know probably almost as much about the history of the Methodist Episcopal Church as the congregation itself does.

A few years ago I had the privilege of working with your pastor in compiling the records of this church and of the other churches in our Township. That kind of compilation was made necessary for the reason that in the old days, when our churches were founded, the only statistics relating to births and marriages and deaths were to be found in the registers of the several churches.

Unfortunately, of course, although our own Township dates back for nearly two hundred and fifty years, the religious life of this particular community did not begin in an organized way until after the Revolution. Before that time there wasn't any Hyde Park.

There was a district of the County of Dutchess that was known as the Krum Elbow Precinct and across Krum Elbow Creek there was a country place that belonged to Dr. John Bard that was known as Hyde Park. But this community, until after the Revolution, went by various names, among others as De Cantillon's Landing and Stoutensburg's Store, and various other appellations.

In the pre-Revolutionary days, as far as the record shows, there was no religious life in this community, although it had been settled far back in the year 1698; that is to say, there was no religious life except for an occasional wandering Quaker preacher who came hither from

Millbrook or Pine Plains and held a meeting perhaps once every three months or so over on what you and I know today as Quaker Lane.

It was not until 1789 that the people in this community who belonged to various churches got together and decided that they ought to have a Meeting House; and thus in 1789 there was organized the Stoutensburg Religious Society, an association of men and women who wanted a place in which to worship.

As a result, there was put up the first church and what afterwards became Hyde Park Building. I suppose it was a very tiny structure because it seated only forty-eight persons; but the interesting thing about that church in 1789 was that at the meeting of the people who organized it, a resolution was passed which said that the church shall be open to every good and well-recommended preacher and to every Christian society.

In other words, it was a church for all of the divisions of the Protestant faith. There were not many Baptists here in those days, they tell us, but there were Methodists, there were Dutch Reform followers, there were Presbyterians and Protestant Episcopalians and, for a number of years, in fact for a whole generation, this entire community worshipped in this house of the Religious Society.

A generation later, in 1811, the Protestant Episcopal Church was organized; and then there came the Methodist Episcopal Church for which, as I remember the date, the first meeting was held in 1832.

As a result of that first meeting Mr. Albertson, for whom Albertson Street has been named - that was somewhat before I was born - gave the lot of land on which the first church building was erected in 1833. But even then they did not have the funds or the congregation was insufficient to have one preacher, as they called them in those days, and so they got what we call today a lay leader, whose name was Slack, Alonzo S. Slack.

Before he became a pastor he came to the original church and conducted services every other Sunday. A little later on, when he had become a member of the Ministry, Mr. Slack came here as the first pastor of the church and he has been succeeded, as you and I know, by a long line of noble and unselfish men down to the present day.

My own association with this church goes back to a very, very early period, in the early eighties.

I remember one day, on my way home, I passed a little house that was occupied by that splendid old couple, Mr. and Mrs. John Clay, and Mrs. John Clay invited me in to give me a piece of gingerbread; and that was when I discovered that there was another church in the village besides my own. So Mrs. Clay was responsible for my first association with Methodism, and it was done with a piece of gingerbread.

Through all these years I have seen this church grow in health and strength because, after all, back there in the eighties it was not nearly so important a factor in the life of the community as it is today.

I like to think also of the advent of other Churches in this Village from time to time - the Dutch Reform Church growing out of that original old Religious Society that was organized in 1789; this church; the Protestant Episcopal Church; the Baptist Church; and the Catholic Church. I like also to go back to the origins of religion in this community.

Religion in those days, a hundred and fifty years ago, was a community affair; I am inclined to think that during the intervening time religion, to a large extent, ceased to be a community affair. When I was a boy, let us be quite frank, there was not the same association, the same teamwork, the same cooperation between churches in this community or of any other community that you and I find today.

It is not only the spirit of these times, but it seems to me that it is fundamentally a matter of common sense, that in our religious worship we should work together instead of flying off on different tangents and different angles, pulling apart instead of pulling together as a unified whole.

During these latter years there has been a splendid change for the better in this regard. We find today the ministers of the different churches sitting amicably side by side on the same platform. More than that, we find them meeting with each other from time to time to try to help solve the community problems together...

Therefore, when we come, for example, to the question of relief, before extending Federal assistance to States or to communities, we ask the question: Have the people in this community done their share? Mind you, there are many ways in which a community can do its share. They can do it through their taxing powers. They can do it through their constituted authorities, the officials of the village or township. But also, they can do an enormous amount of work for the relief of suffering humanity through their churches.

So the first question we ask, quite frankly, in every case, is whether the community has done its share through its officials and its churches...The churches are doing their share; and the men and women and children who make up the congregations of the churches have shown a splendid spirit in these days.

It is an interesting fact that although the national income from 1929 down to the summer of this year fell off by a very large percentage, nevertheless the receipts of the churches of the American communities fell off by a much smaller percentage. In other words, we have faith in our churches and our churches have faith in us.

I am very happy to take part in the one hundredth anniversary of the Methodist Episcopal Church of Hyde Park. I, with you, am proud not only of its history, but of the splendid work that it has done in this community during the full century.

I am happy in the thought that during the one hundred years that lie ahead of us, it is going to continue to do splendid work for the community, and that it is going to do that hand in hand with the other churches of the community. That is the kind of American spirit that is going to bring us over the top.

In closing, may I say one word: The problems which we all face - the problems of so - called economics, the problems that are called monetary problems, the problems of unemployment, the problems of industry and agriculture - we shall not succeed in solving unless the people of this country hold the spiritual values of the country just as high as they do the economic values.

I am very sure that the spirit in which we are approaching those difficult tasks and the splendid cooperation which has been shown, are going to be exemplified in the lives of all the people calling themselves Christians who believe in God and uphold the works of the Church.

ADDRESS TO THE NATIONAL CONFERENCE OF CATHOLIC CHARITIES, GREETING CARDINAL HAYES OCTOBER 4, 1933

IN THE MIDST of problems of material things, in the machine age of invention, of finance, of international suspicion and renewed armaments, every one of us must gain satisfaction and strength in the knowledge that social justice is becoming an evergrowing factor and influence in almost every part of the world today. With every passing year I become more confident that humanity is moving forward to the practical application of the teachings of Christianity as they affect the individual lives of men and women everywhere.

It is fitting that this annual National Conference of Catholic Charities should celebrate also, at the same time, the centennial of the Society of St. Vincent de Paul. I like to remember the day a hundred years ago, the taunt of atheists, the taunt of the enemies of the Christian religion in the Paris of 1833, when they demanded of the churches, "Show us your works." Yes, I like to remember it because of the acceptance of that challenge, and the decision to show that Christianity was not dead, and that the deeds of Christians were in accordance with their faith.

This one Society, this past year, in their task of visitation and relief of the poor in their own homes and in hospitals and institutions, aided more than one hundred and fifty thousand families within the borders of our country; and, with other great organizations of men and women connected with all the churches in all the land, it is working with similar unselfishness for the alleviation of human suffering and the righting of human wrong. When I think of this I am confirmed in my deep belief that God is marching on.

Monsignor Keegan has mentioned the fact that seven months ago this very day, standing at the portals of the capitol at Washington, about to assume the responsibilities of the Presidency, I told the people of America that we were going to face facts, no matter how hard and how difficult those facts might be, and that it was my firm belief that the only thing we had to fear was fear itself...

The Federal Government has inaugurated new measures of relief on a vast scale, but the Federal Government cannot, and does not intend to, take over the whole job. Many times we have insisted that every community and every State must first do its share.

Out of this picture we are developing a new science of social treatment and rehabilitation - working it out through an unselfish partnership, a partnership between great church and private social service agencies and the agencies of Government itself...

No governmental organization in all history has been able to keep the human touch to the same extent as church and private effort. Government can do a great many things better than private associations or citizens, but in the last analysis, success in this kind of personal work in which you are engaged depends upon personal contact between neighbor and neighbor.

The other reason lies in the fact that the people of the United States still recognize, and, I believe, recognize with a firmer faith than ever before, that spiritual values count in the long run more than material values.

Those people in other lands, and I say this advisedly, those in other lands who have sought by edict or by law to eliminate the right of mankind to believe in God and to practice that belief, have, in every known case, discovered sooner or later that they are tilting in vain against an inherent, essential, undying quality, indeed necessity, of the human race - a quality and a necessity which in every century have proved an essential to permanent progress - and I speak of religion.

Clear thinking and earnest effort and sincere faith will result in thoroughgoing support throughout the whole Nation of efforts such as yours. The spirit of our people has not been blunted; it has not been daunted. It has come through the trials of these days unafraid. We have ventured and we have won; we shall venture further and we shall win again. Yes, the traditions of a great people have been enriched. In our measures of recovery and of relief we have preserved all that is best in our history and we are building thereon a new structure-strong and firm and permanent.

I can never express in words what the loyalty and trust of the Nation have meant to me. Not for a moment have I doubted that we would climb out of the valley of gloom. Always I have been certain that we would conquer, because the spirit of America springs from faith - faith in the beloved institutions of our land, and a true and abiding faith in the divine guidance of God.

REMARKS AT WASHINGTON COLLEGE, CHESTERTOWN, MARYLAND, ON RECEIVING AN HONORARY DEGREE OCTOBER 21, 1933

I REMEMBER THAT when I was a boy in school in Massachusetts, Bishop Phillips Brooks made to my class a remark I shall never forget. He said: "You boys will be good citizens just as long as you remember your boyhood ideals."...

But at the same time, the old-fashioned boyhood ideals, the old-fashioned principles, are going to keep the country going...

I have been very greatly honored in being made an alumnus of the College; and I breathe the same prayer that George Washington made to the College nearly a century and a half ago, that the Creator of the Universe will look down on the College and give it His benediction. Let me tell you simply and from the bottom of my heart that I am proud to have come, proud of the honor; and I wish you Godspeed in the years to come.

COMMUNICATIONS WITH MAXIM LITVINOV, PEOPLE'S COMMISSAR FOR FOREIGN AFFAIRS, UNION OF SOVIET SOCIALIST REPUBLICS NOVEMBER 16, 1933

MY DEAR MR. President Roosevelt:

In reply to your letter of November 16, 1933, I have the honor to inform you that the Government of the Union of Soviet Socialist Republics as a fixed policy accords...the following rights...supported by the following law:

The school is separated from the Church. Instruction in religious doctrines is not permitted in any governmental and common schools, nor in private teaching institutions where general subjects are taught. Persons may give or receive religious instruction in a private manner. (Decree of Jan. 23, 1918, art. 9.)...

I am, my dear Mr. President,
Very sincerely yours,
MAXIM LITVINOV
People's Commissar for Foreign Affairs,
Union of Soviet Socialist Republics

My dear Mr. Litvinov:

As I have told you in our recent conversations, it is my expectation that after the establishment of normal relations between our two countries many Americans will wish to reside temporarily or permanently within the territory of the Union of Soviet Socialist Republics, and I am deeply concerned that they should enjoy in all respects the same freedom of conscience and religious liberty which they enjoy at home.

As you well know, the Government of the United States, since the foundation of the Republic, has always striven to protect its nationals, at home and abroad, in the free exercise of liberty of conscience and religious worship, and from all disability or persecution on account of their religious faith or worship.

And I need scarcely point out that the rights enumerated below are those enjoyed in the United States by all citizens and foreign nationals and by American nationals in all the major countries of the world.

The Government of the United States, therefore, will expect that nationals of the United States of America within the territory of the Union of Soviet Socialist Republics will be allowed to conduct without annoyance or molestation of any kind religious services and rites of a ceremonial nature, including baptismal, confirmation, communion, marriage and burial rites, in the English language, or in any other language which is customarily used in the practice of the religious faith to which they belong, in churches, houses, or other buildings appropriate for such service, which they will be given the right and opportunity to lease, erect or maintain in convenient situations.

We will expect that nationals of the United States will have the right to collect from their co-religionists and to receive from abroad voluntary offerings for religious purposes; that they will be entitled without restriction to impart religious instruction to their children, either singly or in groups, or to have such instruction imparted by persons whom they may employ for such purpose; that they will be given and protected in the right to bury their dead according to their religious customs in suitable and convenient places established for that purpose, and given the right and opportunity to lease, lay out, occupy and maintain such burial grounds subject to reasonable sanitary laws and regulations.

We will expect that religious groups or congregations composed of nationals of the United States of America in the territory of the Union of Soviet Socialist Republics will be given the right to have their spiritual needs ministered to by clergymen, priests, rabbis or other ecclesiastical functionaries who are nationals of the United States of America, and that such clergymen, priests, rabbis or other ecclesiastical functionaries will be protected from all disability or persecution and will not be denied entry into the territory of the Soviet Union because of their ecclesiastical status.

I am, my dear Mr. Litvinov,
Very sincerely yours,
FRANKLIN D. ROOSEVELT

ADDRESS DELIVERED AT SAVANNAH, GEORGIA NOVEMBER 18, 1933

WHILE WE ARE celebrating the planting of the Colony of Georgia, we remember that if the early settlers had been content to remain on the coast, there would have been no Georgia today. It was the spirit of moving forward that led to the exploration of the great domain of Piedmont and the mountains, that drove the Western border of this Colony to the very banks of the Mississippi River itself.

Yet, all through those great years of the pioneer, we must remember that there were the doubting Thomases, there was the persistent opposition of those who feared change, of those who wanted to let things alone....

Furthermore, my friends, I am confident that in a State like Georgia, which had its roots in religious teachings and religious liberty, a State in which the first Sunday School was established, there must be satisfaction to know that from now on any American sojourning among the great Russian people will be free to worship God in his own way...

Let me, in closing, read to you a very short passage from a message delivered a generation ago by a great son of a great Georgia mother, Theodore Roosevelt. He said:

"Materially we must strive to secure a broader economic opportunity for all men so that each shall have a better chance to show the stuff of which he is made. Spiritually and ethically we must strive to bring about clean living and right thinking. We appreciate that the things of the body are important; but we appreciate also that the things of the soul are immeasurably more important."

THANKSGIVING DAY PROCLAMATION
NOVEMBER 21, 1933

I, FRANKLIN D. ROOSEVELT, President of the United States of America, do set aside and appoint Thursday, the thirtieth day of November, 1933, to be a Day of Thanksgiving for all our people.

May we on that day in our churches and in our homes give humble thanks for the blessings bestowed upon us during the year past by Almighty God.

May we recall the courage of those who settled a wilderness, the vision of those who founded the Nation, the steadfastness of those who in every succeeding generation have fought to keep pure the ideal of equality of opportunity and hold clear the goal of mutual help in time of prosperity as in time of adversity.

May we ask guidance in more surely learning the ancient truth that greed and selfishness and striving for undue riches can never bring lasting happiness or good to the individual or to his neighbors.

May we be grateful for the passing of dark days; for the new spirit of dependence one on another; for the closer unity of all parts of our wide land; for the greater friendship between employers and those who toil; for a clearer knowledge by all Nations that we seek no conquests and ask only honorable engagements by all peoples to respect the lands and rights of their neighbors; for the brighter day to which we can win through by seeking the help of God in a more unselfish striving for the common bettering of mankind.

In witness whereof, I have hereunto set my hand and caused the seal of the United States to be affixed.

RADIO ADDRESS ON MARYLAND TERCENTENARY CELEBRATION, GREETING GOVERNOR RITCHIE NOVEMBER 22, 1933

AND SO MY friends, I hope that this 300-year anniversary of the founding of Maryland which will go on from now through the year 1934 will be a success not only for those who partake in it, but also will be a reminder to people throughout the United States of the great fight that Lord Baltimore made three centuries ago for religious freedom in America.

GREETINGS ON THE FORTY-FIFTH ANNIVERSARY OF THE LORD'S DAY ALLIANCE, MR. JOHN H. WILLEY, 156 FIFTH AVENUE, NEW YORK CITY DECEMBER 4, 1933

I EXTEND CONGRATULATIONS and best wishes on the occasion of the Forty-fifth Anniversary of the Lord's Day Alliance of the United States.

The object of your organization is, in my opinion, a very worthy one, and the efforts of its members toward the successful attainment of such a goal, are deserving of the highest praise. It is my sincere hope that this work may be carried on with even greater success through future years.

ADDRESS TO THE FEDERAL COUNCIL OF CHURCHES OF CHRIST IN AMERICA DECEMBER 6, 1933

I AM HONORED by the privilege of speaking to the delegated representatives of twenty-five Christian denominations assembled here on the twenty-fifth anniversary of the Federal Council of Churches of Christ in America. In this quarter of a century you have surrendered no individual creed, but at the same time you have been creating a much-needed union that seeks to better the social and moral conditions of all the people of America.

During a quarter of a century more greatly controlled by the spirit of conquest and greed than any similar period since the American and the French Revolutions you have survived and grown. You have come through to the threshold of a new era in which your churches and the other churches - Gentile and Jewish - recognize and stand ready to lead in a new war of peace - the war for social justice.

Christianity was born in and of an era notable for the great gulf that separated the privileged from the underprivileged of the world of two thousand years ago - an era of lines of demarcation between conquerors and conquered; between caste and caste; between warring philosophies based on the theories of logicians rather than on practical humanities. The early churches were united in a social ideal.

Although through all the centuries we know of many periods when civilization has slipped a step backward, yet I am confident that over the sum of the centuries we have gained many steps for every one we have lost.

Now, once more, we are embarking on another voyage into the realm of human contacts. That human agency which we call government is seeking through social and economic means the same goal which the churches are seeking through social and spiritual means.

If I were asked to state the great objective which Church and State are both demanding for the sake of every man and woman and child in this country, I would say that that great objective is "a more abundant life."

The early Christians challenged the pagan ethics of Greece and of Rome; we are wholly ready to challenge the pagan ethics that are represented in many phases of our boasted modern civilization...

We recognize the right of the individual to seek and to obtain his own fair wage, his own fair profit, in his own fair way - just so long as in the doing of it he does not push down or hold down his own neighbor. And at the same time, we are at one in calling for collective effort on broad lines of social planning - a collective effort which is wholly in accord with the social teachings of Christianity.

This new generation of ours stands ready to help us. They may not be as ready as were their fathers and mothers to accept the outward requirements or even many of the ancient observances of the several churches, yet I truly believe that these same churches can find in them a stronger support for the fundamentals of social betterment than many of the older generation are willing to concede...

This new generation, for example, is not content with preachings against that vile form of collective murder-lynch law - which has broken out in our midst anew. We know that it is murder, and a deliberate and definite disobedience of the Commandment, "Thou shalt not kill." We do not excuse those in high places or in low who condone lynch law...

Toward that new definition of prosperity the churches and the Governments, while wholly separate in their functioning, can work hand in hand. Government can ask the churches to stress in their teaching the ideals of social justice, while at the same time government guarantees to the churches - Gentile and Jewish - the right to worship God in their own way.

The churches, while they remain wholly free from even the suggestion of interference in Government, can at the same time teach their millions of followers that they have the right to demand of the Government of their own choosing, the maintenance and furtherance of "a more abundant life." State and Church are rightly united in a common aim. With the help of God, we are on the road toward it.

STATEMENT TO THE FEDERATION OF WOMEN'S CLUBS DECEMBER 14, 1933

WE HAVE THE opportunity of improving conditions and making our country a better home, materially and spiritually, for more than 120,000,000 people. To do this will require the concerted aid and continued efforts of many forces - of Government, Federal, State and local; of social, spiritual, industrial and financial agencies.

CHRISTMAS AMNESTY PROCLAMATION DECEMBER 23, 1933

DURING THE WORLD War, a large number of persons were convicted under the Espionage Act and the Selective Service Act of giving utterance to sentiments adverse to the prosecution of the War and to the enforcement of the draft. They have paid the penalty...Accordingly I have issued a Christmas Amnesty Proclamation, extending a full pardon to all persons who were convicted of such war-time offenses

CHRISTMAS GREETING TO THE NATION
DECEMBER 24, 1933

WE IN THE Nation's capital are gathered around this symbolic tree celebrating the coming of Christmas; in spirit we join with millions of others, men and women and children, throughout our own land and in other countries and continents, in happy and reverent observance of the spirit of Christmas.

For me and for my family it is the happiest of Christmases.

To the many thousands of you who have thought of me and have sent me greetings, and I hope all of you are hearing my voice, I want to tell you how profoundly grateful I am. If it were within my power so to do I would personally thank each and every one of you for your remembrance of me, but there are so many thousands of you that that happy task is impossible.

Even more greatly, my happiness springs from the deep conviction that this year marks a greater national understanding of the significance in our modern lives of the teachings of Him whose birth we celebrate. To more and more of us the words "Thou shalt love thy neighbor as thyself" have taken on a meaning that is showing itself and proving itself in our purposes and daily lives.

May the practice of that high ideal grow in us all in the year to come.

I give you and send you one and all, old and young, a Merry Christmas and a truly Happy New Year.

And so, for now and for always "God Bless Us Every One."

CHRISTMAS GREETING TO THE ARMY AND NAVY
DECEMBER 24, 1933

MY CHRISTMAS GREETINGS and good wishes to the officers and men of the Army and Navy. I am proud of you.

ROOSEVELT, Commander-in-Chief

CHRISTMAS GREETINGS TO AMERICAN
DIPLOMATIC OFFICERS
DECEMBER 24, 1933

AS THE YEAR draws to a holiday pause before its close, I take much pleasure in sending out to you and through you to your personal and official family, and to the Foreign Service staffs my heartiest good wishes. Your loyal and intelligent cooperation with us in Washington has made these recent months of our association a source of great satisfaction and encouragement to me in this important period of our country's development.

In offering my best greetings for Christmas and the New Year, I look forward in confident anticipation to continuing mutual cooperation during 1934.

ANNUAL MESSAGE TO CONGRESS
JANUARY 3, 1934

THROUGH CAREFULLY PLANNED flood control, power development and land-use policies in the Tennessee Valley and in other, great watersheds, we are seeking the elimination of waste, the removal of poor lands from agriculture and the encouragement of small local industries, thus furthering this principle of a better balanced national life...

I look forward, however, to the time in the not distant future, when annual appropriations, wholly covered by current revenue, will enable the work to proceed under a national plan.

Such a national plan will, in a generation or two, return many times the money spent on it; more important, it will eliminate the use of inefficient tools, conserve and increase natural resources, prevent waste, and enable millions of our people to take better advantage of the opportunities which God has given our country.

RADIO ADDRESS TO THE BOY SCOUTS OF AMERICA FEBRUARY 10, 1934

I AM HAPPY to participate in the 24th Anniversary Celebration of our organization, the Boy Scouts of America. Nearly a million of us are mobilized at this time in all parts of the country as a part of the program for this week of celebration. Home and farm patrols and troops of farm boys are joining with their brother scouts in the big cities.

In front of the City Hall in San Francisco - and it is nine o'clock in the morning there - thousands of scouts join with other thousands in the Hippodrome in New York in carrying on the cause of world-wide brotherhood in Scouting.

As most of you know, Scouting has been one of my active interests for many years. I have visited hundreds of Troops in their home towns and in their camps. I know therefore from personal experience the things we do and stand for as Scouts. We have ideals. We are a growing organization. We believe that we are accomplishing fine American results not only for our own membership, but also for our families, our communities and our Nation.

Summed up in one sentence, the aim of Scouting is to build up better citizenship. I believe that we are contributing greatly to that objective.

I am especially happy today to extend personal greetings and congratulations to the Scouts and Leaders who have earned the President's award for progress in the year 1933, as a part of the Ten-Year Program. It is appropriate that we are planning for a celebration of our Silver Jubilee, the Twenty-fifth Anniversary of the Boy Scouts of America, which will culminate in a great national Jamboree here in the Nation's capital in the summer of 1935.

Of course it would be physically impossible for us to have the whole membership of the Boy Scouts of America, a million strong, come to Washington at one time, but I much hope that it will be possible to have every nook and cranny of our Nation represented.

As a preliminary to our Silver Jubilee, and in line with the emphasis of service for others which we have always stressed, I suggest to you that it is time once more for us to do a National Good Turn.

As many of you know, we are doing everything possible in this emergency to help suffering humanity. I called upon the Federal Emergency Relief Administrator, Mr. Harry L. Hopkins, to tell me what kind of National Good Turn would be of the greatest service.

He has recommended that during the balance of the month of February every troop and every Scout do everything possible in their separate localities to collect such household furnishings, bedding and clothes as people may be able to share as gifts to those who greatly need them.

Therefore, I ask you, under the direction of your own local officers, and in conference with the representatives of the Federal Relief Administration and other local social agencies, to gather up such of this material as may be available for distribution.

I am confident that the American people will generously cooperate and respond. Indeed, I am hoping that in many cases they will telephone or send letters to the local Scout offices to offer their help to carry through this National Good Turn.

I have already received offers of cooperation from Governors of States, from mayors and other community leaders. May you carry out this new service and rededicate yourselves to the Scout Oath.

I ask you to join with me and the Eagle Scouts and our President and Chief Scout Executive who are here with me in the White House in giving again the Scout Oath.

All stand!
Give the Scout sign!
Repeat with me the Scout Oath!
"On my honor I will do my best:
To do my duty to God and my country
and to obey the Scout Law;
To help other people at all times;
To keep myself physically strong, mentally awake,
and morally straight."

LETTER TO COLONEL ALVA J. BRASTED, CHIEF OF CHAPLAINS, U.S.A., WAR DEPARTMENT, WASHINGTON, D. C. FEBRUARY 13, 1934

THE GREAT TEACHER said: "I come that ye may have life and that ye may have it more abundantly." The object of all our striving should be to realize that "abundant life."

The supreme values are spiritual. The hope of the world is that character which, built upon the solid rock, withstands triumphantly all the storms of life.

To build this exemplary character is our great task. Without it the abundant life cannot be realized, and the best citizens and best soldiers of a country are those who have put on the armor of righteousness.

Chaplains of the military and naval services and clergymen everywhere who by word and life are advancing the cause of idealism and true religion are doing a commendable work, one that is absolutely essential to the life of the Nation.

LETTER ON BROTHERHOOD DAY TO DR. ROBERT A. ASHWORTH, NEW YORK, N.Y. APRIL 28, 1934

I HAVE JUST learned of the proposed observance of Brotherhood Day by the National Conference of Jews and Christians and I am deeply interested in its possibilities.

This occasion presents an opportunity for concerted thinking on a vital problem of national welfare; it should help us all in our efforts to rise above ancient and harmful suspicions and prejudices and to work together as citizens of American democracy. Good neighborliness, good citizenship and plain common sense in everyday relationships are potential fruits of such a nationwide observance.

ADDRESS AT A MEMORIAL TO WILLIAM JENNINGS BRYAN MAY 3, 1934

NO SELFISH MOTIVE touched his public life; he held important office only as a sacred trust of honor from his country; and when he sought a mandate from his fellow citizens the soul of his inspiration was the furtherance of their interests, not his own, not of a group, but of all.

No man of his time was or could have been more constantly in the limelight than he; yet we can look back and scan his record without being able to point to any instance where he took a position that did not accord with his conscience or his belief.

To Secretary Bryan political courage was not a virtue to be sought or attained, for it was an inherent part of the man. He chose his path not to win acclaim but rather because that path appeared clear to him from his inmost beliefs. He did not have to dare to do what to him seemed right; he could not do otherwise.

It was my privilege to know William Jennings Bryan when I was a very young man. Years later both of us came to the Nation's capital to serve under the leadership of Woodrow Wilson...

It was Mr. Bryan who said: "I respect the aristocracy of learning, I deplore the plutocracy of wealth but I thank God for the democracy of the heart."

Many years ago he also said: "You may dispute over whether I have fought a good fight; you may dispute over whether I have finished my course; but you cannot deny that I have kept the faith."

We who are assembled here today to accept this memorial in the capital of the Republic can well agree that he fought a good fight; that he finished his course; and that he kept the faith.

MOTHER'S DAY PROCLAMATION
MAY 3, 1934

WHEREAS BY HOUSE Joint Resolution 263, approved and signed by President Wilson on May 8, 1914, the second Sunday in May of each year has been designated as Mother's Day for the expression of our love and reverence for the mothers of our country...

Now, therefore, I, Franklin D. Roosevelt, President of the United States of America, do hereby call upon our citizens to express on Mother's Day, Sunday, May 13, 1934, our love and reverence for motherhood:

(a) By the customary display of the United States flag on all Government buildings, homes, and other suitable places;

(b) By the usual tokens and messages of affection to our mothers; and

(c) By doing all that we can through our churches, fraternal and welfare agencies for the relief and welfare of mothers and children who may be in need of the necessities of life.

LETTER ON THE ONE HUNDREDTH ANNIVERSARY OF THE BIRTH OF CARDINAL GIBBONS, ADDRESSED TO ARCHBISHOP MICHAEL J. CURLEY, BALTIMORE, MARYLAND
MAY 21, 1934

IN MY RADIO address last November on the Maryland Tercentenary Celebration, I expressed the hope that the celebration "will also be a reminder to people throughout the United States of the great fight that Lord Baltimore made three centuries ago for religious freedom in America."...

Loyal, steadfast to his own religious faith, a foremost leader in its councils, Cardinal Gibbons during his long life ever extended the gift of freedom, which he himself so highly appreciated, unto all of his fellow citizens, no matter what their religious faith might be.

ADDRESS AT GETTYSBURG
MAY 30, 1934

ON THESE HILLS of Gettysburg two brave armies of Americans once met in contest.

Not far from here, in a valley likewise consecrated to American valor, a ragged Continental Army survived a bitter winter to keep alive the expiring hope of a new Nation; and near to this battlefield and that valley stands that invincible city where the Declaration of Independence was born and the Constitution of the United States was written by the fathers. Surely, all this is holy ground...

In those days, it was an inspired prophet of the South who said: "My brethren, if we know one another, we will love one another." The tragedy of the Nation was that the people did not know one another because they had not the necessary means of visiting one another.

Since those days, two subsequent wars, both with foreign Nations, have measurably allayed and softened the ancient passions. It has been left to us of this generation to see the healing made permanent...

Today, we have many means of knowing each other - means that at last have sounded the doom of sectionalism. It is, I think, as I survey the picture from every angle, a simple fact that the chief hindrance to progress comes from three elements which, thank God, grow less in importance with the growth of a clearer understanding of our purposes on the part of the overwhelming majority.

FIRESIDE CHAT
JUNE 28, 1934

I HAVE POINTED out to the Congress that we are seeking to find the way once more to well-known, long-established but to some degree forgotten ideals and values. We seek the security of the men, women and children of the Nation...While I was in France during the War our boys used to call the United States "God's country." Let us make it and keep it "God's country."

REMARKS IN HAWAII,
GREETING GOVERNOR POINDEXTER
JULY 28, 1934

IN A FINE old prayer for our country are found these words: "Fashion into one happy people those brought hither out of many kindreds and tongues." That prayer is being answered in the Territory of Hawaii.

REMARKS AT THE SITE OF
BONNEVILLE DAM, OREGON
AUGUST 3, 1934

I WANT TO tell you from the bottom of my heart what a privilege it is to come here and see this great work at first hand. May it go on with God's blessing and with your blessings.

ADDRESS DELIVERED AT GREEN BAY, WISCONSIN, GREETING GOV. SCHMEDEMAN AUGUST 9, 1934

WE ARE BUT carrying forward the fundamentals behind the pioneering spirit of the fathers when we apply the pioneering methods to the better use of vast land and water resources - what God has given us to use as trustees not only for ourselves but for future generations...

Confidence is returning...to the fair and sincere bankers and financiers and business men, big and little, who now, for the first time, find Government cooperating with them in new attempts to put the Golden Rule into the temples of finance...

In this modern world, the spreading out of opportunity ought not to consist of robbing Peter to pay Paul...

We who support this New Deal do so because it is a square deal and because it is essential to the preservation of security and happiness in a free society such as ours. I like its definition by a member of the Congress. He said:

"The new deal is an old deal - as old as the earliest aspirations of humanity for liberty and justice and the good life. It is as old as Christian ethics, for basically its ethics are the same."

NEW YEAR'S GREETING TO AMERICAN JEWS AUGUST 13, 1934

I AM HAPPY, at this festival season of Rosh Hashanah, to renew my good wishes to my fellow citizens of Jewish faith throughout the land.

It is a suitable opportunity to pause and, by dedicating ourselves anew to the responsibilities of the present day, to continue the work which, in common with all Americans, we have undertaken toward realizing the promise of the years which lie before us.

TELEGRAM OF CONGRATULATIONS TO THE NEW COMMANDER-IN-CHIEF OF THE SALVATION ARMY, GENERAL EVANGELINE BOOTH, LONDON, ENGLAND SEPTEMBER 4, 1934

PLEASE ACCEPT MY sincere congratulations on your election as General of the Salvation Army throughout the world. In these troubled times it is particularly important that the leadership of all good forces shall work for the amelioration of human suffering and for the preservation of the highest spiritual ideals.

Through your efforts as Commander-in-Chief of the Salvation Army in the United States, you have earned the gratitude and admiration of millions of your countrymen. I am confident that, under your guidance, the Salvation Army will go steadily forward in service to the unfortunate of every land.

ADDRESS TO THE CONFERENCE ON THE MOBILIZATION FOR HUMAN NEEDS SEPTEMBER 28, 1934

THE CHURCH GROUPS and the social groups organized on private lines, whether they act separately or jointly through Community Chests, or in any other way, are an essential part of the structure of our life.

THANKSGIVING DAY PROCLAMATION
NOVEMBER 15, 1934

I, FRANKLIN D. ROOSEVELT, President of the United States of America, hereby designate Thursday, the twenty-ninth day of November, 1934, as a Day of Thanksgiving for the people of the Nation.

Thus to set aside in the autumn of each year a day on which to give thanks to Almighty God for the blessings of life is a wise and reverent custom, long cherished by our people. It is fitting that we should again observe this custom.

During the past year we have been given courage and fortitude to meet the problems which have confronted us in our national life. Our sense of social justice has deepened. We have been given vision to make new provisions for human welfare and happiness, and in a spirit of mutual helpfulness we have cooperated to translate vision into reality.

More greatly have we turned our hearts and minds to things spiritual. We can truly say, "What profiteth it a Nation if it gain the whole world and lose its own soul."

With gratitude in our hearts for what has already been achieved, may we, with the help of God, dedicate ourselves anew to work for the betterment of mankind.

REMARKS AT CLINCH RIVER BELOW
THE NORRIS DAM
NOVEMBER 16, 1934

ALL OF YOU who are working here at this great dam project and all of the good people throughout the Tennessee Valley who are working on the rest of this great program some day will be known as veterans...All I can say to you is "Godspeed the work."

PRESS CONFERENCE, WARM SPRINGS, GEORGIA
NOVEMBER 23, 1934

NOW, THERE WAS no reason in God's world why the Mississippi Power Company could not have gone to Corinth and said the same thing - no reason in the world...

It could have done that same thing. But it was the Tennessee Valley Authority that went down and sold the idea to the people in that county and said, "Let us have a uniform power rate.

ADDRESS TO THE CONFERENCE ON CRIME
DECEMBER 10, 1934

THIS CAN COME only through expert service in marshalling the assets of home, school, church, community and other social agencies, to work in common purpose with our law enforcement agencies.

CHRISTMAS GREETING TO THE NATION
DECEMBER 24, 1934

THIS IS THE second year that I have joined with you on this happy occasion. Then, as now, with millions of others we celebrate the happy observance of Christmas.

The year toward which we looked then with anticipation and hope has passed. We have seen fulfilled many things that a year ago were only hopes. Our human life thus goes on from anticipation and hope to fulfillment. This year again we are entitled to new hopes and new anticipations.

For all those who can hear but not see this gathering, let me explain that here before us in the park in front of the White House is the monument of a man who will live forever as the embodiment of courage - Andrew Jackson.

His was a long, long life in the public service, distinguished at all times by a chivalrous meeting of problems and difficulties that attended that service, a fast belief in people and a profound love for them. His patriotism was unstained and unafraid. Carved into that monument is his expression of the necessity for union. That message grows in importance with the years.

In these days it means to me a union not only of the States but a union of the hearts and minds of the people in all the States and their many interests and purposes, devoted with unity to the human welfare of our country.

Just across the street is the house he occupied one hundred years ago, the house the people of the country have built for their Presidents. From its windows I see this monument to this man of courage. It is an inspiration to me, as it should be to all Americans.

And so let us make the spirit of Christmas of 1934 that of courage and unity. It is the way to greater happiness and wellbeing. That is, I believe, an important part of what the Maker of Christmas would have it mean.

In this sense, the Scriptures admonish us to be strong and of good courage, to fear not, to dwell together in Unity.

I wish you one and all, here and everywhere, a very, very Merry Christmas.

CHRISTMAS GREETING TO THE FOREIGN
DIPLOMATIC SERVICE
DECEMBER 24, 1934

TOWARD THE CLOSE of my second year in office, I send to you and to the members of the Foreign Service in the country of your residence, as well as to your family, personal and official, my cordial Christmas and New Year's greetings.

ANNUAL MESSAGE TO CONGRESS
JANUARY 4, 1935

THE LESSONS OF history, confirmed by the evidence immediately before me, show conclusively that continued dependence upon relief induces a spiritual and moral disintegration fundamentally destructive to the national fiber. To dole out relief in this way is to administer a narcotic, a subtle destroyer of the human spirit...

Such people, in the days before the great depression, were cared for by local efforts - by States, by counties, by towns, by cities, by churches and by private welfare agencies. It is my thought that in the future they must be cared for as they were before. I stand ready through my own personal efforts, and through the public influence of the office that I hold, to help these local agencies to get the means necessary to assume this burden...

Beyond the material recovery, I sense a spiritual recovery as well. The people of America are turning as never before to those permanent values that are not limited to the physical objectives of life. There are growing signs of this on every hand. In the face of these spiritual impulses we are sensible of the Divine Providence to which Nations turn now, as always, for guidance and fostering care.

MESSAGE TO THE BOY SCOUTS OF AMERICA ON THEIR TWENTY-FIFTH ANNIVERSARY FEBRUARY 8, 1935

AS I REVIEW the record of these twenty-five years of Scouting in America, I am impressed with the extent of the volunteer service we have rendered.

We as a Nation are proud of the fact that in addition to our splendid system of education and of other services made available through funds secured by taxation, there are in each community so many well-organized and efficiently administered agencies which supplement the work of Government and make available additional opportunities which strengthen the best objectives of the home, the church and the school.

LETTER ON THE PRESIDENT'S ANCESTORS TO PHILIP SLOMOVITZ, ESQ., EDITOR, THE DETROIT JEWISH CHRONICLE, DETROIT, MICHIGAN MARCH 7, 1935

ALL I KNOW about the origin of the Roosevelt family in this country is that all branches bearing the name are apparently descended from Claes Martenssen Van Roosevelt, who came from Holland sometime before 1648 - even the year is uncertain.

Where he came from in Holland I do not know, nor do I know who his parents were. There was a family of the same name on one of the Dutch Islands and some of the same name living in Holland as lately as thirty or forty years ago, but, frankly, I have never had either the time or the inclination to try to establish the line on the other side of the ocean before they came over here, nearly three hundred years ago.

In the dim distant past they may have been Jews or Catholics or Protestants. What I am more interested in is whether they were good citizens and believers in God. I hope they were both.

STATEMENT ON SIGNING PAN-AMERICAN UNION TREATY APRIL 15, 1935

THE TREATY PROVIDES for the protection of historic monuments, museums, scientific, artistic, religious and cultural institutions in time of peace as well as in time of war.

FIRESIDE CHAT APRIL 28, 1935

WE HAVE IN the darkest moments of our national trials retained our faith in our own ability to master our destiny. Fear is vanishing and confidence is growing on every side, faith is being renewed in the vast possibilities of human beings to improve their material and spiritual status through the instrumentality of the democratic form of government. That faith is receiving its just reward. For that we can be thankful to the God who watches over America.

PRESS CONFERENCE MAY 31, 1935

YOU AND I know human nature. Fundamentally it comes down to this. In the long run can voluntary processes on the part of business bring about the same practical results that were attained under N.R.A.? I mean the good results. Of course there have been some bad ones.

But I mean the good results. Can it be done by voluntary action on the part of business?

Can we go ahead as a Nation with the beautiful theory, let us say, of some of the press, "At last the rule of Christ is restored. Business can do anything it wants and business is going to live up to the Golden Rule so marvelously that all of our troubles are ended." It is a school of thought that is so delightful in its naivete.

ADDRESS TO THE GRADUATES OF THE UNITED STATES MILITARY ACADEMY JUNE 12, 1935

I EXTENDED TO each and every one of you who graduate today my congratulations and best wishes. As Commander-in-Chief of the Army of the United States I tell you that I am proud of you and wish you Godspeed.

REMARKS TO STATE WORKS PROGRESS ADMINISTRATORS JUNE 17, 1935

WE CANNOT DISCRIMINATE in any of the work we are conducting either because of race or religion or politics.

STATEMENT ON RELIGIOUS STATUS OF AMERICANS IN MEXICO JULY 16, 1935

THE PRESIDENT STATED that he is in entire sympathy with all people who make it clear that the American people and the Government believe in freedom of religious worship not only in the United States, but also in other Nations.

GREETING BY TELEPHONE TO THE BI-CENTENNIAL CELEBRATION OF SAINTE GENEVIEVE, MISSOURI AUGUST 22, 1935

THE HISTORY OF the town of Sainte Genevieve eloquently testifies to the fortitude of those pioneers who built their homes on the western bank of the Mississippi and wrested minerals from the hills, furs from the forest, and a plentiful harvest from the plain; who merged their varied nationalities in a mighty effort to carve an American Nation out of the Western wilderness.

We admire that Christian courage which refused to be daunted by Indian depredations and massacres, by a gradual change in the course of the Mississippi threatening the destruction of the settlement, or by the disastrous flood of 1785.

In due course, through the rugged efforts of your predecessors, the hostile Indians were pacified; and the restless Mississippi, far from annihilating the community, provoked a providential removal of the church and other buildings to a better site where the village could expand and flourish.

These triumphs over affliction are characteristic of the spirit of our early Americans. Although the problems which confront us today are of a different sort, I am confident that you have not lost the stalwart qualities of frontier days.

It is with a full appreciation of your past that, on this occasion of your Bi-Centennial Celebration, I extend to you my hearty wishes for a happy and prosperous future.

RADIO ADDRESS TO THE
YOUNG DEMOCRATIC CLUBS OF AMERICA
AUGUST 24, 1935

WE HAVE NO right to speak slightingly of the heritage, spiritual and material, that comes down to us. There are lessons that it teaches that we abandon only at our own peril. "Hold fast to that which is permanently true" is still a counsel of wisdom...

If fifty thousand employees spoke with fifty thousand voices, there would be a modern Tower of Babel.

REMARKS AT THE CELEBRATION OF THE
FIFTIETH ANNIVERSARY OF
STATE CONSERVATION AT LAKE PLACID
SEPTEMBER 14, 1935

THESE ARE SOME of the things that Conservation has to look forward to, and in the meantime the spreading of the gospel of conservation is something that we are succeeding in accomplishing.

The people in the last two years have become more and more conscious of the practical economic effect of what we are doing. They are becoming more and more conscious of the value to themselves - city dwellers and country dwellers - in protecting these great assets of nature that God has given us.

LETTER TO THE CLERGY OF AMERICA
SEPTEMBER 23, 1935

YOUR HIGH CALLING brings you intimate daily contact not only with your own parishioners, but with people generally in your community. I am sure you see the problems of your people with wise and sympathetic understanding.

Because of the grave responsibilities of my office, I am turning to representative clergymen for counsel and advice, feeling confident that no group can give more accurate or unbiased views.

I am particularly anxious that the new social security legislation just enacted, for which we have worked so long, providing for old-age pensions, aid for crippled children and unemployment insurance, shall be carried out in keeping with the high purposes with which this law was enacted.

It is also vitally important that the works program shall be administered to provide employment at useful work, and that our unemployed as well as the Nation as a whole may derive the greatest possible benefits.

I shall deem it a favor if you will write me about conditions in your community. Tell me where you feel our Government can better serve our people. We can solve our many problems, but no one man or single group can do it. We shall have to work together for the common end of better spiritual and material conditions for the American people.

May I have your counsel and your help? I am leaving on a short vacation, but will be back in Washington in a few weeks and I will deeply appreciate your writing to me.

GREETINGS TO THE AMERICAN PROTESTANT HOSPITAL ASSOCIATION, ADDRESSING REVEREND CHARLES JARRELL, D.D., PRESIDENT, NEW JEFFERSON HOTEL, ST. LOUIS, MISSOURI SEPTEMBER 25, 1935

IT IS WITH pleasure that I send my personal greetings to the American Protestant Hospital Association meeting in annual convention at St. Louis...

Generous American people have always shown a disposition to help the afflicted and to make life happier for an ever-increasing percentage of the population.

Our hospitals, and particularly those administered by non-profit religious organizations, symbolize better than any other institution the depth as well as the dynamic quality of this national characteristic.

ADDRESS AT SAN DIEGO EXPOSITION, SAN DIEGO, CALIFORNIA, GREETING GOVERNOR MERRIAM AND MAYOR BENBOUGH OCTOBER 2, 1935

THE INEVITABLE OVERTOOK us and during more than three years of increasing hardship we came to understand the ultimate national need for more than the necessities and pleasures of life; that which is spiritual in us came forward and taught us to seek security of the spirit - that peace of mind, that confidence in the future, that deep contentment which make life not only possible but full and complete...

In the first emergency action of those days we provided direct relief because a human situation confronted us, but, as rapidly as we could, recognizing that the moral and spiritual fiber of the American people should not be sapped by the narcotic of idleness, we undertook to substitute work for the dole...

In the United States we regard it as axiomatic that every person shall enjoy the free exercise of his religion according to the dictates of his conscience. Our flag for a century and a half has been the symbol of the principles of liberty of conscience, of religious freedom and of equality before the law; and these concepts are deeply ingrained in our national character.

It is true that other Nations may, as they do, enforce contrary rules of conscience and conduct. It is true that policies may be pursued under flags other than our own, but those policies are beyond our jurisdiction.

Yet in our inner individual lives we can never be indifferent, and we assert for ourselves complete freedom to embrace, to profess and to observe the principles for which our flag has so long been the lofty symbol.

As it was so well said by James Madison, over a century ago: "We hold it for a fundamental and inalienable truth that religion and the manner of discharging it can be directed only by reason and conviction, not by force or violence."...

In the two years and a half of my Presidency, this Government has remained constant in following this policy of our own choice. At home we have preached, and will continue to preach, the gospel of the good neighbor.

STATEMENT ON THE FOUR HUNDREDTH ANNIVERSARY OF THE PRINTING OF THE ENGLISH BIBLE OCTOBER 6, 1935

THE FOUR HUNDREDTH anniversary of the printing of the first English Bible is an event of great significance. It challenges the reverent attention of English-speaking peoples the world over.

To that day, October 4, 1535, when Myles Coverdale, an Augustinian Friar, later the Bishop of Exeter, produced this Book in the common vernacular, we trace not only a measurable increase in the cultural value and influence of this greatest of books, but a quickening in the widespread dissemination of those moral and spiritual precepts that have so greatly affected the progress of Christian civilization.

The part that William Tyndale played in this English translation is generally acknowledged by the historian. It is also evident that there were others who made valuable contributions to the monumental undertaking. Independent of and apart from the devotion of these zealous translators, the work they did marks the beginning of one of the great epochs in the history of English-speaking peoples.

It would be difficult to appraise the far-reaching influence of this work and subsequent translations upon the speech, literature, moral and religious character of our people and their institutions. It has done much to refine and enrich our language.

To it may be traced the richest and best we have in our literature. Poetry, prose, painting, music and oratory have had in it their guide and inspiration. In it Lincoln found the rounded euphonious phrases for his Gettysburg address. Speaking of its place in his life, he says: "In regard to the great Book, I have only to say, it is the best gift which God has ever given to man."

One cannot study the story of the rise and development of the men and women who have been and continue to be the pathfinders and benefactors of our people and not recognize the outstanding place the Bible has occupied as the guide and inspiration of their thought and practice.

Apart from their professed allegiance to any particular form of Christian doctrine or creedal expression of faith, they have found in it that which has shaped their course and determined their action.

Look where we will, even in periods that have been marked by apostasy and doubt, still men have found here in these sacred pages that which has refreshed and encouraged them as they prosecuted their pilgrimage and sought for higher levels of thinking and living.

In the formative days of the Republic the directing influence the Bible exercised upon the fathers of the Nation is conspicuously evident.

To Washington it contained the sure and certain moral precepts that constituted the basis of his action. That which proceeded from it transcended all other books, however elevating their thought. To his astute mind moral and religious principles were the "indispensable supports" of political prosperity, the "essential pillars of civil society."

Learned as Jefferson was in the best of the ancient philosophers, he turned to the Bible as the source of his higher thinking and reasoning. Speaking of the lofty teachings of the Master, he said: "He pushed His scrutinies into the heart of man; erected His tribunal in the region of his thoughts, and purified the waters at the fountain head."

Beyond this he held that the Bible contained the noblest ethical system the world has known. His own compilation of the selected portions of this Book, in what is known as "Jefferson's Bible," bears evidence of the profound reverence in which he held it.

Entirely apart from these citations of the place the Bible has occupied in the thought and philosophy of the good and the great, it is the veneration in which it has been and is held by vast numbers of our people that gives it its supreme place in our literature.

No matter what the accidents and chances of life may bring in their train, no matter what the changing habits and fashions of the world may effect, this Book continues to hold its unchallenged place as the most loved, the most quoted and the most universally read and pondered of all the volumes which our libraries contain.

It has withstood assaults, it has resisted and survived the most searching microscopic examination, it has stood every test that could be applied to it and yet it continues to' hold its supreme place as the Book of books. There have been periods when it has suffered stern and searching criticism, but the hottest flame has not destroyed its prevailing and persistent power.

We cannot read the history of our rise and development as a Nation, without reckoning with the place the Bible has occupied in shaping the advances of the Republic. Its teaching, as has been wisely suggested, is ploughed into the very heart of the race.

Where we have been truest and most consistent in obeying its precepts we have attained the greatest measure of contentment and prosperity; where it has been to us as the words of a book that is sealed, we have faltered in our way, lost our range finders and found our progress checked.

It is well that we observe this anniversary of the first publishing of our English Bible. The time is propitious to place a fresh emphasis upon its place and worth in the economy of our life as a people.

As literature, as a book that contains a system of ethics, of moral and religious principles, it stands unique and alone. I commend its thoughtful and reverent reading to all our people. Its refining and elevating influence is indispensable to our most cherished hopes and ideals.

MESSAGE TO THE FIFTH ANNUAL WOMEN'S CONFERENCE OCTOBER 17, 1935

A FALLING STANDARD in the incomes of average Americans, the dragging of innocent children from homes into factories, the problems of delinquency that arise from social conditions, the destruction of workers' morale by unemployment, the effects of poverty and dependency in old age, widespread preventable diseases, unnecessary industrial warfare, and, most of all, that failure of reason which permits and wages modern war - all of these challenging factors in modern society throw upon the women of the Nation a material and spiritual burden of the greatest significance.

REMARKS AT THE CITADEL, CHARLESTON, SOUTH CAROLINA OCTOBER 23, 1935

I SHALL ALWAYS bear with me a very happy recollection...of my opportunity once more to see this historic city, to see those delightful and splendid old homes - homes that belong not just to you who are fortunate to live in Charleston, but homes and churches and public buildings that belong to all of us Americans, all of us who care for the great traditions of the United States.

GREETING TO CATHOLIC WAR VETERANS, REVEREND E. J. HIGGINS, NATIONAL CHAPLAIN, CATHOLIC WAR VETERANS, LONG ISLAND CITY, NEW YORK OCTOBER 30, 1935

THERE IS SOMETHING very heartening in the message of goodwill which you, as National Chaplain of the Catholic War Veterans, addressed to me in an open letter through the medium of Station WLWL. It comes to me as a voice of confidence and of hope for a better world.

As Commander-in-Chief, I welcome the pledge of fealty from a body of veterans who have served in their country's defense and who, knowing the ardors and the heartaches and the misery of war, dedicate themselves anew to the arts of peace; for peace, too, has its own victories no less valorous than those of war.

May I make humble acknowledgment of your generous sentiments concerning my leadership? Happily we are now emerging from the years of depression but I want you to understand how reassuring it is to receive a pledge of faith such as you convey in the name of the Catholic War Veterans.

Ours will be the victory if we set ourselves resolutely to the performance of those spiritual and corporal acts of mercy which have ever been the salvation of men and of Nations. With organizations like yours marshaled in a mighty crusade for peace, we may look forward to a time, let us hope, not far distant, when under the Providence of God, war shall be no more and peace shall be the heritage of men of good will.

ADDRESS AT ARLINGTON NATIONAL CEMETERY NOVEMBER 11, 1935

THE PAST AND the present unite in prayer that America will ever seek the ways of peace, and by her example at home and abroad speed the return of good-will among men.

THANKSGIVING DAY PROCLAMATION NOVEMBER 12, 1935

I, FRANKLIN D. ROOSEVELT, President of the United States of America, hereby designate Thursday, the twenty-eighth of November, 1935, as a Day of National Thanksgiving.

In traversing a period of national stress our country has been knit together in a closer fellowship of mutual interest and common purpose. We can well be grateful that more and more of our people understand and seek the greater good of the greater number.

We can be grateful that selfish purpose of personal gain, at our neighbor's loss, less strongly asserts itself. We can be grateful that peace at home is strengthened by a growing willingness to common counsel. We can be grateful that our peace with other Nations continues through recognition of our own peaceful purpose.

But in our appreciation of the blessings that Divine Providence has bestowed upon us in America, we shall not rejoice as the Pharisee rejoiced. War and strife still live in the world. Rather, must America by example and in practice help to bind the wounds of others, strive against disorder and aggression, encourage the lessening of distrust among peoples and advance peaceful trade and friendship.

The future of many generations of mankind will be greatly guided by our acts in these present years. We hew a new trail.

Let us then on the day appointed offer our devotions and our humble thanks to Almighty God and pray that the people of America will be guided by Him in helping their fellow men.

LETTER ON POLICY REGARDING RELIGIOUS ACTIVITIES IN MEXICO TO MR. MARTIN H. CARMODY, SUPREME KNIGHT, KNIGHTS OF COLUMBUS, NEW HAVEN, CONNECTICUT NOVEMBER 13, 1935

WITHOUT COMMENTING UPON the language of your communication under acknowledgment, and without reference to the accuracy of the statements or conclusions which you advance, I shall inform you once more of the attitude of this Administration in the matter of the policy pursued by the Government of Mexico toward religious activities in that Republic.

The right of United States citizens resident or traveling in foreign countries to worship freely, to conduct services within their houses, or within appropriate buildings maintained for that purpose, is desired by this Government. There has not been brought to this Government during the past year a single complaint by any United States citizen that such opportunities in Mexico have been refused them.

In respect to the rights enjoyed by Mexican citizens living in Mexico, it has been the policy of this Administration to refrain from intervening in such direct concerns of the Mexican Government. That policy of non-intervention I shall continue to pursue.

While this Government does not assume to undertake any accurate determination of what the facts in such domestic concerns of other Governments may be, this policy of non-intervention, however, can in no sense be construed as indifference on our part. I repeat what I stated publicly in San Diego, California, on October 2nd, last:

"Our national determination to keep free of foreign wars and foreign entanglements cannot prevent us from feeling deep concern when ideals and principles that we have cherished are challenged. In the United States we regard it as axiomatic that every person shall enjoy the free exercise of his religion according to the dictates of his conscience. Our flag for a century and a half has been the symbol of the principles of liberty of conscience, of religious freedom and equality before the law; and these concepts are deeply ingrained in our national character.

"It is true that other Nations may, as they do, enforce contrary rules of conscience and conduct. It is true that policies that may be pursued under flags other than our own are beyond our jurisdiction.

Yet in our inner individual lives we can never be indifferent, and we assert for ourselves complete freedom to embrace, to profess and to observe the principles for which our flag has so long been the lofty symbol. As it was so well said by James Madison, 'We hold it for a fundamental and inalienable truth that religion and the manner of discharging it can be directed only by reason and conviction, not by force or violence.'"

This statement, I now reiterate to you.

Inasmuch as you have referred in your letter under acknowledgment to the policy pursued in such matters as this by previous Administrations and have mentioned specifically the Administration of President Theodore Roosevelt, it may not be inappropriate to call to your attention the statement of former President Theodore Roosevelt contained in his Annual Message to the Congress of December 6, 1904:

"...Ordinarily it is very much wiser and more useful for us to concern ourselves with striving for our own moral and material betterment here at home than to concern ourselves with trying to better the conditions of things in other Nations.

We have plenty of sins of our own to war against, and under ordinary circumstances we can do more for the general uplifting of humanity by striving with heart and soul to put a stop to civic corruption, to brutal lawlessness and violent race prejudices here at home than by passing resolutions about wrongdoing elsewhere."

You and I abhor equally, I trust, religious intolerance, whether at home or abroad. For my own part, however, I decline to permit this Government to undertake a policy of interference in the domestic concerns of foreign

Governments and thereby jeopardize the maintenance of peaceful conditions.

ADDRESS ON RECEIVING AN HONORARY DEGREE FROM NOTRE DAME UNIVERSITY DECEMBER 9, 1935

THERE CAN BE no true national life either within a Nation itself, or between that Nation and other Nations, unless there be the specific acknowledgment of, and the support of organic law to, the rights of man. Supreme among those rights we, and now the Philippine Commonwealth, hold to be the rights of freedom of education and freedom of religious worship.

This university from which we send our welcome to the new Commonwealth exemplifies the principles of which I speak.

Through the history of this great Middle West - its first explorers and first missionaries - Joliet, Marquette, La Salle, Hennepin - its lone eagle, Father Badin, who is buried here - its apostolic Father Sorin, founder of the University of Notre Dame - its zealous missionaries of other faiths - its pioneers of varied nationalities - all have contributed to the upbuilding of our country because all have subscribed to those fundamental principles of freedom - freedom of education, freedom of worship.

Long ago, George Mason, in the Virginia Declaration of Rights, voiced what has become one of the deepest convictions of the American people:

"Religion, or the duty which we owe to our Creator, and the manner of discharging it, can be directed only by reason and conviction, not by force or violence; and therefore all men are equally entitled to the free exercise of religion according to the dictates of conscience."...

Of their own initiative, by their own appreciation, the people of the Philippine Commonwealth have now also championed them before all the world.

Through the favor of Divine Providence may they be blessed as a people with prosperity. May they grow in grace through their own Constitution to the peace and well-being of the whole world.

Let me say, as I leave you, that I am happy to be here today, that I am proud of the great distinction which you have conferred upon me, that I was more touched than anything else by the little word of the President of Notre Dame when he said that I will be in your prayers. I appreciate that. I trust that I may be in your prayers.

ADDRESS ON RECEIVING THE 1935 AWARD FOR DISTINGUISHED SERVICE TO AGRICULTURE, CHICAGO, ILLINOIS DECEMBER 9, 1935

THE MEASURE TO which we turned to stop the decline and rout of American agriculture originated in the aspirations of the farmers themselves, expressed through the several farm organizations...

We sought to stop the rule of tooth and claw that threw farmers into bankruptcy or turned them virtually into serfs, forced them to let their buildings, fences and machinery deteriorate, made them rob their soil of its God-given fertility, deprived their sons and daughters of a decent opportunity on the farm.

To those days, I trust, the organized power of the Nation has put an end forever...

The thing that we are all seeking is justice - justice in the common - sense interpretation of that word - the interpretation that means "Do unto your neighbors as you would be done by." That interpretation means justice against exploitation on the part of those who do not care much for the lives, the happiness and the prosperity of their neighbors...

In these present days we have seen and are seeing, not a re-birth of material prosperity alone; of greater significance to our national future is that spiritual reawakening, that deeper thinking and understanding that has come to our land...

We strive for the United States of America, and if we shall succeed, as by God's help we will, America will point the way toward a better world.

CHRISTMAS GREETING TO THE NATION DECEMBER 24, 1935

ONCE MORE THE most joyous of all days draws near and again it is my great privilege on this blessed Eve of the Nativity to wish the American people everywhere a Merry Christmas.

This is the third time that I have joined in these Christmas Eve festivities. We are gathered together in a typical American setting in the park here in front of the White House. Before me and around me is an American assemblage - men and women of all ages, youths and maidens, young children who know nothing about the cares of life - all jubilant with joyous expectation.

The night is falling and the spirit of other days, too, broods over the scene. Andrew Jackson looks down upon us from his prancing steed; and the four corners of the square in which we are gathered around a gaily lit Christmas tree are guarded by the figures of intrepid leaders in the Revolutionary War -Von Steuben, the German; Kosciusko, the Pole; and Lafayette and Rochambeau from the shores of France.

This is in keeping with the universal spirit of the festival we are celebrating; for we who stand here among our guardians out of the past and from far shores are, I suppose, as diverse in blood and origin as are the uncounted millions throughout the land to whom these words go out tonight.

But around the Manger of the Babe of Bethlehem "all Nations and kindreds and tongues" find unity. For the spirit of Christmas knows no race, no creed, no clime, no limitation of time or space.

The spirit of Christmas breathes an eternal message of peace and good-will to all men.

We pause therefore on this Holy Night and, laying down the burdens and the cares of life and casting aside the anxieties of the common day, rejoice that nineteen hundred years ago, heralded by angels, there came into the world One whose message was of peace, who gave to all mankind a new commandment of love.

In that message of love and of peace we find the true meaning of Christmas.

And so I greet you with the greeting of the Angels on that first Christmas at Bethlehem which, resounding through centuries, still rings out with its eternal message: "Glory to God in the highest, and on earth peace, good-will to men."

ANNUAL MESSAGE TO CONGRESS
JANUARY 3, 1936

WE HAVE SOUGHT by every legitimate means to exert our moral influence against repression, against intolerance, against autocracy and in favor of freedom of expression, equality before the law, religious tolerance and popular rule...

The principle that they would instill into government if they succeed in seizing power is well shown by the principles which many of them have instilled into their own affairs..."By their fruits ye shall know them."...

I cannot better end this message on the state of the Union than by repeating the words of a wise philosopher at whose feet I sat many, many years ago.

"Fear not, view all the tasks of life as sacred, have faith in the triumph of the ideal, give daily all that you have to give, be loyal and rejoice whenever you find yourselves part of a great ideal enterprise. You, at this moment, have the honor to belong to a generation whose lips are touched by fire. You live in a land that now enjoys the blessings of peace...The human race now passes through one of its great crises...a new call for men to carry on the work of righteousness, of charity, of courage, of patience, and of loyalty."

ANDREW JACKSON DAY DINNER ADDRESS, WASHINGTON, D.C. JANUARY 8, 1936

NO PARTY OF reaction, no candidates of reaction can fulfill the hope and the faith of that everlasting spirit. It is the sacred duty of us who are vested with the responsibility of leadership to justify the expectations of the young men and women of the United States...

May a double portion of Old Hickory's heroic spirit be upon us tonight. May we be inspired by the power and the glory and the justice of his rugged and fearless life.

LETTER OF APPRECIATION TO LOUIS STANCOURT, ESQ., LONG ISLAND, NEW YORK FEBRUARY 8, 1936

IT IS MOST of all because you give me the blessings of the unknown men whose voices seem never to be heard, because you rightly believe that I do try, as best I may, to understand the human and the spiritual problems of the millions in our great land who are loyal to our common ideals and who want to hold their heads high.

RADIO ADDRESS ON BROTHERHOOD DAY
FEBRUARY 23, 1936

I AM MOST happy to speak to you from my own home on the evening of a Sabbath Day which has been observed in so many of your home communities as Brotherhood Day.

The National Conference of Jews and Christians has set aside a day on which we can meet, not primarily as Protestants or Catholics or Jews but as believing Americans; a day on which we can dedicate ourselves not to the things which divide but to the things which unite us. I hope that we have begun to see how many and how important are the things on which we are united. Now, of all times, we require that kind of thinking.

There are honest differences of religious belief among the citizens of your town as there are among the citizens of mine. It is a part of the spirit of Brotherhood Day, as it is a part of our American heritage, to respect those differences. And it is well for us to remember that this America of ours is the product of no single race or creed or class.

Men and women - your fathers and mine - came here from the far corners of the earth with beliefs that widely varied. And yet each, in his own way, laid his own special gift upon our national altar to enrich our national life. From the gift that each has given, all have gained.

This is no time to make capital out of religious disagreement, however honest. It is a time, rather, to make capital out of religious understanding. We who have faith cannot afford to fall out among ourselves.

The very state of the world is a summons to us to stand together. For as I see it, the chief religious issue is not between our various beliefs. It is between belief and unbelief. It is not your specific faith or mine that is being called into question - but all faith.

Religion in wide areas of the earth is being confronted with irreligion; our faiths are being challenged. It is because of that threat that you and I must reach across the lines between our creeds, clasp hands, and make common cause.

To do that will do credit to the best of our religious tradition. It will do credit, also, to the best in our American tradition. The spiritual resources of our forbears have brought us a long way toward the goal which was set before the Nation at its founding as a Nation.

Yet I do not look upon these United States as a finished product. We are still in the making. The vision of the early days still requires the same qualities of faith in God and man for its fulfillment.

No greater thing could come to our land today than a revival of the spirit of religion - a revival that would sweep through the homes of the Nation and stir the hearts of men and women of all faiths to a reassertion of their belief in God and their dedication to His will for themselves and for their world. I doubt if there is any problem - social, political or economic - that would not melt away before the fire of such a spiritual awakening.

I know of no better way to kindle such a fire than through the fellowship that an occasion like this makes possible. For Brotherhood Day, after all, is an experiment in understanding; a venture in neighborliness.

I like to think of our country as one home in which the interests of each member are bound up with the happiness of all. We ought to know, by now, that the welfare of your family or mine cannot be bought at the sacrifice of our neighbor's family; that our well-being depends, in the long run, upon the wellbeing of our neighbors.

The good neighbor idea - as we are trying to practice it in international relationships - needs to be put into practice in our community relationships. When it is we may discover that the road to understanding and fellowship is also the road to spiritual awakening. At our neighbor's fireside we may find new fuel for the fires of faith at our own hearthsides.

It would be a fitting thing for an organization such as the National Conference of Jews and Christians to undertake this kind of project in neighborliness. I should like to see Associations of Good Neighbors in every town and city and in every rural community of our land. Such associations of sincere citizens like-minded as to the underlying principles and ideals would reach across the lines of creed or of economic status.

It would bring together men and women of all stations to share their problems and their hopes and to discover ways of mutual and neighborly helpfulness. Here perhaps is a way to pool our spiritual resources; to find common ground on which all of us of all faiths can stand; and thence to move forward as men and women concerned for the things of the spirit.

ADDRESS AT ROLLINS COLLEGE, FLORIDA, ON RECEIVING AN HONORARY DEGREE MARCH 23, 1936

IF WE ANALYZE what a group is, we find that the family group is the oldest, the smallest, and yet through all the years of change the most important. And there are other groups to which almost every man and woman is tied, connected in some way. They are connected with some form of association - the church, the social circle, the club, the lodge, the labor organization, the neighboring farmers, the political party.

ADDRESS TO THE YOUNG DEMOCRATIC CLUB, BALTIMORE, MARYLAND APRIL 13, 1936

YOUR OBJECTIVE, I take it, in the widest sense is this: an opportunity to make an honest living; a reasonable chance to improve your condition in life as you grow older; a practical assurance against want and suffering in your old age; and with it all the right to participate in the finer things of life - good health, clean amusement, and your share in the satisfactions of the arts, the sciences and religion...

Our country richly endowed today in body, mind and spirit, still has need of many things. But I am certain that one of its chief needs today is the releasing and the enlistment of the spirit of youth.

Do not underestimate the significance of that spirit. Yesterday Christendom celebrated Easter - the anniversary of the Resurrection of Our Lord who, at the beginning of His ministry was thirty years of age and at His death was only thirty-three. Christianity began with youth and, through the last two thousand years, the spirit of youth repeatedly has revitalized it.

Our war for independence was a young man's crusade. Age was on the side of the Tories and the Tories were on the side of the old order. At the Revolution's outbreak George Washington was forty-three, Patrick Henry thirty-eight, Thomas Jefferson whose birthday we are celebrating today was thirty-two and Alexander Hamilton was eighteen.

Our Constitution, likewise, was the creation of young minds. The average age of the men who wrote the Constitution was about forty-four. The qualities of youth are not of a sort that self-satisfied people welcome in 1936 any more than self-satisfied people welcomed them in 1776.

I have used the words "the qualities of youth." Be wise enough, be tolerant enough, you who are young in years, to remember that millions of older people have kept and propose to keep these qualities of youth.

You ought to thank God tonight if, regardless of your years, you are young enough in spirit to dream dreams and see visions - dreams and visions about a greater and finer America that is to be; if you are young enough in spirit to believe that poverty can be greatly lessened; that the disgrace of involuntary unemployment can be wiped out; that class hatreds can be done away with; that peace at home and peace abroad can be maintained; and that one day a generation may possesses this land, blessed beyond anything we now know, blessed with those things - material and spiritual - that make man's life abundant.

If that is the fashion of your dreaming then I say: "Hold fast to your dream. America needs it."

ADDRESS AT THE DEDICATION OF THE NEW DEPARTMENT OF INTERIOR BUILDING, WASHINGTON, D.C. APRIL 16, 1936

SUPPORTED BY AN awakened country, which by now is beginning to realize the truth of the old warnings, we in these later days have devoted our thoughts and energies to the conservation of that God-given wealth. Employing every agency of Government to protect our birthright we have in the past several years made advances far beyond the hopes of earlier-day conservationists.

LETTER OF GREETING ON THE CENTENARY OF THE DEATH OF JAMES MADISON MAY 8, 1936

WE SHOULD NOT overlook, on an occasion like this, certain of Madison's characteristics which are peculiarly American, and particularly his lifelong interest in the education of youth, his consistent defense of civil liberty, and his advocacy of religious tolerance and freedom...

It seems to me particularly fitting that one hundred years after his death we should recall the following words, which show his attachment to the Union and his fervent belief that the people of the United States constitute a Nation with common interests and a common purpose:

"May it not be regarded as among the Providential blessings to these States, that their geographical relations, multiplied as they will be by artificial channels of intercourse, give such additional force to the many obligations to cherish that union which alone secures their peace, their safety, and their prosperity?"

LETTER OF GREETING TO RIGHT REVEREND MONSIGNOR ROBERT FULTON KEEGAN, PRESIDENT, NATIONAL CONFERENCE OF SOCIAL WORK, ATLANTIC CITY, NEW JERSEY MAY 23, 1936

IT IS WITH sincere regret that I find myself unable to be at the 1936 meeting of the National Conference of

Social Work. I have great concern for the work of social welfare agencies and the efforts of social workers to make this country a more neighborly place in which to live. Cognizant, therefore, of the value of your deliberations and proceedings, I assure you of my deep interest in the high purposes for which you are convened.

The National Conference of Social Work is indeed an expression of the social conscience of America. Its members have consecrated their lives to the bringing about of a better social order wherein men and women shall have greater opportunity to enjoy the blessings of life. Many of us are accustomed to appealing for the cause of humanity.

Let us remember that humanity is not society; humanity is just plain folks. Some of our so-called leaders have made the mistake of looking upon men and women as economic and social units. Logically, therefore, they speak of men and women as individuals, just as they would of other things - of animals or plants or atoms.

In matters of social welfare we should keep sight of the fact that we are not dealing with "units," "individuals" or with "economic men." We are dealing with persons. Human personality is something sacred. It enjoys the light of reason and liberty. It grows by rising above material things and wedding itself to spiritual ideals.

Our social order is worthy of human beings only in so far as it recognizes the inherent value of human personality. Our cities, our States and our Nations exist not for themselves but for men and women. We cannot be satisfied with any form of society in which human personality is submerged.

To you as President of the Conference and to all who participate I send my deepest and most heartfelt congratulations.

REMARKS IN ROCKPORT, ARKANSAS
JUNE 10, 1936

I AM VERY happy to have come here to take part in this religious service. It means a great deal to me.

This particular spot has seen much history. It has seen many famous men pass through here on their way west. It has seen Americans through many generations, but remember that in all those days, and in this one, religion has taken part in everything that has occurred.

I always remember that in the earliest days of the white settlement of North America, in the days of the landing at Plymouth, the colonization of Jamestown and the founding of New Amsterdam, the first thing that the earliest colonists did when they set foot on shore was to hold a religious service.

It seemed to be in our American blood. And so, as the Nation developed and as men moved across the Alleghenies and across the Mississippi, religion went hand in hand with them.

I am glad to think that in these more recent days the spiritual qualities of the American people are keeping pace with the progress of the more material civilization. And that is why, you good people who live in this section of Arkansas, I ask you always to keep that spiritual faith and to remember the early days when your ancestors brought religion across the Mississippi.

REMARKS AT THE UNVEILING OF THE ROBERT E. LEE MEMORIAL STATUE, DALLAS, TEXAS
JUNE 12, 1936

I AM VERY happy to take part in this unveiling of the statue of General Robert E. Lee.

All over the United States we recognize him as a great leader of men, as a great general. But, also, all over the United States I believe that we recognize him as something much more important than that. We recognize Robert E. Lee as one of our greatest American Christians and one of our greatest American gentlemen.

ADDRESS AT GEORGE ROGERS CLARK MEMORIAL, VINCENNES, INDIANA, GREETING GOVERNOR MCNUTT AND GOVERNOR HORNER JUNE 14, 1936

EVENTS OF HISTORY take on their due proportions only when viewed in the light of time. With every passing year the capture of Vincennes, more than a century and a half ago when the Thirteen Colonies were seeking their independence, assumes greater and more permanent significance.

I come, as you know, from the Valley of the Hudson; and the first grave danger, as the War of the Revolution progressed, lay in the effort of the British, with their Indian allies, to drive a wedge from Canada through the Valley of Lake Champlain and the Valley of the Mohawk, to meet the British frigates from the City of New York at the head of navigation on the Hudson River. If this important offensive in the year 1777 had been successful,

New England would have been cut off from the States lying south of New York, and by holding the line of the Hudson River the British, without much doubt, could have conquered first one half and then the other half of the divided Colonies. That was our first great crisis.

The defeat and surrender of General Burgoyne at Saratoga became recognized as the definite turning point of the military operations of the Revolution.

But there was another great danger. Danger lay thereafter not in the immediate defeat of the Colonies, but rather in their inability to maintain themselves and grow after their independence had been won. The records of history show that the British planned a definite hemming-in process, whereby the new Nation would be strictly limited in area and in activity to the territory lying south of Canada and east of the Allegheny Mountains.

Toward this end they conducted military operations on an important scale west of the Alleghenies, with the purpose, which was at first successful, of driving back eastward across the mountains all those Americans who, before the Revolution, had crossed into what is now Ohio and Michigan and Indiana and Illinois and Kentucky and Tennessee.

In that year, 1778, the picture of this Western country was dark indeed. The English held all the region northwest of the Ohio, and their Indian allies were burning cabins and driving fleeing families back across the mountains south of the river. Indeed there were only three forts that remained in all of Kentucky, and their fall seemed inevitable.

In that moment, against the dark background, rose the young Virginian, George Rogers Clark. Out of despair and destruction he brought concerted action. With a flash of genius, the twenty-six-year-old leader conceived a campaign - a brilliant masterpiece of military strategy. Working with the good-will of the French settlers through these States, and overawing the Indians by what perhaps we can call sheer bravado, he swept through to Kaskaskia and other towns of the Illinois country.

But the menace of the regular British forces remained. Colonel Henry Hamilton, the British Commander of the Northwest, had come down from Detroit.

He seized and fortified Vincennes. Fort Sackville, where we stand today, as long as it remained uncaptured, made Clark's position untenable. His desperate resolution to save his men and the Northwest by a mid-winter march and an attack by riflemen on a fort manned by the King's own regiment and equipped with cannon marked the heroic measure of the man.

It is worth repeating the story that the famous winter march began at Kaskaskia with a religious service. To Father Pierre Gibault, and to Colonel Francis Vigo, a patriot of Italian birth, next to Clark himself, the United States is indebted for the saving of the Northwest Territory. And it was in the little log church, predecessor of yonder Church of Saint Francis Xavier, that Colonel Hamilton surrendered Vincennes to George Rogers Clark.

It is not a coincidence that this service in dedication of a noble monument takes place on a Sunday morning. Governor McNutt and I, aware of the historic relationship of religion to this campaign of the Revolution, and to the later Ordinance of 1787, have understood and felt the appropriateness of today.

Clark had declared at Kaskaskia before he began his famous march, that all religions would be tolerated in America. Eight years later the Ordinance of 1787, which established the territory northwest of the Ohio River, provided that "no person demeaning himself in a peaceable and orderly manner shall ever be molested on account of his mode of worship or for religious sentiments in the said territory."

And the Ordinance went on to declare further that "religion, morality and knowledge being necessary to good government and the happiness of mankind, schools and the means of education shall forever be encouraged."

It seems to me that one hundred and forty-nine years later the people of the United States, in every part thereof, could reiterate and continue to strive for the principle that religion, morality and knowledge are necessary to good government and the happiness of mankind.

Today religion is still free within our borders; it must ever remain so.

Today morality means the same thing as it meant in the days of George Rogers Clark, though we must needs apply it to many, many situations of which George Rogers Clark never dreamt. In his day among the pioneers there were jumpers of land claims; there were those who sought to swindle their neighbors, even though they were all poor in this world's goods and lived in sparsely settled communities.

Today among our teeming millions there are still those who by dishonorable means seek to obtain the possessions of their unwary neighbors.

Our modern civilization must constantly protect itself against moral defectives whose objectives are the same, but whose methods are more subtle than those of their prototypes of a century and a half ago. We do not change our form of free government when we arm ourselves with new weapons against new devices of crime and cupidity.

Today, as in 1787, we have knowledge; but it is a vastly wider knowledge...

George Rogers Clark did battle against the tomahawk and the rifle. He saved for us the fair land that lay between the mountains and the Father of Waters. His task is not done. Though we fight with weapons unknown to him, it is still our duty to continue the saving of this fair land.

May the Americans who, a century and a half from now, celebrate at this spot the three hundredth anniversary of the heroism of Clark and his men, think kindly of us for the part we are taking today in preserving the Nation of the United States.

ACCEPTANCE SPEECH FOR THE RENOMINATION FOR THE PRESIDENCY, PHILADELPHIA, PENNSYLVANIA JUNE 27, 1936

PHILADELPHIA IS A good city in which to write American history. This is fitting ground on which to reaffirm the faith of our fathers; to pledge ourselves to restore to the people a wider freedom; to give to 1936 as the founders gave to 1776 - an American way of life.

That very word freedom, in itself and of necessity, suggests freedom from some restraining power. In 1776 we sought freedom from the tyranny of a political autocracy - from the eighteenth century royalists who held special privileges from the crown.

It was to perpetuate their privilege that they governed without the consent of the governed; that they denied the right of free assembly and free speech; that they restricted the worship of God; that they put the average man's property and the average man's life in pawn to the mercenaries of dynastic power; that they regimented the people...

For too many of us the political equality we once had won was meaningless in the face of economic inequality. A small group had concentrated into their own hands an almost complete control over other people's property, other people's money, other people's labor - other people's lives. For too many of us life was no longer free; liberty no longer real; men could no longer follow the pursuit of happiness...

The defeats and victories of these years have given to us as a people a new understanding of our Government and of ourselves. Never since the early days of the New England town meeting have the affairs of Government been so widely discussed and so clearly appreciated. It has been brought home to us that the only effective guide for the safety of this most worldly of worlds, the greatest guide of all, is moral principle.

We do not see faith, hope and charity as unattainable ideals, but we use them as stout supports of a Nation fighting the fight for freedom in a modern civilization.

Faith - in the soundness of democracy in the midst of dictatorships.

Hope - renewed because we know so well the progress we have made.

Charity - in the true spirit of that grand old word. For charity literally translated from the original means love, the love that understands, that does not merely share the wealth of the giver, but in true sympathy and wisdom helps men to help themselves.

We seek not merely to make Government a mechanical implement, but to give it the vibrant personal character that is the very embodiment of human charity.

We are poor indeed if this Nation cannot afford to lift from every recess of American life the dread fear of the unemployed that they are not needed in the world. We cannot afford to accumulate a deficit in the books of human fortitude.

In the place of the palace of privilege we seek to build a temple out of faith and hope and charity.

It is a sobering thing, my friends, to be a servant of this great cause. We try in our daily work to remember that the cause belongs not to us, but to the people. The standard is not in the hands of you and me alone. It is carried by America. We seek daily to profit from experience, to learn to do better as our task proceeds.

Governments can err, Presidents do make mistakes, but the immortal Dante tells us that divine justice weighs the sins of the cold-blooded and the sins of the warm-hearted in different scales.

Better the occasional faults of a Government that lives in a spirit of charity than the consistent omissions of a Government frozen in the ice of its own indifference.

There is a mysterious cycle in human events. To some generations much is given. Of other generations much is expected. This generation of Americans has a rendezvous with destiny.

In this world of ours in other lands, there are some people, who, in times past, have lived and fought for freedom, and seem to have grown too weary to carry on the fight. They have sold their heritage of freedom for the illusion of a living. They have yielded their democracy.

I believe in my heart that only our success can stir their ancient hope. They begin to know that here in America we are waging a great and successful war. It is not alone a war against want and destitution and economic demoralization. It is more than that; it is a war for the survival of democracy. We are fighting to save a great and precious form of government for ourselves and for the world.

ADDRESS AT THE HOME OF THOMAS JEFFERSON, MONTICELLO, VIRGINIA JULY 4, 1936

IT WAS SYMBOLIC that Thomas Jefferson should live on this mountain-top of Monticello. On a mountain-top all paths unite. And Jefferson was the meeting point of all the vital forces of his day.

There are periods in history when one man seems great because those who stand beside him are small. Jefferson was great in the presence of many great and free men.

When we read of the patriots of 1776 and the fathers of the Constitution, we are taken into the presence of men who caught the fire of greatness from one another, and who all became elevated above the common run of mankind.

The source of their greatness was the stirring of a new sense of freedom. They were tasting the first fruits of self-government and freedom of conscience. They had broken away from a system of peasantry, away from indentured servitude.

They could build for themselves a new economic independence. Theirs were not the gods of things as they were, but the gods of things as they ought to be. And so, as Monticello itself so well proves, they used new means and new models to build new structures.

Of all the builders of those days it is perhaps generally conceded that Benjamin Franklin and Thomas Jefferson possessed what may be roughly described as the most fertile minds. Franklin was stranger to no science, to no theory of philosophy, to no avenue of invention. Jefferson had those qualities in equal part; and with greater opportunity in the days of peace which followed the

Revolution, Jefferson was enabled more fully to carry theory into practice.

Farmer, lawyer, mechanic, scientist, architect, philosopher, statesman, he encompassed the full scope of the knowledge of his time; and his life was one of the richest diversity. To him knowledge and ideal were fuel to be used to feed the fires of his own mind, not just wood to be left neatly piled in the woodbox.

More than any historic home in America, Monticello appeals to me as an expression of the personality of its builder. In the design, not of the whole alone, but of every room, of every part of every room, in the very furnishings which Jefferson devised on his own drawing board and made in his own workshop, there speaks ready capacity for detail and, above all, creative genius.

He was a great gentleman. He was a great commoner. The two are not incompatible.

He applied the culture of the past to the needs and the life of the America of his day. His knowledge of history spurred him to inquire into the reason and justice of laws, habits and institutions. His passion for liberty led him to interpret and adapt them in order to better the lot of mankind.

Shortly before taking the office of President he wrote to a friend, "I have sworn on the Altar of God eternal hostility against every form of tyranny over the mind of man." His life served that consecration. Constantly he labored to enlarge the freedom of the human mind and to destroy the bondage imposed on it by ignorance, poverty and political and religious intolerance.

On one day of his long life he gave to the world a Declaration of Independence on behalf of political freedom for himself and his fellow Americans. But his Declaration of Independence for the human mind was a continuing achievement, renewed and reiterated every day of his whole life.

One hundred and sixty years have passed since the Fourth of July, 1776. On that day, Thomas Jefferson was thirty-three years old. His imagination, his enthusiasm and his energy, the qualities that youth offers in every generation, were symbolic of that generation of men, who not only made a Nation in the wealth of their imagination and energy, but, because their youthful wings had not been clipped, were able to grow with the Nation and guide it in wisdom throughout their lives.

Through all the intervening years, America has lived and grown under the system of government established by Jefferson and his generation. As Nations go, we live under one of the oldest continuous forms of democratic government in the whole world. In that sense we are old.

But the world has never had as much human ability as it needs; and a modern democracy in particular needs, above all things, the continuance of the spirit of youth. Our problems of 1936 call as greatly for the continuation of imagination and energy and capacity for responsibility as did the age of Thomas Jefferson and his fellows.

Democracy needs now, as it found then, men developed, through education, to the limit of their capacity for ultimate responsibility. Emergencies and decisions in our individual and community and national lives are the stuff out of which national character is made. Preparation of the mind, preparation of the spirit of our people for such emergencies, for such decisions, is the best available insurance for the security and development of our democratic institutions.

Was the spirit of such men as Jefferson the spirit of a Golden Age gone now, and never to be repeated in our history? Was the feeling of fundamental freedom which lighted the fire of their ability a miracle we shall never see again?

That is not my belief. It is not beyond our power to re-light that sacred fire. There are no limitations upon the Nation's capacity to obtain and maintain true freedom, no limitations except the strength of our Nation's desire and determination.

On the hillside below where we stand is the tomb of Thomas Jefferson. He was given many high offices in State and Nation. But the words recorded above his grave, chosen by himself, are only these:

"HERE WAS BURIED THOMAS JEFFERSON, AUTHOR OF THE DECLARATION OF AMERICAN INDEPENDENCE, OF THE STATUTE OF VIRGINIA FOR RELIGIOUS FREEDOM, AND FATHER OF THE UNIVERSITY OF VIRGINIA."

The honors which other men had given him were unimportant; the opportunities he had given to other men to become free were all that really counted.

REMARKS AT THE ROOSEVELT HOME CLUB CELEBRATION, HYDE PARK, NEW YORK JULY 11, 1936

I RECEIVED IN Washington a letter from a small town in the Middle West. There were four hundred voters in the town. The letter was signed by three hundred and ninety of them...The three hundred and ninety signatures expressed the idea to me that the finest thing that has happened to their town was the building of a new schoolhouse.

To them that schoolhouse had been the great need of that town, and it was the one thing that they and their wives and children wanted. They had not been able to raise the money to build it out there. Nobody would take their bond;

no bank would lend it to them except, perhaps, at a very high rate of interest. It was an honest, God-fearing community...

The result was that the Federal Government made them the loan, and gave them a portion of the cost of the building in what we call "work relief." The building was built and the town feels just as proud of that little schoolhouse as the seven million people who live in New York City feel about their Triborough Bridge...

And so, as Mr. Wilson has so well put it in the prayer, I cannot help feeling that the undertaking heart goes with equal strength and equal importance with the understanding of the problem itself.

REMARKS AT THE GREAT LAKES EXPOSITION, CLEVELAND, OHIO AUGUST 14, 1936

I HAVE BEEN especially desirous of seeing the work that was caused, not by a depression, not by man, but by what we used to call in the old days "an act of God." That is why I have been visiting some of the flood areas in the East and shall visit more. That is why I am going out to the great drought area of the West...

ADDRESS AT CHAUTAUQUA, NEW YORK AUGUST 14, 1936

BUT ALL THE wisdom of America is not to be found in the White House or in the Department of State; we need the meditation, the prayer, and the positive support of the people of America who go along with us in seeking peace.

GREETING TO THE Y.M.C.A. SENT TO MR. C. R. MEASE, CHAIRMAN, FOUNDER'S DAY COMMITTEE, NEWARK, NEW JERSEY
AUGUST 19, 1936

AS AN EXPRESSION of man's highest aspirations, religion has been universal among people throughout all history. Worship has played a fundamental role in all social evolution.

Growing out of the work of the churches and enlarging the field of church activity, the Young Men's Christian Association developed as an institution where emphasis was placed essentially upon Christianity in action rather than upon Christian beliefs and Christian modes of thought. Young men found in it a place where they could carry out their Christian impulses.

It is difficult to imagine what a difference it would have made if no organization such as the Y.M.C.A. had been developed in this country. Down through the decades the Y.M.C.A. has grown strong. It has adjusted itself to the changing needs of the times. During this recent depression it has done valiant service in providing programs of guidance, education, and recreation for the millions of unemployed young men who have stood in great need of such programs.

I am glad to join with the many friends of the Y.M.C.A. in paying tribute to Sir George Williams, the founder of this great organization. His life should be an inspiration to the boys and young men who find in the Y.M.C.A. the preparation for the social leadership which they are to assume in the future.

FIRESIDE CHAT
SEPTEMBER 6, 1936

IN A PHYSICAL and a property sense, as well as in a spiritual sense, we are members one of another.

ADDRESS AT THE GREEN PASTURES RALLY,
CHARLOTTE, NORTH CAROLINA
SEPTEMBER 10, 1936

GREEN PASTURES! WHAT a memory those words call forth! In all our schooling, in every part of the land, no matter to what church we happen to belong, the old Twenty-third Psalm is in all probability better known to men, women and children than any other poem in the English language.

And in this great lyric, what do we best remember? Two lines:

"He maketh me to lie down in green pastures; He leadeth me beside the still waters."

It does not greatly matter whether that symbol of an ideal of human physical and spiritual happiness was written in its original three thousand or five thousand or ten thousand years ago. It might have been written as well in the twentieth century of the Christian era...

The ancient psalmist did not use the parable of the merchants' camel train or the royal palace or the crowded bazaar of the East. He had, in his day, as we have today, the problems of competing trade and social crowding; and I venture to suggest that long before the Christian era, the ancient civilizations of the East were confronted with problems of social economics which, though small in point of human numbers and small in point of worldly goods, were still, by comparison, as potent in their effect and as difficult in their solution as the extraordinarily similar problems of social economics that face us in this country today.

Be it remembered then, that those kings and prophets reverted, just as we do today, to the good earth and the still waters when they idealized security of the body and mind...

Green pastures! Millions of our fellow Americans, with whom I have been associating in the past two weeks, out on the Great Plains of America, live with prayers and hopes for the fulfillment of what those words imply.

Still waters! Millions of other Americans, with whom I also have been associated of late, live with prayers and hopes either that the floods may be stilled-floods that bring with them destruction and disaster to fields and flocks, to homesteads and cities - or else they look for the Heaven-sent rains that will fill their wells, their ponds and their peaceful streams...

So much for the green pastures and the still waters in their more literal physical terms. Those ancient words apply, however, with equal force to men and women and children. Your life and mine, though we work in the mill or in the office or in the store, can still be a life in green pastures and beside still waters...

I trust, therefore, that you will likewise agree that better conditions on the farms, better conditions in the factories, better conditions in the homes of America are leading us to that beautiful spiritual figure of the old psalmist - green pastures and still waters.

GREETING ON 74TH ANNIVERSARY OF EMANCIPATION PROCLAMATION, RIGHT REV.

WRIGHT, JR., BISHOP, AFRICAN METHODIST EPISCOPAL CHURCH, NEW YORK CITY SEPTEMBER 16, 1936

I APPRECIATED THE opportunity of extending greetings to all those who are planning to participate in the celebration of the Seventy-fourth Anniversary of the issuance of the Preliminary Proclamation of Emancipation by President Lincoln.

It is an occasion for recalling the great progress which Negroes have made as citizens of our Republic. It also is an occasion for remembering that in the truest sense freedom cannot be bestowed, it must be achieved; and that there must be constant vigilance if it is to be maintained.

The record which our Negro citizens have made in their own personal and racial development and their contribution to the material advancement of our country and to the promotion of its ideals are well known.

I heartily congratulate them on their record, and hope that in the future, as in the past, they will continue to show intelligence, industry and fortitude in striving for the best our Democracy offers.

ADDRESS AT THE HARVARD UNIVERSITY TERCENTENARY CELEBRATION, GREETING PRESIDENT CONANT SEPTEMBER 18, 1936

IN THE WORDS of Euripides: "There be many shapes of mystery. And many things God makes to be, Past hope or fear. And the end men looked for cometh not, And a path is there where no man sought. So hath it fallen here."...

WELCOME TO CONFERENCE ON THE PERU-ECUADOR BOUNDARY DISPUTE
SEPTEMBER 30, 1936

YOU ARE DOUBLY welcome to the United States and to this capital. You are very welcome because of your high purposes and you are equally welcome as distinguished representatives of our two sister Republics. I wish you Godspeed in your mission of peace.

ADDRESS AT ST. PAUL, MINNESOTA, GREETING SEN. SHIPSTEAD AND CHIEF JUSTICE DEVANEY
OCTOBER 9, 1936

PEACE DEPENDS UPON the acceptance of the principle and practice of the good neighbor. That practice is founded on the Golden Rule, and must be fortified by cooperation of every kind between Nations...

Confident in the practical wisdom of the ends we seek, with full faith that it will serve in a practical way for peace on earth and good-will between men and Nations, we shall continue on our way.

ADDRESS AT OMAHA, NEBRASKA
OCTOBER 10, 1936

WE KNEW THAT our soil had been recklessly impoverished by crops which did not pay. Because we stand committed to a philosophy of continuous plenty, we have set ourselves resolutely against waste - waste that comes from unneeded production, waste that imperils the Nation's future by draining away the abundance with which God has enriched our soil...

In all our plans we are guided, and will continue to be guided, by the fundamental belief that the American farmer, living on his own land, remains our ideal of self-reliance and of spiritual balance - the source from which the reservoirs of the Nation's strength are constantly renewed.

ADDRESS AT WICHITA, KANSAS
OCTOBER 13, 1936

WHAT THAT ADMINISTRATION has done since 1933 to clear up the debris which had been left over by twelve years of neglect need not be repeated; you all know it.

You know what the "devil-take-the-hindmost" policy of the nineteen-twenties brought down upon our heads. You know that the vast speculative gains of a few were made without any regard to the deep injuries which they were causing to the great masses of our people...

Add to that one more objective: that all Americans may have full opportunity for education, for reasonable leisure and recreation, for the right to carry on representative Government and for freedom to worship God in their own way...

In the whole of the Western Hemisphere, all the way from the North Pole to the South Pole, we have preached, and we have gained recognition of, the doctrine of the good neighbor.

We have extended the right hand of fellowship. Many Nations of the earth have taken that outstretched hand. We propose, of course, no interference with the affairs of other Nations. We seek only by force of our own example to spread the gospel of peace throughout the world.

ADDRESS AT KANSAS CITY, MISSOURI
OCTOBER 13, 1936

AS WE TAKE STOCK, we recognize that the most priceless of our human assets are the young men and women of America - the raw material out of which the United States must shape its future. Nature's deepest instinct is the concern in every parent's heart for the welfare of the children.

It is a law of nature which equals even the instinct for the preservation of life itself. Indeed it is part of that law, for without the preservation of youth, the race itself would perish. And so, the highest duty of any Government is to order public affairs so that opportunities for youth shall be made ever broader and firmer.

We Americans have never lost our sense of this obligation. To a greater degree than any other peoples we have sought to give each rising generation a little better chance in life than the one that preceded it.

The little red schoolhouse for the education of the young, and the church for the training of their spiritual qualities, have always been the first structures to rise in every new settlement, as our ancestors pushed new frontiers through the wilderness. The school is the last expenditure upon which America should be willing to economize...

America has lost a good many things during the depression. Some of them needed to go; I am glad that they have gone.

We have lost, for example, that false sense of values that puts financial success above every other kind of achievement.

We have lost a little of our cocksureness, a little of the bumptiousness which the Pharisee had when he thanked God that he was not as other people. We have lost something of that feeling that ours is an "every-man-for-himself" kind of society, in which the law of the jungle is law enough.

But many things we have saved - things worth saving. We have saved our morale. We have preserved our belief in American institutions. In this world of ours where some Nations have taken perilous detours, we have faced our problems and have met them with a democracy. Within that democracy we are determined to keep on solving them.

We have saved above all our faith in the future - a faith under which America has only begun to march.

REAR-PLATFORM REMARKS AT
EMPORIA, KANSAS
OCTOBER 13, 1936

THANK THE LORD, we are going into this election with a smile on our faces.

ADDRESS AT PROVIDENCE, RHODE ISLAND
OCTOBER 21, 1936

MY FRIENDS, HERE I am back in Rhode Island and glad to be here. I am glad that Governor Greene spoke of Rhode Island and Providence Plantations as the cradle of religious liberty.

ADDRESS DEDICATING CHEMISTRY BUILDING,
HOWARD UNIVERSITY, WASHINGTON, D. C.
OCTOBER 26, 1936

I HAVE BEEN greatly interested in learning a moment ago from the Chairman of the Executive

Committee that the origin of Howard University was in a house of prayer...

Its founding, many years ago, as an institution for the American Negro was a significant occasion. It typified America's faith in the ability of man to respond to opportunity regardless of race or creed or color.

ADDRESS ON THE OCCASION OF THE FIFTIETH ANNIVERSARY OF THE STATUE OF LIBERTY OCTOBER 28, 1936

FIFTY YEARS AGO our old neighbor and friend from across the sea gave us this monument to stand at the principal eastern gateway to the New World...

Then came one of the great ironies of history. Rulers needed to find gold to pay their armies and increase their power over the common men. The seamen they sent to find that gold found instead the way of escape for the common man from those rulers. What they found over the Western horizon was not the silk and jewels of Cathay but mankind's second chance - a chance to create a new world after he had almost spoiled an old one.

And the Almighty seems purposefully to have withheld that second chance until the time when men would most need and appreciate liberty, the time when men would be enlightened enough to establish it on foundations sound enough to maintain it.

For over three centuries a steady stream of men, women and children followed the beacon of liberty which this light symbolizes. They brought to us strength and moral fiber developed in a civilization centuries old but fired anew by the dream of a better life in America. They brought to one new country the cultures of a hundred old ones.

It has not been sufficiently emphasized in the teaching of our history that the overwhelming majority of those who came from the Nations of the Old World to our American shores were not the laggards, not the timorous, not the failures.

They were men and women who had the supreme courage to strike out for themselves, to abandon language and relatives, to start at the bottom without influence, without money and without knowledge of life in a very young civilization. We can say for all America what the Californians say of the Forty-Niners: "The cowards never started and the weak died by the way."

Perhaps Providence did prepare this American continent to be a place of the second chance. Certainly, millions of men and women have made it that. They adopted this homeland because in this land they found a home in which the things they most desired could be theirs - freedom of opportunity, freedom of thought, freedom to worship God. Here they found life because here there was freedom to live.

It. is the memory of all these eager seeking millions that makes this one of America's places of great romance. Looking down this great harbor I like to think of the countless numbers of inbound vessels that have made this port. I like to think of the men and women who, with the break of dawn off Sandy Hook, have strained their eyes to the west for a first glimpse of the New World.

They came to us - most of them - in steerage. But they, in their humble quarters, saw things in these strange horizons which were denied to the eyes of those few who traveled in greater luxury.

They came to us speaking many tongues - but a single language, the universal language of human aspiration.

How well their hopes were justified is proved by the record of what they achieved. They not only found freedom in the New World, but by their effort and devotion they made the New World's freedom safer, richer, more far-reaching, more capable of growth.

Within this present generation, that stream from abroad has largely stopped. We have within our shores today the materials out of which we shall continue to build an even better home for liberty.

We take satisfaction in the thought that those who have left their native land to join us may still retain here their affection for some things left behind - old customs, old language, old friends. Looking to the future, they wisely choose that their children shall live in the new language and in the new customs of this new people.

And those children more and more realize their common destiny in America. That is true whether their forebears came past this place eight generations ago or only one.

The realization that we are all bound together by hope of a common future rather than by reverence for a common past has helped us to build upon this continent a unity unapproached in any similar area or population in the whole world.

For all our millions of square miles, for all our millions of people, there is a unity in language and speech, in law and in economics, in education and in general purpose, which nowhere finds its match.

It was the hope of those who gave us this Statue and the hope of the American people in receiving it that the Goddess of Liberty and the Goddess of Peace were the same.

The grandfather of my old friend the French Ambassador, and those who helped him make this gift possible, were citizens of a great sister Republic established on the principle of the democratic form of government. Citizens of all democracies unite in their desire for peace. Grover Cleveland recognized that unity of purpose on this spot fifty years ago.

He suggested that liberty enlightening the world would extend her rays from these shores to every other Nation.

Today that symbolism should be broadened. To the message of liberty which America sends to all the world must be added her message of peace.

Even in times as troubled and uncertain as these, I still hold to the faith that a better civilization than any we have known is in store for America and by our example, perhaps, for the world.

Here destiny seems to have taken a long look. Into this continental reservoir there has been poured untold and untapped wealth of human resources. Out of that reservoir, out of the melting pot, the rich promise which the New World held out to those who came to it from many lands is finding fulfillment.

The richness of the promise has not run out. If we keep the faith for our day as those who came before us kept the faith for theirs, then you and I can smile with confidence into the future.

It is fitting, therefore, that this should be a service of rededication to the liberty and the peace which this Statue symbolizes. Liberty and peace are living things. In each generation - if they are to be maintained - they must be guarded and vitalized anew.

We do only a small part of our duty to America when we glory in the great past. Patriotism that stops with that is a too-easy patriotism - a patriotism out of step with the patriots themselves. For each generation the more patriotic part is to carry forward American freedom and American peace by making them living facts in a living present.

To that we can, we do, rededicate ourselves.

ADDRESS AT HARRISBURG, PENNSYLVANIA
OCTOBER 29, 1936

IF MODERN GOVERNMENT is to justify itself, it must see to it that human values are not mangled and destroyed. You and I know that that is sound morality and good religion...

When we came to Washington in 1933 it was our fundamental belief that faith without works is dead.

ADDRESS AT CAMDEN, NEW JERSEY
OCTOBER 29, 1936

AFTER THE CRASH, and after the long years of despair which followed it, one prayer went up from the American people - they wanted something to tie to - they sought stability because they knew that without stability they could not have security.

ADDRESS AT MADISON SQUARE GARDEN,
NEW YORK CITY
OCTOBER 31, 1936

WRITTEN THERE IN large letters are the names of countless other Americans of all parties and all faiths, Americans who had eyes to see and hearts to understand, whose consciences were burdened because too many of their fellows were burdened, who looked on these things four years ago and said, "This can be changed. We will change it."...

For twelve years this Nation was afflicted with hear-nothing, see-nothing, do-nothing Government. The Nation looked to Government but the Government looked away. Nine mocking years with the golden calf and three long years of the scourge!

Nine crazy years at the ticker and three long years in the breadlines! Nine mad years of mirage and three long years of despair! Powerful influences strive today to restore that kind of government with its doctrine that that Government is best which is most indifferent.

For nearly four years you have had an Administration which instead of twirling its thumbs has rolled up its sleeves. We will keep our sleeves rolled up.

We had to struggle with the old enemies of peace - business and financial monopoly, speculation, reckless banking, class antagonism, sectionalism, war profiteering.

They had begun to consider the Government of the United States as a mere appendage to their own affairs. We know now that Government by organized money is just as dangerous as Government by organized mob...

The fraudulent nature of this attempt is well shown by the record of votes on the passage of the Social Security Act. In addition to an overwhelming majority of Democrats in both Houses, seventy-seven Republican Representatives voted for it and only eighteen against it and fifteen Republican Senators voted for it and only five against it. Where does this last-minute drive of the Republican leadership leave these Republican Representatives and Senators who helped enact this law?...

You and I will continue to refuse to accept that estimate of our unemployed fellow Americans. Your Government is still on the same side of the street with the Good Samaritan and not with those who pass by on the other side...

"Peace on earth, good will toward men" - democracy must cling to that message. For it is my deep conviction that democracy cannot live without that true religion which gives a nation a sense of justice and of moral purpose. Above our political forums, above our market places stand the altars of our faith - altars on which burn the fires of devotion that maintain all that is best in us and all that is best in our Nation.

We have need of that devotion today. It is that which makes it possible for government to persuade those who are mentally prepared to fight each other to go on instead, to work for and to sacrifice for each other.

That is why we need to say with the Prophet: "What doth the Lord require of thee - but to do justly, to love mercy and to walk humbly with thy God." That is why the recovery we seek, the recovery we are winning, is more than economic. In it are included justice and love and humility, not for ourselves as individuals alone, but for our Nation. That is the road to peace.

REMARKS AT POUGHKEEPSIE, NEW YORK
NOVEMBER 2, 1936

BUT, IN THE last analysis, the problem before the voters of the country, not only tomorrow but next year and the year after that, is whether they want to vote for those people who they believe will carry out that expression of a greater physical and mental and spiritual security for the people of this country.

RADIO GREETING TO 21 AMERICAN REPUBLICS
NOVEMBER 7, 1936

TODAY THE DELEGATION of the United States to the Inter-American Conference for the Maintenance of Peace and the delegations of several other American Republics are sailing from New York for Buenos Aires, and I am taking this opportunity to wish them Godspeed and at the same time to send a word of greeting to the peoples of the twenty-one American Nations...

I feel confident that on the solid foundation of inter-American friendship, equality, and unity the Conference at Buenos Aires will be able to take further steps for the maintenance of peace, thus insuring the continuance of conditions under which it will be possible, nay, inevitable, for the economic, social, cultural, and spiritual life of the Nations of this Hemisphere to reach full growth.

THANKSGIVING DAY PROCLAMATION
NOVEMBER 12, 1936

I, FRANKLIN D. ROOSEVELT, President of the United States of America, hereby designate Thursday, the twenty-sixth day of November, 1936, as a day of national thanksgiving.

The observance of a day of general thanksgiving by all the people is a practice peculiarly our own, hallowed by usage in the days before we were a nation and sanctioned through succeeding years.

Having safely passed through troubled waters, it is our right to express our gratitude that Divine Providence has vouchsafed us wisdom and courage to overcome adversity. Our free institutions have been maintained with no abatement of our faith in them. In our relations with other peoples we stand not aloof but make resolute effort to promote international friendship and, by the avoidance of discord, to further world peace, prosperity, and happiness.

Coupled with our grateful acknowledgment of the blessings it has been our high privilege to enjoy, we have a deepening sense of our solemn responsibility to assure for ourselves and our descendants a future more abundant in faith and in security.

Let us, therefore, on the day appointed, each in his own way, but together as a whole people, make due expression of our thanksgiving and humbly endeavor to follow in the footsteps of Almighty God.

ADDRESS BEFORE A JOINT SESSION OF THE NATIONAL CONGRESS AND THE SUPREME COURT OF BRAZIL AT RIO DE JANEIRO NOVEMBER 27, 1936

ECONOMICALLY WE SUPPLY each other's needs; intellectually we maintain a constant, a growing exchange of culture, of science, and of thought; spiritually the life of each can well enrich the life of all.

ADDRESS TO THE INTER-AMERICAN CONFERENCE FOR THE MAINTENANCE OF PEACE, BUENOS AIRES, ARGENTINA DECEMBER 1, 1936

PEACE COMES FROM the spirit and must be grounded in faith...

But this faith of the Western World will not be complete if we fail to affirm our faith in God.

In the whole history of mankind, far back into the dim past before man knew how to record thoughts or events, the human race has been distinguished from other forms of life by the existence, the fact, of religion.

Periodic attempts to deny God have always come and will always come to naught.

In the constitution and in the practice of our Nations is the right of freedom of religion. But this ideal, these words, presuppose a belief and a trust in God.

The faith of the Americas, therefore, lies in the spirit. The system, the sisterhood, of the Americas is impregnable so long as her Nations maintain that spirit.

In that faith and spirit we will have peace over the Western World. In that faith and spirit we will all watch and guard our Hemisphere. In that faith and spirit may we also, with God's help, offer hope to our brethren overseas.

CHRISTMAS GREETING TO THE NATION
DECEMBER 24, 1936

I HAVE BEEN reading the Christmas Carol to my family, in accordance with our old custom. On this eve of Christmas I want to quote to you the pledge of old Scrooge when, after many vicissitudes, he had come to understand in his heart the great lesson and the great opportunity of Christmastide.

"I will honor Christmas in my heart and try to keep it all the year. I will live in the Past, the Present and the Future. The Spirits of all Three shall strive within me. I will not shut out the lessons that they teach."

And at the end of the story is this glorious passage:

"Scrooge was better than his word. He did it all and infinitely more; and to Tiny Tim, who did NOT die, he was a second father. He became as good a friend, as good a master and as good a man as the good old city knew, or any other good old city, town or borough in the good old world.

Some people laughed to see the alteration in him, but he let them laugh and little heeded them; for he was wise enough to know that nothing ever happened on this globe for good, at which some people did not have their fill of laughter in the outset. His own heart laughed; and that was good enough for him."

The teaching of the Sermon on the Mount is as adequate to the needs of men and of Nations today as when it was first proclaimed among the hills above the Sea of Galilee. In such measure as its spirit is accepted men and nations may lay claim to be seekers after peace on earth.

We of the Western Hemisphere have this year rendered special tribute to the spirit of Christmas, for we have pledged anew our faith in the arbitrament of reason and the practice of friendship. To that faith we bear witness tonight. May that faith make us happy today and tomorrow and through all the coming year.

PRESS CONFERENCE
DECEMBER 29, 1936

Q: CAN WE LOOK for a specific recommendation from you some time early in the Session on this proposal?

THE PRESIDENT; I am not a prophet or the son of a prophet. . . .

ANNUAL MESSAGE TO CONGRESS
JANUARY 6, 1937

THE TIMES REQUIRED the confident answer of performance to those whose instinctive faith in humanity made them want to believe that in the long run democracy would prove superior to more extreme forms of Government as a process of getting action when action was wisdom, without the spiritual sacrifices which those other forms of Government exact.

SECOND TERM
JANUARY 20, 1937-JANUARY 19, 1941

SECOND INAUGURAL ADDRESS
JANUARY 20, 1937

WE OF THE Republic pledged ourselves to drive from the temple of our ancient faith those who had profaned it; to end by action, tireless and unafraid, the stagnation and despair of that day...

We are beginning to wipe out the line that divides the practical from the ideal; and in so doing we are fashioning an instrument of unimagined power for the establishment of a morally better world...

For these reasons I am justified in believing that the greatest change we have witnessed has been the change in the moral climate of America...

It is not in despair that I paint you that picture. I paint it for you in hope - because the Nation, seeing and understanding the injustice in it, proposes to paint it out. We are determined to make every American citizen the subject of his country's interest and concern; and we will never regard any faithful, law-abiding group within our borders as superfluous.

The test of our progress is not whether we add more to the abundance of those who have much; it is whether we provide enough for those who have too little...

While this duty rests upon me I shall do my utmost to speak their purpose and to do their will, seeking Divine guidance to help us each and every one to give light to them that sit in darkness and to guide our feet into the way of peace.

LETTER TO JAMES P. DAWSON, THE NEW YORK TIMES, ON THE OCCASION OF THE BASEBALL WRITERS ASSOCIATION OF AMERICA FOURTEENTH ANNUAL DINNER JANUARY 23, 1937

BUT WHILE NOT there in person I shall be with you in spirit, as will millions of other Americans who follow through the sports writers of the Nation not only baseball, but football, boxing, track and field sports, golf, tennis, winter sports - when there is winter - and many other games through which, as participants or spectators, we as a people benefit physically, mentally and morally.

GREETING TO THE UNITED PALESTINE APPEAL, ADDRESSING DOCTOR STEPHEN S. WISE, UNITED PALESTINE APPEAL, WASHINGTON, D.C. FEBRUARY 6, 1937

PLEASE CONVEY MY good wishes to the men and women gathering in Washington for the National Conference for Palestine which has been summoned by the United Palestine Appeal.

The American people, ever zealous in the cause of human freedom, have watched with sympathetic interest the effort of the Jews to renew in Palestine the ties of their ancient homeland and to reestablish Jewish culture in the place where for centuries it flourished and whence it was carried to the far corners of the world.

This year marks the twentieth anniversary of the Balfour Declaration, the keystone of contemporary reconstruction activities in the Jewish homeland.

Those two decades have witnessed a remarkable exemplification of the vitality and vision of the Jewish pioneers in Palestine. It should be a source of pride to Jewish citizens of the United States that they, too, have had a share in this great work of revival and restoration.

It gives me great pleasure to send all who are participating in your deliberations my hearty felicitations and warmest personal greetings.

FIRESIDE CHAT
MARCH 9, 1937

THE COURTS, HOWEVER, have cast doubts on the ability of the elected Congress to protect us against catastrophe by meeting squarely our modern social and economic conditions...

I hope that you have re-read the Constitution of the United States in these past few weeks. Like the Bible, it ought to be read again and again...

The Court has more and more often and more and more boldly asserted a power to veto laws passed by the Congress and State Legislatures in complete disregard of this original limitation...

The Court has been acting not as a judicial body, but as a policy-making body...

There is no basis for the claim made by some members of the Court that something in the Constitution has compelled them regretfully to thwart the will of the people...

The Court in addition to the proper use of its judicial functions has improperly set itself up as a third House of the Congress-a super-legislature, as one of the justices has called it-reading into the Constitution words and implications which are not there, and which were never intended to be there...

We have, therefore, reached the point as a Nation where we must take action to save the Constitution from the Court and the Court from itself. We must find a way to take an appeal from the Supreme Court to the Constitution itself. We want a Supreme Court which will do justice under the Constitution - not over it. In our Courts we want a government of laws and not of men...

I want - as all Americans want - an independent judiciary as proposed by the framers of the Constitution. That means a Supreme Court that will enforce the Constitution as written - that will refuse to amend the Constitution by the arbitrary exercise of judicial power-amendment by judicial say-so...

We must have Judges who will retain in the Courts the judicial functions of a court, and reject the legislative powers which the courts have today assumed...

In forty-five out of the forty-eight States of the Union, Judges are chosen not for life but for a period of years...

Our difficulty with the Court today rises not from the Court as an institution but from human beings within it. We cannot yield our constitutional destiny to the personal judgment of a few men who, being fearful of the future, would deny us the necessary means of dealing with the present...

This proposal of mine will not infringe in the slightest upon the civil or religious liberties so dear to every American.

RADIO GREETING ON ST. PATRICK'S DAY, WARM SPRINGS, GEORGIA MARCH 17, 1937

OBSERVING THE 17TH of March are your brothers of the other old societies-the Friendly Sons of St. Patrick in the City of New York, the Friendly Sons of St. Patrick in Philadelphia, the Hibernian Society in Baltimore and the Hibernian Society of Charleston.

In all these generations your Societies have lived up to the noble legend "non sibi sed aliis"- not for yourselves but for others. You have aided your own members, and many others who might be deserving of your charity. You have aided not Irishmen alone or the descendants of Irishmen - you have contributed greatly to the good of your communities as a whole.

I have a particular tenderness for St. Patrick's Day for, as some of you know, it was on the seventeenth of March, 1905, that a Roosevelt wedding took place in New York City with the accompaniment of bands playing their way up Fifth Avenue to the tune of "The Wearin' of the Green."

On that occasion New York had two great attractions - the St. Patrick's Day Parade, and President Theodore Roosevelt, who had come from Washington to give the bride away. I might add that it was wholly natural and logical that in the spotlight of these two simultaneous attractions the bride and the bridegroom were almost entirely overlooked and left in the background...

Yes, I am always thrilled by St. Patrick's Day, the day that Irishmen the world over garner to their hearts and souls their tenderest memories, recall the ancient glories of Erin and renew their allegiance to the great Apostle of fifteen hundred years ago. Through all the vicissitudes of these fifteen centuries, through tramplings and burnings, through war and slaughter, in times of plenty and in times of famine-Ireland, and the descendants of Ireland, have been faithful to the heritage of St. Patrick.

The same devotion and steadfastness to the cause of liberty within the homeland itself, has accompanied the sons and daughters of Ireland wherever they have gone, even to the far corners of the earth.

Our own country owes a great debt to them for their contribution to its upbuilding. They have borne arms in our wars both in the colonial and the national periods. In commerce, agriculture, and industry, in the arts and sciences, in literature, in the professions and in the councils of state they have shown special aptitude and outstanding talent...

"Not for ourselves but for others." That motto can well be the inspiration of all of us - not alone for the fine purposes of charity, but also for our guidance in our public and private service. Selfishness is without doubt the greatest danger that confronts our beloved country today. Good old St. Patrick - and may he ever be with us was the epitome of unselfishness. May we follow in his footsteps through all of the years.

LETTER ON RELIGIOUS TOLERANCE MR. MICHAEL WILLIAMS, THE CALVERT ASSOCIATES, NEW YORK CITY MARCH 30, 1937

THE LESSON OF religious toleration - a toleration which recognizes complete liberty of human thought, liberty of human conscience - is one which, by precept and example, must be inculcated in the hearts and minds of all Americans if the institutions of our democracy are to be maintained and perpetuated.

We must recognize the fundamental rights of man. There can be no true national life in our democracy unless we give unqualified recognition to freedom of religious worship and freedom of education. We have not forgotten, nor ever shall forget, the noble service in the cause of religious toleration rendered by the Calverts in Maryland three centuries ago.

It gives me pleasure, therefore, to learn that The Commonweal, organ of the Calvert Associates, has arranged to celebrate in St. Patrick's Cathedral next Monday the three hundred third anniversary of the founding of Maryland, and Maryland's part in the establishment of religious liberty in America.

I have learned also with peculiar satisfaction that The Commonweal believes that rarely before in our history have prospects for achieving permanent harmony among the various elements composing our Nation been so propitious as at the present time.

I rejoice in this assurance. I pledge myself at this solemn commemoration, with all the resources at my command, to work for so happy a consummation. My prayer shall ever be that this Nation, under God, may vindicate through all coming time the sanctity of the right of all within our borders to the free exercise of religion according to the dictates of conscience.

GREETING TO THE EDITORIAL BOARD OF THE CHRISTIAN SCIENCE MONITOR, BOSTON, MASSACHUSETTS, ON ITS EFFORTS FOR PEACE APRIL 10, 1937

AT BUENOS AIRES last December the twenty-one American Republics reaffirmed their faith in and support of the peaceful way of international living, and they gave practical testimony to their adherence to the ideals of democratic government and the Christian honoring of their solemn obligations.

The preservation of peace needs the devoted support of newspapers throughout the world, and it is encouraging to find The Christian Science Monitor devoting itself further to the enlargement of understanding between the English-speaking peoples on this historic occasion.

ADDRESS TO THE GOVERNING BOARD OF THE PAN AMERICAN UNION
APRIL 14, 1937

DEMOCRACY CANNOT THRIVE in an atmosphere of international insecurity. Such insecurity breeds militarism, regimentation and the denial of freedom of speech, of peaceful assemblage and of religion.

STATEMENT ON A REPORT BY THE NATIONAL RESOURCES COMMITTEE
JULY 12, 1937

MORE THAN JOBS and investment are affected by technical change: Family, church, community, state and all industry are subject to its influence.

STATEMENT ON THE DEATH OF SENATOR JOSEPH T. ROBINSON
JULY 14, 1937

OF HIM WELL may it be said: He has fought a good fight; he has finished his course; he has kept the faith.

ADDRESS AT THE CORNERSTONE LAYING CEREMONIES FOR THE NEW FEDERAL TRADE COMMISSION BUILDING JULY 12, 1937

MAY THIS PERMANENT home of the Federal Trade Commission stand for all time as a symbol of the purpose of the Government to insist on a greater application of the Golden Rule to the conduct of corporations and business enterprises in their relationship to the body politic.

RADIO ADDRESS ON THE DEDICATION OF THE AMERICAN MONUMENT AT MONTFAUCON, FRANCE AUGUST 1, 1937

WE, OF THIS country, have not forgotten nor could we ever forget the aid given us by France in the dark days of the American Revolution.

Our historic friendship finds apt expression in the quotation from a letter which Washington wrote to Rochambeau, and which is inscribed on the base of our monument to the great Frenchman: "We have been contemporaries and fellow-laborers in the cause of liberty, and we have lived together as brothers should do, in harmonious friendship."

Many things have gone into the making of the France which we revere and with whose culture we find ourselves in close communion. All of the past speaks to us in the living present, and out of the shadows of a thousand years emerge the glory and the achievement which are France.

These things we remember today, nor do we forget the living France: the green fields around Montfaucon, with broad farms and contented dwellers on the soil; the villages and cities with their artists and artisans - all these make and preserve the France we hail today.

To the preservation of this civilization American soldiers and sailors contributed' their lives and lie buried on this and other battlefields. They died brothers-in-arms with Frenchmen. And in their passing America and France gained deeper devotion to the ideals of democracy.

In their name, for their sake, I pray God no hazard of the future may ever dissipate or destroy that common ideal. I greet the Republic of France, firm in the confidence that a friendship as old as the American nation will never be suffered to grow less.

ADDRESS AT ROANOKE ISLAND, NORTH CAROLINA
AUGUST 18, 1937

UNTIL RECENT YEARS history was taught as a series of facts and dates. Today we are beginning to look more closely into the events which preceded those great social and economic and political changes which have deeply affected the known history of the world.

For example, most of us older people learned of Columbus' voyages and how America came to be named - and we jumped from there in our North American history to the founding of Jamestown and of Plymouth - 1492 to 1607 - with mere passing reference to Roanoke and perhaps to the voyage of Verazzano.

It has always been a pet theory of mine that many other voyages of exploration and of trade took place in that century along our American shores. We know that during the same period the Spaniards established great colonies throughout the West Indies, at Panama and other points in

Central America, and extended their cities, their religious institutions and even their universities to both the east and west coasts of South America.

It is unbelievable that white men did not come scores of times to what is today the Atlantic Seaboard of the United States. Some day, perhaps, a closer search of the records of the seafaring towns of Britain and France and Flanders and Holland and Scandinavia will rediscover discoverers. Perhaps even it is not too much to hope that documents in the old country and excavations in the new may throw some further light, however dim, on the fate of the "Lost Colony" and Roanoke and Virginia Dare.

If we are to understand the full significance of the early explorations and the early settlements, if we are to understand the kind of world upon which Virginia Dare opened her eyes on that far-away August day in 1587, we must ask why Western Europe came to the New World.

It was in part because the era was an era of restless action. Under the Renaissance men experienced great awakenings; they were fired with restless energy to burst the narrow bounds of the medieval conception of the Universe, to fare forth on voyages of exploration and conquest.

Many of those who sailed in immense discomfort, in tiny ships, across the Atlantic, were adventurers, some of them seeking riches, some seeking fame, some impelled by the mere spirit of unrest. But most of the people who came in the early days to America - the men, the women and the children - came hither seeking something very different, seeking an opportunity which they could not find in their homes of the old world.

We hear of the gentlemen of title, who, on occasion, came to the Colonies, and we hear of the gentlemen of wealth who helped to fit out the expeditions.

But it is a simple fact which cannot too often be stressed that an overwhelming majority of those who came to the Colonies from England and Scotland and Ireland and Wales and France and Holland and Sweden belonged to what our British cousins would, even today, call "the lower middle classes."

The opportunity they sought was something they did not have at home - opportunity freely to exercise their own chosen form of religion, opportunity to get into an environment where there were no classes, opportunity to escape from a system which still contained most of the elements of Feudalism.

This is said not in derogation of those pioneers. It is rather in praise of them. They had the courage, physically and mentally, by deed and word, to seek better things, to try to capture ideals and hopes forbidden to them by the laws and rulers of their own home lands.

It is well, too, that we bear in mind that in all the pioneer settlements democracy, and not feudalism, was the rule. The men had to take their turn standing guard at the stockade raised against the Indians. The women had to take their turn husking corn stored for the winter supply of the community. In other words, they were all working for the life and success of the community.

Rules of conduct had to be established to keep private greed or personal misconduct in check. I fear very much that if certain modern Americans, who protest loudly their devotion to American ideals, were suddenly to be given a comprehensive view of the earliest American colonists and their methods of life and government, they would promptly label them socialists. They would forget that in these pioneer settlements were all the germs of the later American Constitution.

They would forget, too, that throughout the days that intervened between Roanoke and Jamestown and Plymouth, and the time of the American Revolution itself, practical democracy was carried on in the lives of the inhabitants of nearly every community in the Thirteen Colonies. It is true that as commerce developed in the seaboard cities, and as a few great landed estates were set up here and there, a school of thought parallel with the same school of thought in England made great headway.

It was this policy which came into the open in the Constitutional Convention of 1787; for in that Convention there were some who wanted a King, there were some who wanted to create titles, and there were many, like Alexander Hamilton, who sincerely believed that suffrage and the right to hold office should be confined to persons of property and persons of education.

We know, however, that although this school persisted, with the assistance of the newspapers of the day, during the first three National Administrations, it was eliminated for many years at least under the leadership of President Thomas Jefferson and his successors. His was the first great battle for the preservation of democracy. His was the first great victory for American democracy.

In the half century that followed there was constant war between those who, like Andrew Jackson, believed in a democracy conducted by and for a complete cross-section of the population, and those who, like the Directors of the Bank of the United States and their friends in the United States Senate, believed in the conduct of government by a self-perpetuating group at the top of the ladder.

That this was the clear line of demarcation - the fundamental difference of opinion in regard to American institutions - is proved by an amazingly interesting letter which Lord Macaulay wrote in 1857 to an American friend....

"Your constitution is all sail and no anchor...Either some Caesar or Napoleon will seize the reins of government with a strong hand, or your Republic will be...laid waste by Barbarians in the twentieth century as the Roman Empire was in the fifth."

That, my friends, with all due respect to Lord Macaulay, is an excellent representation of the cries of alarm which rise today from the throats of American Lord Macaulays. They tell you that America drifts toward the Scylla of dictatorship on the one hand, or the Charybdis of anarchy on the other...

They do not believe in democracy - I do. My anchor is democracy - and more democracy. And, my friends, I am of the firm belief that the Nation, by an overwhelming majority, supports my opposition to the vesting of supreme power in the hands of any class...

Under democratic government the poorest are no longer necessarily the most ignorant part of society. I agree with the saying of one of our famous statesmen who devoted himself to the principle of majority rule: "I respect the aristocracy of learning; I deplore the plutocracy of wealth; but thank God for the democracy of the heart."

I seek no change in the form of American government. Majority rule must be preserved as the safeguard of both liberty and civilization.

GREETING TO THE INSTITUTE OF HUMAN
RELATIONS, ADDRESSED TO DOCTOR EVERETT
R. CLINCHY, THE NATIONAL CONFERENCE OF
JEWS AND CHRISTIANS, NEW YORK CITY
AUGUST 20, 1937

I AM GLAD to learn that the Institute of Human Relations to be held under the auspices of the National Conference of Jews and Christians proposes to concern itself this year with the consideration of an American public opinion which shall maintain and develop democracy. Few subjects could be of more vital interest at this particular time. The very theme of the Institute: "Public Opinion in a Democracy" is stimulating as well as inspiring.

The whole structure of democracy rests upon public opinion. Indeed under a government which functions through democratic institutions we are ruled by public opinion. Only through the full and free expression of public opinion can the springs of democracy be renewed and its institutions kept alive and capable of functioning.

There are among us some who are a little too complacent these days in the assertion that democracy as a system of government is challenged abroad. Can we be too sure that it is not distrusted right here within our own gates by a small minority, powerful and articulate, which, paying lip service to democracy, seeks by every means within its power to thwart the will of the majority? Let us not forget that eternal vigilance is the price of liberty.

We have today three powerful agencies in the creation of public opinion: the press, motion pictures, radio. Ours then is the duty to see that these agencies through adherence to the highest ideals of truth, justice and fair play are maintained as public agencies for the creation of wholesome relationships among the various cultural, religious, racial and economic interest groups which make up the American people.

The sum of these complex and composite interests constitutes what we mean by American democracy.

Our own Nation for its own guidance and for the guidance of other peoples if they will follow it has ever held aloft the torch of human freedom - freedom of press, of speech, of conscience, of assembly.

Ours is the duty; and the National Conference of Jews and Christians through this forthcoming Institute of Human Relations can be a potent agency in guaranteeing that our torch of freedom shall never be lowered. Rather must we strive by every legitimate means to increase the light of that torch that its rays may extend ever farther - that its splendor may be seen by all men.

LABOR DAY STATEMENT BY THE PRESIDENT
SEPTEMBER 5, 1937

THE GOVERNMENT HASs committed itself to a very definite program in the advancement of the economic, industrial and spiritual welfare of our people.

GREETING TO THE AMERICAN LEGION, ADDRESSED TO HARRY W. COLMERY, NATIONAL COMMANDER, THE AMERICAN LEGION, INDIANAPOLIS, INDIANA
SEPTEMBER 13, 1937

THERE ARE FEW more exalted sentiments than those embodied in the preamble to our Legion Constitution: For God and Country; to uphold and defend the Constitution of the United States; to foster and perpetuate Americanism; to maintain law and order; to inculcate a sense of individual obligation to the Community, State and Nation; to combat the autocracy of both the classes and the masses; to make right the master of might; to promote peace and good will on earth; to safeguard and transmit to posterity the principles of justice, freedom and democracy.

ADDRESS ON CONSTITUTION DAY, WASHINGTON, D.C. SEPTEMBER 17, 1937

I BELIEVE THAT these things can be done under the Constitution, without the surrender of a single one of the civil and religious liberties it was intended to safeguard...

Modern history proves that reforms too long delayed or denied have jeopardized peace, undermined democracy and swept away civil and religious liberties...

No one cherishes more deeply than I the civil and religious liberties achieved by so much blood and anguish through the many centuries of Anglo-American history.

ADDRESS AT ANTIETAM BATTLEFIELD, MARYLAND SEPTEMBER 17, 1937

I CAME INTO the world seventeen years after the close of the war between the States, the results of that war and of the difficult years that followed it do not make me think of it as history.

And today, seventy-five years after the critical battle of Antietam, there are still many among us who can remember it. It is, therefore, an American battle which thousands of Americans, middle-aged and old, can still visualize as bearing some relationship to their own lives.

We know that Antietam was one of the decisive engagements of the Civil War because it marked the first effort of the Confederacy to invade the North - tactically a drawn battle, but actually a factor of vital importance to the final result because it spelled the failure of the attempt.

Whether we be old or young, it serves us little to discuss again the rights and the wrongs of the long four years war between the states. We can but wish that the war had never been. We can and we do revere the memory of the brave men who fought on both sides. We can and we do honor those who fell on this and other fields.

But we know today that it was best, for the generation of Americans who fought the war and for the generations of Americans who have come after them, that the conflict did not end in a division of our land into two nations. I like to think that it was the will of God that we remain one people.

ADDRESS AT TIMBERLINE LODGE
SEPTEMBER 28, 1937

I AM VERY keen about travel, not only personally - you know that - but also about travel for as many Americans as can possibly afford it, because those Americans will be getting to know their own country better; and the more they see of it, the more they will realize the privileges which God and nature have given to the American people.

ADDRESS AT GRAND FORKS, NORTH DAKOTA
OCTOBER 4, 1937

I RECEIVED THE other day a letter from one of the only two living former members of the Supreme Court of the United States...

He goes on to speak of what we are doing by introducing into our national life and legislation something at least of the influence of the Golden Rule.

ADDRESS AT CHICAGO
OCTOBER 5, 1937

I HAVE BEEN greeted by tens of thousands of Americans who have told me in every look and word that their material and spiritual well-being has made great strides forward in the past few years...

Those who cherish their freedom and recognize and respect the equal right of their neighbors to be free and live in peace, must work together for the triumph of law and moral principles in order that peace, justice and confidence may prevail in the world. There must be a return to a belief in the pledged word, in the value of a signed treaty. There must be recognition of the fact that national morality is as vital as private morality.

A bishop wrote me the other day: "It seems to me that something greatly needs to be said in behalf of ordinary humanity against the present practice of carrying the horrors of war to helpless civilians, especially women and children.

It may be that such a protest might be regarded by many, who claim to be realists, as futile, but may it not be that the heart of mankind is so filled with horror at the present needless suffering that that force could be mobilized in sufficient volume to lessen such cruelty in the days ahead. Even though it may take twenty years, which God forbid, for civilization to make effective its corporate protest against this barbarism, surely strong voices may hasten the day."

There is a solidarity and interdependence about the modern world, both technically and morally, which makes it impossible for any nation completely to isolate itself from economic and political upheavals in the rest of the world, especially when such upheavals appear to be spreading and not declining. There can be no stability or peace either within nations or between nations except under laws and moral standards adhered to by all...

If civilization is to survive the principles of the Prince of Peace must be restored.

RADIO ADDRESS IN HONOR OF GENERAL KRZYZANOWSKI OF POLAND OCTOBER 11, 1937

IN THE EPIC struggle of the human race to govern itself Poland for centuries has been the champion of freedom. Through stress and storm, whether her sun shone brightly or suffered long though temporary eclipse, she has ever fought to hold aloft the torch of human liberty.

The American people and the people of Poland have maintained a friendship based upon this common spiritual ideal...

We as a Nation seek spiritual union with all who love freedom.

REMARKS AT THE DEDICATION OF THE POST OFFICE AT POUGHKEEPSIE, N.Y. OCTOBER 13, 1937

THE PEOPLE, EVEN in those days, were talking about freedom of religion and freedom of the press, just as they are rightly doing it today.

The Clintonian faction insisted that the Constitution should not be ratified because it had no Bill of Rights in it. The Hamiltonian faction, to which incidentally, my great, great grandfather belonged as a member of the Convention, said that it did not make much difference.

138   *THE FAITH OF FDR*

It took leadership on the part of the Dutchess County delegates to suggest a compromise, the compromise that the State of New York should ratify the Federal Constitution in full faith and confidence that the Bill of Rights would be put in at the earliest possible moment. That is how we New Yorkers came to be a part of the Union and that is one reason why, at the first opportunity, a Bill of Rights was put in.

GREETING TO THE NATIONAL FOREIGN TRADE COUNCIL CONVENTION OCTOBER 30, 1937

I AM SURE that the National Foreign Trade Convention will continue to assist the Government in carrying forward the trade agreements program, a program based upon the principle of equality of treatment which expresses the Golden Rule.

PROCLAMATION 2260 ON THANKSGIVING DAY NOVEMBER 9, 1937

I, FRANKLIN D. ROOSEVELT, President of the United States of America, hereby designate Thursday, the twenty-fifth day of November 1937 as a day of National Thanksgiving.

The custom of observing a day of public thanksgiving began in Colonial times and has been given the sanction of national observance through many years. It is in keeping with all of our traditions that we, even as our fathers in olden days, give humble and hearty thanks for the bounty and the goodness of Divine Providence.

The harvests of our fields have been abundant and many men and women have been given the blessing of stable employment.

A period unhappily marked in many parts of the world by strife and threats of war finds our people enjoying the blessing of peace. We have no selfish designs against other nations.

We have been fortunate in devoting our energies and our resources to constructive purposes and useful works. We have sought to fulfill our obligation to use our national heritage by common effort for the common good.

Let us, therefore, on the day appointed forego our usual occupations and, in our accustomed places of worship, each in his own way, humbly acknowledge the mercy of God from whom comes every good and perfect gift.

CHRISTMAS GREETING TO THE NATION
DECEMBER 24, 1937

LAST NIGHT BEFORE I went to sleep I chanced to read in an evening paper a story by a columnist which appeals to me so much as a Christmas sermon that this afternoon, on the occasion of lighting the National Christmas Tree in Lafayette Square in front of the White House, I am going to read to you from it. Here is his parable:

We were sitting in a high room above the chapel, and although it was Christmas Eve, my good friend the dominie seemed curiously troubled. And that was strange, for he was a man extremely sensitive to the festivities of his faith.

The joys and sorrows of Jesus were not to him events of a remote past but more current and living happenings than the headlines in the newspapers. At Christmas he seems actually to hear the voice of the herald angels.

My friend is an old man, and I have known him for many years, but this was the first time the Nativity had failed to rouse him to an ecstasy. He admitted that something was wrong. "Tomorrow," he said, "I must go down into that chapel and preach a Christmas sermon. And I must speak of peace and good will toward men. I know you think of me as a man too cloistered to be of any use to my community. And I know that our world is one of war and hate and enmity.

"And you, my young friend, and others keep insisting that before there can be brotherhood there must be the bashing of heads. You are all for good will to men, but you want to note very many exceptions. And I am still hoping and praying that in the great love of God the final seal of interdiction must not be put on even one. You may laugh at me, but right now I am worrying about how Christmas came to Judas Iscariot."

It is the habit of my friend when he is troubled by doubts to reach for the Book, and he did so now. He smiled and said, "Will you assist me in a little experiment?"

I will close my eyes and you hold out the Bible to me. I will open it at random and run my fingers down a page. You read me the text which I blindly select."

I did as he told me, and he happened on the twenty-sixth chapter of St. Matthew and the twenty-fifth verse. I felt sorry for him, for this was no part of the story of the birth of Christ but instead an account of the great betrayal.

"Read what it says," commanded the dominie. And I read, "Then Judas, which betrayed him, answered and said, 'Master, is it I?' He' said unto him, 'Thou hast said.'"

My friend frowned, but then he looked at me in triumph. "Now I remember. My hand is not as steady as it used to be. You should have taken the lower part of my finger and not the top. Read the twenty-seventh verse. It is not an eighth of an inch away. Read what it says."

And I read, "And He took the cup, and gave thanks, and gave it to them, saying, 'Drink ye all of it.'"

"Mark that!" cried the old man exultantly. "Not even to Judas, the betrayer, was the wine of life denied. I can preach my Christmas sermon now, and my text will be, 'Drink ye all of it.' Good will toward men means good will to every last son of God. Peace on earth means peace to Pilate, peace to the thieves on the cross and peace to poor Iscariot."

I was glad, for he had found Christmas, and I saw by his face that once more he heard the voice of the herald angels.

LETTER OF GREETING TO THE UNITED METHODIST COUNCIL, ADDRESSED TO BISHOP ERNEST LYNN WALDORF, UNITED METHODIST COUNCIL ON THE FUTURE OF FAITH AND SERVICE, CHICAGO, ILLINOIS
JANUARY 17, 1938

IN A WORLD perplexed by doubt and fear and uncertainty, there is need for a return to religion, religion as exemplified in the Sermon on the Mount.

We need more and more a consciousness of the fact that in the highest and the noblest sense we are our brother's keeper and I want to reiterate the belief I have already affirmed many times that there is not a problem, social, political or economic, that would not find full solution in the fire of a religious awakening.

So it seems to me that your purpose in making a study of the needs, privileges and opportunities of the day in which we live in order that religion may have its rightful

142   *THE FAITH OF FDR*

place in the solution of our problems, points a way fruitful in promise of effective results.

Today when we see religion challenged in wide areas of the earth we who hold to old ideals of the Fatherhood of God and the Brotherhood of Man must be steadfast and united in bearing unceasing witness to our faith in things of the spirit.

In that faith I wish you and your co-workers Godspeed. You are the sowers of the seed. May God bless the harvest.

RADIO ADDRESS FOR THE FIFTH BIRTHDAY BALL FOR CRIPPLED CHILDREN JANUARY 29, 1938

TODAY THE MAJOR fight of medicine and science is being directed against two other scourges, the toll of which is unthinkably great - cancer and infantile paralysis... In both fields the fight. is again being conducted with national unity - and we believe with growing success....

One touch of nature makes the whole world kin. And that kinship, which human suffering evokes, is perhaps the closest of all, for we know that those who work to help the suffering find true spiritual fellowship in that labor of love.

So, although no word of mine can add to the happiness we share in this great service in which we are all engaged, I do want to tell you all how deeply I appreciate everything you have done. Thank you all and God bless you all.

REMARKS TO VISITING PROTESTANT MINISTERS, HEADED BY DR. OSCAR F. BLACKWELDER OF THE LUTHERAN CHURCH OF THE REFORMATION, PRESIDENT OF THE WASHINGTON MINISTERIAL

UNION, VISITING THE WHITE HOUSE, WASHINGTON, D.C. JANUARY 31, 1938

I AM GRATEFUL to you for this wonderful expression of faith - of faith and works. I am glad that you referred to what I said in 1934 about the need of spiritual reawakening in the country.

I do not know how you gentlemen feel, but I cannot help feeling myself, from the testimony that comes to me day by day, that there has been definite and distinct progress towards a spiritual reawakening in the four years which have passed since I spoke in 1934. I receive evidences of this from all our Protestant Churches; I get it from Catholic priests and from Jewish rabbis, as well.

It is a very significant thing that this awakening has come about in America. It makes me realize more fully that we do have, in addition to the duty we owe to our own people, an additional duty to the rest of the world. Things have been going on in other countries - things which are not spiritual in any sense of the word - and that is putting it mildly.

I must make a confession: I did not realize until the last few years how much influence America has in the world. I did not really, deep down in my heart, believe very much in church missions in other lands.

Today I do. I have seen what the American church missions have accomplished in many countries, not only on the religious side but on the side of health and of education. After all, the three of them tie in very definitely together. We call what we have been doing "human security" and "social justice." In the last analysis all of those terms can be described by one word; and that is "Christianity."

We have made great progress at home. I believe, in making that progress, we have had a great influence in other nations of the world. We have gone far in these years toward a greater human security and a greater social justice.

We don't want to stop that progress. We want to keep on. We have a task, not only for four years or eight years or twenty years to come - but a task that lasts through all eternity. As long as we continue to make the progress we are making, we can look for a safer and better America in our own lifetime.

You good people have been working toward that end. You have been rendering a great service to your Government.

We still have a long way to go. Whether we like it or not, we have to think about the average man, woman and child in the United States. We are doing just that; and they appreciate it. That is one reason why the Churches are stronger today than they were four years ago. If we can continue to make the same progress in the next several years as we have in the past, we can feel we have been good and faithful servants.

I appreciate your coming here and all I can say is God bless you; keep up the good work.

RADIO GREETING TO THE
BOY SCOUTS OF AMERICA
FEBRUARY 7, 1938

ON THIS TWENTY-EIGHTH birthday of the Boy Scouts of America we should be especially thankful for a youth movement which seeks merely to preserve such simple fundamentals as physical strength, mental alertness and moral straightness.

PROCLAMATION 2276 ON THE BIRTHDAY OF THOMAS JEFFERSON MARCH 21, 1938

I, FRANKLIN D. ROOSEVELT, President of the United States of America, do hereby call upon officials of the Government to display the flag of the United States on all Government buildings on April 13, 1938, and on April 13 of each succeeding year,

And do invite the people of the United States to observe the day in schools, churches, and other suitable places, with appropriate ceremonies in commemoration of the birth of Thomas Jefferson.

PRESS CONFERENCE WITH EDITORS AND PUBLISHERS OF TRADE PAPERS. WASHINGTON, D.C. APRIL 8, 1938

NOW, OUT WEST, in one or two factories that we know of, they are working people sixty hours a week since the NRA went out. I call that unfair competition. Whenever you start to get a wages and hours bill, the Congressman for that particular district gets a piteous plea, "For God's sake don't do anything or you won't go back to Congress." So, he tries to get an amendment to take care of his district. That is pure selfishness...

We have six or seven map-printing establishments right here in Washington, and some through the country. Do you think that Congress can ever be induced to consolidate them?...

Yet they have all agreed that somebody ought to do it. Well, there isn't anybody to do it, unfortunately, except the President. A year ago they thought that the idea was perfectly grand, but today they find that it is giving him certain powers. I don't want the powers, God knows. If the thing does not go through, I will rock along all right.

MESSAGE TO CONGRESS ON STIMULATING RECOVERY APRIL 14, 1938

THE DRIVING FORCE of a Nation lies in its spiritual purpose, made effective by free, tolerant but unremitting national will.

FIRESIDE CHAT APRIL 14, 1938

I HAD HOPED to be able to defer this talk until next week because, as we all know, this is Holy Week. But what I want to say to you, the people of the country, is of such immediate need and relates so closely to the lives of human beings and the prevention of human suffering that I have felt that there should be no delay.

In this decision I have been strengthened by the thought that by speaking tonight there may be greater peace of mind and the hope of Easter may be more real at firesides everywhere, and that it is not inappropriate to encourage peace when so many of us are thinking of the Prince of Peace.

PRESS CONFERENCE WITH MEMBERS OF THE ASSOCIATED CHURCH PRESS, WASHINGTON, D.C. APRIL 20, 1938

ON THE REORGANIZATION Bill...what we want to do is to put it on the same kind of an efficient basis that we would run an industrial plant, or a private charity, or even the financial end of a church...

But, all of a sudden, there broke out - I don't know who started it, but I do know who carried it on; and one was the gentleman from near Detroit who talks on the air.

He claimed that this was an attack on the educational system of the Nation, whereupon, immediately, the Members of the Congress, the House and the Senate, were flooded with telegrams that this bill would give the President of the United States a chance to grab all the church schools of the Nation, the Protestant church schools and the Parochial schools, although I don't know what the President of the United States was going to do with them when he did grab them...

Let me tell you about Iowa: I have a Chinese friend who was in college with me. He is a merchant in Canton, but I hear from him once a year. I got a letter from him the other day.

"Do you remember me telling you about my brother away in the interior, about three hundred miles southwest of Hankow? He was very prosperous, with an awfully nice home and a fine family. He had always been a pacifist. He has opposed a Chinese Army to protect the Nation of China. He said, 'We are so big, there is nobody that would dare to trouble us.' I have never agreed with my brother."

It is a Christian family. And the other day he said, "I am very sorry to tell you that my brother and his wife and four children were killed." They lived in the Iowa of China. Those planes came over and dropped a bomb on the house where they were cooling off.

They killed three hundred people in the near-by village, and two minutes later they were gone. They had wiped out one of the rural communities of the Iowa of China. He never thought it could happen, I never thought it would happen, and his brother in Canton never thought it would happen.

GREETING TO THE WORLD'S CHRISTIAN ENDEAVOR CONVENTION IN MELBOURNE, AUSTRALIA, ADDRESSED TO REV. DANIEL A. POLING, D.D., PHILADELPHIA, PENNSYLVANIA JUNE 15, 1938

THERE IS SOMETHING inspiring and soul-stirring about the very scope of the Tenth World's Christian Endeavor Convention to be held in Melbourne, Australia. The fact that Christians from all parts of the world are to make a far journey to Melbourne demonstrates that the message of the Nazarene is a vital and compelling force in the lives of millions of men and women.

This is most reassuring in a world in which the forces of greed and avarice and a disregard of fundamental human rights have brought disaster and despair where peace and plenty and true happiness should reign supreme. We regret that sorrow and heavy burdens are the possession of many; but we do not abandon hope.

I have said, and I desire to reiterate it to this body of Christians gathered from many lands, that what this weary world most needs is a revival of the spirit of religion. Would that such a revival could sweep the nations today and stir the hearts of men and women of all faiths to a reassertion of their belief in the Providence of God and the brotherhood of man. I doubt if there is in the world a single problem, whether social, political, or economic, which would not find ready solution if men and nations would rule their lives according to the plain teaching of the Sermon on the Mount.

In sending my greetings to the Tenth World's Christian Endeavor Convention may I express the hope that its deliberations will turn the hearts and minds of men and women everywhere toward this great but simple truth.

ADDRESS AT THE TERCENTENARY CELEBRATION, WILMINGTON, DELAWARE JUNE 27, 1938

IN THE SUCCEEDING centuries tens of thousands of others have come to our shores and added their strength and their fine qualities of good citizenship to the American nation. In every phase of our history, in every endeavor - in commerce and industry, in science and art, in agriculture, in education and religion, in statecraft and government, they have well played their part.

ADDRESS AT THE DEDICATION OF THE MEMORIAL ON THE GETTYSBURG BATTLEFIELD, GETTYSBURG, PENNSYLVANIA JULY 3, 1938

IMMORTAL DEEDS AND immortal words have created here at Gettysburg a shrine of American patriotism. We are encompassed by "The last full measure of devotion" of many men and by the words in which Abraham Lincoln expressed the simple faith for which they died.

ADDRESS TO GOV. DAVEY, SENATOR BULKLEY, CHAIRMAN WHITE AND THE PEOPLE OF THE NORTHWEST TERRITORY, IN MARIETTA, OHIO JULY 8, 1938

LONG BEFORE 1788 there were white men here, "spying out this land of Canaan." An intrepid outpost breed they were - the scouts and the skirmishers of the great American migration. The sight of smoke from neighbors' chimneys might have worried them. But Indians and redcoats did not.

Long before 1788, at Kaskaskia and Vincennes, with scant help from the Seaboard, they had held their beloved wilderness for themselves - and for us - with their own bare hands and their own long rifles. But their symbol is Vincennes, not Marietta.

Here, with all honor to the scouts and the skirmishers, we celebrate the coming of a different type of men and women - the first battalions of that organized army of occupation which transplanted from over the Alleghenies whole little civilizations that took root and grew. They were giving expression to a genius for organized colonization, carefully planned and ordered under law.

The men who came here before 1788 came as Leif Ericson's men to Vineland, in a spirit all of adventure. But the men and women of the Ohio Company who came to Marietta came rather like the men and women of the Massachusetts Bay Company to Boston, an organized society, unafraid to meet temporary adventure, but serious in seeking permanent security for men and women and children and homes.

Many of them were destined to push on; but most came intending to stay. Such people may not be the first to conquer the earth, but they will always be the last to possess it.

Right behind the men and women who established Marietta one hundred and fifty years ago moved that instrument of law and order and cooperation - government. A representative of the national government entered Marietta to administer the Northwest Territory under the famous Northwest Ordinance. And what we are celebrating today is this establishment of the first civil government west of the original thirteen states.

Three provisions of the Northwest Ordinance I always like to remember.

It provided that "no person demeaning himself in a peaceable and orderly manner shall ever be molested on account of his mode of worship or for religious sentiment in the said territory."

It provided that "religion, morality and knowledge being necessary to good government and the happiness of mankind, schools and means of education shall forever be encouraged."

And it provided for the perpetual prohibition of slavery in the Territory.

Free, educated, God-fearing men and women - that is what the thirteen states hoped the new West would exemplify. It has well fulfilled that hope.

ADDRESS AT OKLAHOMA CITY, OKLAHOMA
JULY 9, 1938

DURING THESE PAST six years the people of this Nation have definitely said "yes"-with no "but" about it-to the old Biblical question, "Am I my brother's keeper?" In these six years I sense a growing devotion to the teachings of the Scriptures, to the quickening of religion, to a greater willingness on the part of the individual to help his neighbor and to live less unto and for himself alone.

ADDRESS AT TREASURE ISLAND, SAN
FRANCISCO, GREETING GOV. MERRIAM
JULY 14, 1938

THE YEAR 1939 would go down in history not only as the year of the two great American World's Fairs, but would be a year of world-wide rejoicing if it could also mark definite steps toward permanent world peace. That is the hope and the prayer of the overwhelming number of men and women and children in all the earth today.

ADDRESS AT UNIVERSITY OF GEORGIA, ATHENS AUGUST 11, 1938

YEARS AGO, WHEN I first came to Georgia, I was told by a distinguished citizen of the State that public school education was well provided for because there was a law - or perhaps it was in the State Constitution...Apparently a law or a clause in the Constitution was not enough. What is law without enforcement? Apparently, the Biblical method, the divine method "Let there be light - and there was light" did not work as mere man's dictum.

RADIO ADDRESS ON THE 3RD ANNIVERSARY OF THE SOCIAL SECURITY ACT, WHITE HOUSE, WASHINGTON, D.C. AUGUST 15, 1938

IN THE EARLY days of colonization and through the long years following, the worker, the farmer, the merchant, the man of property, the preacher and the idealist came here to build, each for himself, a stronghold for the things he loved. The stronghold was his home; the things he loved and wished to protect were his family, his material and spiritual possessions.

ADDRESS AT DEDICATION OF INTERNATIONAL BRIDGE, CLAYTON, NEW YORK, GREETING MR. MACKENZIE KING
AUGUST 18, 1938

THE ST. LAWRENCE River is more than a cartographic line between our two countries. God so formed North America that the waters of an inland empire drain into the Great Lakes Basin. The rain that falls in this vast area finds outlet through this single natural funnel, close to which we now stand.

A TRIBUTE ON THE DEATH OF CARDINAL HAYES
SEPTEMBER 4, 1938

I AM DEEPLY sorry to hear of the passing of His Eminence, Cardinal Hayes. I had the privilege of his friendship for many long years. His great spiritual leadership has had a deep influence on our generation, and all of us who knew him, and had sincere affection for him, will feel his loss.

ADDRESS AT DENTON, MARYLAND, GREETING CONGRESSMAN GOLDSBOROUGH AND CONGRESSMAN LEWIS
SEPTEMBER 5, 1938

CLEARER EVERY DAY is the one great lesson of history - the lesson taught by the Master of Galilee - that the only road to peace and the only road to a happier and better civilization is the road to unity - the road called the "Highway of Fellowship."...

You have sent your sons and daughters by the thousands into the industrial world. Your products of farm and fishery go to the greatest city markets of the United

States. And you have never lost the sense of the lasting spiritual values in life.

That is why I have wanted to come here on Labor Day and preach a sermon, if you will, on that ancient text "We are all members one of another."

In order to make that relationship a benefit rather than a curse, in order to keep all of our people abreast of each other and in line with the present, our democratic form of Government must move forward on many fronts at the same time...

It is suggestive to me that Representative Lewis of Maryland has never forgotten that he learned to read and write at the knee of a Christian minister in Sunday School. That is why perhaps he has lived the life of the Good Samaritan - and he has never passed by on the other side...For our own safety we cannot afford to follow those in public life who quote the Golden Rule and take no steps to bring it closer.

MESSAGE TO CZECHOSLOVAKIA, GERMANY, GREAT BRITAIN, AND FRANCE ON WAR THREAT SEPTEMBER 26, 1938

IT IS MY conviction that all people under the threat of war today pray that peace may be made before, rather than after, war.

GREETING TO THE NATIONAL EUCHARISTIC CONGRESS TO HIS EXCELLENCY, ARCHBISHOP RUMMEL OF NEW ORLEANS, LOUISIANA OCTOBER 1, 1938

I SEND HEARTY greetings to you and through you to all who gather within the hospitable borders of the Archdiocese of New Orleans on the occasion of the Eighth

National Eucharistic Congress. I trust that the deliberations will quicken the spiritual life of all who participate and inspire them with new zeal for the work of the Master whom we all serve.

We have just celebrated the one hundred fiftieth anniversary of the adoption of our Federal Constitution, which guarantees freedom of conscience as the cornerstone of all our liberties.

We in this country are upholders of the ideal of democracy in the government of man. We believe with heart and soul that in the long struggle of the human race to attain an orderly society the democratic form of government is the highest achievement. All of our hopes have their basis in the democratic ideal.

Even before the adoption of our Declaration of Independence George Mason, in the Virginia Declaration of Rights, voiced what has become one of the deepest convictions of the American people:

"That religion, or the duty which we owe to our Creator, and the manner of discharging it, can be directed only by reason and conviction, not by force or violence, and therefore all men are equally entitled to the free exercise of religion, according to the dictates of conscience; and that it is the mutual duty of all to practice Christian forbearance, love, and charity towards each other."

We still remain true to the faith of our fathers who established religious liberty when the nation began. We must remember, too, that our forebears in every generation, and wherever they established their homes, made prompt and generous provision for the institutions of religion. We must continue their steadfast reliance upon the Providence of God.

I have said and I repeat to this solemn Eucharistic Congress that no greater blessing could come to our land today than a revival of the spirit of religion. I doubt if there is any problem in the world today - social, political or economic - that would not find happy solution if approached in the spirit of the Sermon on the Mount.

May your prayers hasten the day when both men and nations will bring their lives into conformity with the teaching of Him Who is the Way, the Light and the Truth.

RADIO ADDRESS FOR THE MOBILIZATION FOR HUMAN NEEDS
OCTOBER 14, 1938

I AM CALLING your attention to the past and present generosity of the people of America. That generosity never has failed and please God it never will fail. In full faith and confidence, therefore, I present to you the news that local Community Chest drives will shortly be undertaken in all parts of the country.

LETTER ON THE PALESTINE SITUATION, ADDRESSING THE HONORABLE MILLARD E. TYDINGS, UNITED STATES SENATE
OCTOBER 19, 1938

I FULLY APPRECIATE the concern expressed by you in your letter of October 14, 1938, regarding the Palestine situation.

I have on numerous occasions, as you know, expressed my sympathy in the establishment of a National Home for the Jews in Palestine and, despite the set-backs caused by the disorders there during the last few years, I have been heartened by the progress which has been made and by the remarkable accomplishments of the Jewish settlers in that country.

As I have had occasion to inform a number of Members of Congress within the past few days, we have kept constantly before the British Government, through our Ambassador in London, the interest which the American people have in Palestine and I have every reason to believe that that Government is fully cognizant of public opinion on the matter in this country.

We were assured, in the discussions which took place in London a little more than a year ago, that the British Government would keep us fully informed of any proposals which it might make to the Council of the League of Nations for the modification of the Palestine Mandate.

We expect, therefore, to have the opportunity afforded us of communicating to the British Government our views with respect to any changes in the Mandate which may be proposed as a result of the forthcoming report of the Palestine Partition Commission.

I understand, however, that under the terms of our convention with Great Britain regarding the Palestine Mandate we are unable to prevent modifications in the Mandate. The most we can do is to decline to accept as applicable to American interest any modifications affecting such interests unless we have given our assent to them.

You may be sure that we shall continue to follow the situation with the closest attention.

RADIO ADDRESS TO THE HERALD-TRIBUNE FORUM, GREETING MRS. REID
OCTOBER 26, 1938

THERE CAN BE no peace if humble men and women are not free to think their own thoughts, to express their own feelings, to worship God.

LETTER TO JOSEPH PULITZER, ESQ., EDITOR, THE ST. LOUIS POST-DISPATCH NOVEMBER 2, 1938

HERE IS ONE so fresh one would expect to find dew on the petals: "The greatest measure of centralization and of paternalism in government ever undertaken in this country since the adoption of the Federal Constitution, is undoubtedly the Inter-State Commerce bill."

So spake the same New York Sun, not this week, but fifty-one years ago last February.

Something which brings the past right up to the present is found in this wail: "There is depression, distrust and gloom on every hand," from the New York Herald of April 30, 1893.

This is the way a very old friend reversed English on the approach of the millennium, December 9, 1893:

"There has never been anything more closely approaching monarchy or autocracy than there is in this country today under a so-called Democratic government....It may as well be admitted, as dictators go, (the) President would make a very fair specimen....He is right sometimes, and then we all have occasion to compliment him on his resolution, his dogged persistency, and his utter disregard for what seems to be the prevalent public opinion. Also he is wrong sometimes, and then his partisans have to admit that he is the most mulish and most obstinately wrong-headed man who ever sat in the chair of Washington....The struggle between the would-be dictator and the people of the United States is one which men of all parties may watch with much interest."

New York Daily Tribune felt no better on the day before Christmas of the same year. The writer had prescience, almost the gift of prophecy. Exemplifying the truth of an oft-quoted passage from Ecclesiastes the Tribune said: "Millions are in distress because hundreds of thousands were deluded into believing that a change of party control would give them a larger share of the common prosperity, or misled by an irrational inclination to take the chances of 'A New Deal.'"

I think I ought to add for the record that Ecclesiastes' exact words were: "There is no new thing under the sun."...

At any rate, to the youngster about to embark on a career as a newspaperman the then General Manager of the Associated Press said: "Write factually, truthfully and simply. The American people are sufficiently intelligent, if given the facts, to draw their own conclusions - to form their own opinions."

RADIO ADDRESS ON THE ELECTIONS
NOVEMBER 4, 1938

JUDGE PARTIES AND candidates, not merely by what they promise, but...by the kind of people who finance and promote their campaigns. By their promoters ye shall know them...

The Governor of this State...the preservation of civil and religious liberties - all these precious essentials of civilization are entrusted to him...

Look over the rest of the names on the ballot next Tuesday...Pick them without regard to race, color or creed...

Remember that the Fathers of the American Revolution represented many religions and came from many foreign lands.

Remember that no matter what their origin they all agreed with Benjamin Franklin in that crisis: "We must indeed all hang together or most assuredly we shall all hang separately."

PRESS CONFERENCE
NOVEMBER 5, 1938

THE PRESIDENT: The news of the past few days from Germany has deeply shocked public opinion in the United States. Such news from any part of the world would inevitably produce a similar profound reaction among American people in every part of the nation. I myself could scarcely believe that such things could occur in a twentieth century civilization. With a view to gaining a first-hand picture of the current situation in Germany I asked the Secretary of State to order our Ambassador in Berlin to return at once for report and consultation...

Q: There are reports from London that Mr. Kennedy has made a suggestion to the British Government concerning a place wherein the Jewish refugees would be taken care of.

THE PRESIDENT: I cannot comment on the report, because I know nothing of what has been happening in London. We do know that the Intergovernmental Committee on refugees is at work trying to extend its help to take care of an increasingly difficult situation.

Q: Mr. President, can you tell us whether you feel that there is any place in the world where you could take care of mass emigration of the Jews from Germany - have you given thought to that?

THE PRESIDENT: I have given a great deal of thought to it.

Q: Can you tell us any place particularly desirable?
THE PRESIDENT: No, the time is not ripe for that...

Q: Would you recommend a relaxation of. our immigration restrictions so that the Jewish refugees could be received in this country?

THE PRESIDENT: That is not in contemplation; we have the quota system...

THE PRESIDENT. There is one other factor...there are in this country at the present time...as high as twelve to fifteen thousand refugees from, principally, Germany and Austria - what was Austria - who are in this country on what are called "Visitors' Permits," I think that is the word.

In other words, they are here, not on a quota, but as visitors with proper passports from their own governments. The situation apparently has arisen that, because of a recent decree, those visitors' passports will be canceled as of the thirtieth of December, this year.

Now, as a matter of practical fact, a great many of these people - who are not all Jews by any means, since other religions are included in very large numbers among them - if they were to get back to Germany before the thirtieth of December, a great many of them believe that their treatment on reaching home might be a very serious problem. In other words, it is a question of concentration camps, et cetera and so on. They are not here under a quota so we have a very definite problem as to what to do. I don't know, from the point of view of humanity, that we have a right to put them on a ship and send them back to Germany under the present conditions.

We can legally - the Secretary of Labor can, legally - give six months extensions so that they can stay in this country under the six months extension provision. As I understand it, the law does not say how many six months extensions there can be - it does not limit the number.

So what I told the Secretary of Labor yesterday was that it would be a cruel and inhuman thing to compel them to leave here in time to get back to Germany by the thirtieth of December. I have suggested to Miss Perkins that they be given six months extensions.

Under those extensions they cannot, as I understand it, apply for American citizenship. They are only visitors. Therefore, there being no adequate law on the subject, we shall simply present the facts to the Congress. If the Congress takes no action, these unfortunate people will be allowed to stay in this country.

Q: Will you repeat that, Mr. President?

THE PRESIDENT: They will be allowed to stay in this country under the six months extension law, because I cannot, in any decent humanity, throw them out.

Q: Do you understand that you may at the end of the first six months, extend for another period of six months?

THE PRESIDENT: Yes.

Q: And on and on?

THE PRESIDENT: I think so, but I am not clear about it. Anyway, we are going to present the situation to the Congress when it meets. I have no doubt that the Congress will not compel us to send these twelve or fifteen thousand people back to Germany, any more than the Congress compelled us to send a large number of the refugees of the old Russian regime back to Russia after Russia was taken over.

Q: Are they permitted to work over here?

THE PRESIDENT: Oh, as visitors, a good many of them, for example, are teaching in the universities and colleges.

THANKSGIVING DAY PROCLAMATION
NOVEMBER 19, 1938

I, FRANKLIN D. ROOSEVELT, President of the United States of America, do hereby designate Thursday, the twenty-fourth of November, 1938, as a day of general thanksgiving.

Our Fathers set aside such a day as they hewed a nation from the primeval forest. The observance was consecrated when George Washington issued a Thanksgiving proclamation in the first year of his presidency. Abraham Lincoln set apart "a Day of Thanksgiving and Praise to our beneficent Father who dwelleth in the heavens."

Thus from our earliest recorded history, Americans have thanked God for their blessings. In our deepest natures, in our very souls, we, like all mankind since the earliest origin of mankind, turn to God in time of trouble and in time of happiness. "In God We Trust."

For the blessings which have been ours during the present year we have ample cause to be thankful.

Our lands have yielded a goodly harvest, and the toiler in shop and mill receives a more just return for his labor.

We have cherished and preserved our democracy.

We have lived in peace and understanding with our neighbors and have seen the world escape the impending disaster of a general war.

In the time of our fortune it is fitting that we offer prayers for unfortunate people in other lands who are in dire distress at this our Thanksgiving Season.

Let us remember them in our families and our churches when, on the day appointed, we offer our thanks to Almighty God. May we by our way of living merit the continuance of His goodness.

STATEMENT ON REFUGEES IN PALESTINE
NOVEMBER 23, 1938

IT IS REPORTED here that the number of refugees to be permitted entry into Palestine will be materially increased, and in particular that many children and young people will be given refuge there. I have no means of knowing the accuracy of this report but I hope that it is true.

ADDRESS AT UNIVERSITY OF NORTH CAROLINA, CHAPEL HILL, NORTH CAROLINA, GREETING PRESIDENT GRAHAM, THE CAROLINA POLITICAL UNION, AND GOVERNOR HOEY
DECEMBER 5, 1938

IT IS ONLY the possessors of "headline" mentality that exaggerate or distort the true objectives of those in this Nation whether they be the president of the University of North Carolina or the President of the United States, who, with Mr. Justice Cardozo, admit the fact of change and seek to guide change into the right channels to the greater glory of God and the greater good of mankind.

You undergraduates who see me for the first time have read your newspapers and heard on the air that I am, at the very least, an ogre - a consorter with Communists, a destroyer of the rich, a breaker of our ancient traditions. Some of you think of me perhaps as the inventor of the economic royalist, of the wicked utilities, of the money changers of the Temple.

You have heard for six years that I was about to plunge the Nation into war; that you and your little brothers would be sent to the bloody fields of battle in Europe; that I was driving the Nation into bankruptcy; and that I breakfasted every morning on a dish of "grilled millionaire."

Actually I am an exceedingly mild mannered person - a practitioner of peace, both domestic and foreign, a believer in the capitalistic system, and for my breakfast a devotee of scrambled eggs...

ADDRESS AT GROUNDBREAKING FOR THOMAS JEFFERSON MEMORIAL, WASHINGTON, D.C. DECEMBER 15, 1938

FOR MORE THAN fifty years, Thomas Jefferson, the third President of the United States, has been recognized by our citizens not only for the outstanding part which he took in the drafting of the Declaration of Independence itself, not only for his authorship of the Virginia statute for religious freedom, but also for the services he rendered in establishing the practical operation of the American Government as a democracy and not as an autocracy.

CHRISTMAS GREETINGS TO DISABLED VETERANS DECEMBER 19, 1938

TO YOU, WHO in time of national peril, have defended your country with courage, fortitude and heroic self-sacrifice, I extend my heartfelt holiday greetings. It is my earnest wish and that of an ever grateful nation that for you and those dear to you this Christmas season will be one of happiness and hope, and that the New Year will see your restoration to comfort and health in a happy nation long destined, in the Providence of God, to remain at peace.

CHRISTMAS GREETINGS TO THE ARMY AND NAVY DECEMBER 24, 1938

IT GIVES ME great pleasure to send my most cordial and hearty Christmas greetings to the Army and the Navy. Events of the past twelve months have served to focus public attention on the national defense and to bring home to all of our people a greater appreciation of the protective missions of our land and sea forces.

The nation is grateful to its democratic armed forces, volunteers to a man, for their whole-hearted devotion to duty. It is my sincere hope that this holiday season will bring happiness and good cheer to all who wear the uniform of our republic.

ADDRESS ON LIGHTING THE COMMUNITY CHRISTMAS TREE, WASHINGTON, D.C. DECEMBER 24, 1938

TONIGHT IS CHRISTMAS Eve. We are gathered again around our Community Tree here in Lafayette Park, across the street from the White House. Darkness has fallen over the Capital but all about us shine a myriad of brilliant lights. All our hearts, warmed by the eternal fire of Christmas rejoice, because new life, new hope, new happiness are in them.

In this setting I wish my fellow countrymen everywhere a Merry Christmas with peace, content and friendly cheer to all. I wish also to thank the thousands who have remembered me and my family this Christmas with individual greetings. We shall always treasure these friendly messages.

At this time let us hope that the boon of peace which we in this country and in the whole Western Hemisphere enjoy under the Providence of God may likewise be vouchsafed to all nations and all peoples. We desire peace. We shall work for peace. We covet neither the lands nor the possessions of any other nation or people.

We of the Western World who have borne witness by works as well as words to our devotion to the cause of peace, ought to take heart tonight from the atmosphere of hope and promise in which representatives of twenty-one free republics are now assembled in the Pan-American Conference at Lima, Peru.

I consider it a happy circumstance that these deliberations will be successfully concluded soon after the birthday of the Prince of Peace. It is indeed a holy season in which to work for good will among men. We derive new strength, new courage for our work from the spirit of Christmas.

We do not expect a new Heaven and a new Earth overnight, but in our own land, and other lands - wherever men of good will listen to our appeal - we shall work as best we can with the instruments at hand to banish hatred, greed and covetousness from the heart of mankind.

And so the pledge I have so often given to my own countrymen I renew before all the world on this glad Christmas Eve, that I shall do whatever lies within my own power to hasten the day foretold by Isaiah, when men "shall beat their swords into plowshares and their spears into pruning hooks; nation shall not lift up sword against nation, neither shall they learn war any more."

ANNUAL MESSAGE TO CONGRESS
JANUARY 4, 1939

STORMS FROM ABROAD directly challenge three institutions indispensable to Americans, now as always. The first is religion. It is the source of the other two - democracy and international good faith.

Religion, by teaching man his relationship to God, gives the individual a sense of his own dignity and teaches him to respect himself by respecting his neighbors.

Democracy, the practice of self-government, is a covenant among free men to respect the rights and liberties of their fellows.

International good faith, a sister of democracy, springs from the will of civilized nations of men to respect the rights and liberties of other nations of men.

In a modern civilization, all three - religion, democracy and international good faith - complement and support each other.

Where freedom of religion has been attacked, the attack has come from sources opposed to democracy. Where democracy has been overthrown, the spirit of free worship has disappeared. And where religion and democracy have vanished, good faith and reason in international affairs have given way to strident ambition and brute force.

An ordering of society which relegates religion, democracy and good faith among nations to the background can find no place within it for the ideals of the Prince of Peace. The United States rejects such an ordering, and retains its ancient faith.

There comes a time in the affairs of men when they must prepare to defend, not their homes alone, but the tenets of faith and humanity on which their churches, their governments and their very civilization are founded. The defense of religion, of democracy and of good faith among nations is all the same fight. To save one we must now make up our minds to save all.

We know what might happen to us of the United States if the new philosophies of force were to encompass the other continents and invade our own. We, no more than other nations, can afford to be surrounded by the enemies of our faith and our humanity. Fortunate it is, therefore, that in this Western Hemisphere we have, under a common ideal of democratic government, a rich diversity of resources and of peoples functioning together in mutual respect and peace.

That Hemisphere, that peace, and that ideal we propose to do our share in protecting against storms from any quarter. Our people and our resources are pledged to secure that protection. From that determination no American flinches...

We have learned that God-fearing democracies of the world which observe the sanctity of treaties and good faith in their dealings with other nations cannot safely be indifferent to international lawlessness anywhere. They cannot forever let pass, without effective protest, acts of aggression against sister nations - acts which automatically undermine all of us...

Above all, we have made the American people conscious of their interrelationship and their interdependence. They sense a common destiny and a common need of each other. Differences of occupation, geography, race and religion no longer obscure the nation's fundamental unity in thought and in action...

Dictatorship, however, involves costs which the American people will never pay: The cost of our spiritual values. The cost of the blessed right of being able to say what we please. The cost of freedom of religion. The cost of seeing our capital confiscated.

The cost of being cast into a concentration camp. The cost of being afraid to walk down the street with the wrong neighbor. The cost of having our children brought up, not as free and dignified human beings, but as pawns molded and enslaved by a machine...

Once I prophesied that this generation of Americans had a rendezvous with destiny. That prophecy comes true. To us much is given; more is expected.

This generation will "nobly save or meanly lose the last best hope of earth...The way is plain, peaceful, generous, just - a way which if followed the world will forever applaud and God must forever bless."

LETTER ON THE 6TH OBSERVANCE OF BROTHERHOOD DAY TO DR. EVERETT R. CLINCHY, NATIONAL CONFERENCE OF CHRISTIANS AND JEWS, NEW YORK CITY JANUARY 5, 1939

THE SIXTH OBSERVANCE of Brotherhood Day under the auspices of the National Conference of Christians and Jews during the week of Washington's Birthday, 1939, gives emphasis to principles that are fundamental in the American way of life.

Never has it been more essential that our people of every national origin, race or faith should proclaim those civic ideals that they hold in common and engage together in those activities that reflect their common social aims.

Here in the United States, while maintaining the right to differ in our creeds, all groups must unite in maintaining for all, the liberties guaranteed by the American Constitution and in cultivating that mutual respect, friendship and cooperation across dividing lines, which will bind us together as a nation.

It is my hope that the observance of Brotherhood Day this year will advance these ideals.

ADDRESS AT THE JACKSON DAY DINNER
JANUARY 7, 1939

THIS NEW GENERATION, since the war, believes more than did its fathers in the precept "I am my brother's keeper." It believes in realities, economic and spiritual realities.

RADIO ADDRESS ON THE SIXTH BIRTHDAY BALL
FOR CRIPPLED CHILDREN
JANUARY 30, 1939

I SHOULD LIKE to say just a word about the National Foundation for Infantile Paralysis. Not yet two years old, it is a mature and efficient organization working industriously to perform its functions with but one objective - the banishment of infantile paralysis...

With my thanks to all of my countrymen goes from the depths of my soul a prayer that God will bless the work and the workers. The good cause must go on.

REMARKS TO TRUSTEES OF THE FRANKLIN D.
ROOSEVELT LIBRARY, INC., WASHINGTON, D.C.
FEBRUARY 4, 1939

SOME OF US not long ago, in September, listened on a Monday afternoon, at two o'clock, to the personal voice of the leader of the German State, who made an amazing speech in the Sports Palace.

The next day the American people, at the same hour, heard the quite sober, appealing and rather pathetic voice of Neville Chamberlain telling his democracy and a great many other democracies the story that the English-speaking peoples had to tell.

RADIO ADDRESS ON THE TWENTY-NINTH ANNIVERSARY OF THE BOY SCOUTS OF AMERICA FEBRUARY 8, 1939

THESE BOYS, SO full of promise for the future, are a national asset and therefore should be regarded as a national trust. Ours is the duty to inculcate in the Scout mind those simple but fundamental principles which embrace strength of body, alertness of mind and, above these and growing out of them, that sense of moral responsibility upon which all sound character rests...

As one who has long been active in Scout work and who feels a special responsibility as Honorary President of the Boy Scouts of America, I like to think that faithful observance of the Scout Oath constitutes an excellent preliminary training in the duties of citizenship.

ADDRESS ON THE ONE HUNDRED AND FIFTIETH ANNIVERSARY OF THE CONGRESS MARCH 4, 1939

IN THAT BILL of Rights lies another vast chasm between our representative democracy and those reversions to personal rule which have characterized these recent years.

Jury trial: do the people of our own land ever stop to compare that blessed right of ours with some processes of trial and punishment which of late have reincarnated the so-called "justice" of the dark ages?

The taking of private property without due compensation: would we willingly abandon our security against that in the face of the events of recent years?

The right to be safe against unwarrantable searches and seizures: read your newspapers and rejoice that our firesides and our households are still safe.

Freedom to assemble and petition the Congress for a redress of grievances: the mail and the telegraph bring daily proof to every Senator and every Representative that that right is at the height of an unrestrained popularity.

Freedom of speech: yes, that, too, is unchecked for never in all history has there been so much of it on every side of every subject. It is indeed a freedom which, because of the mildness of our laws of libel and slander, goes unchecked except by the good sense of the American people.

Any person is constitutionally entitled to criticize and call to account the highest and the lowest in the land - save only in one exception. For be it noted that the Constitution of the United States itself protects Senators and Representatives and provides that "for any speech or debate in either House they shall not be questioned in any other place." And that immunity is most carefully not extended to either the Chief Justice of the United States or the President.

Freedom of the press: I take it that no sensible man or woman believes that it has been curtailed or threatened or that it should be. The influence of the printed word will always depend on its veracity; and the nation can safely rely on the wise discrimination of a reading public which with the increase in the general education is well able to sort truth from fiction. Representative democracy will never tolerate suppression of true news at the behest of government.

Freedom of religion: that essential of the rights of mankind everywhere goes back also to the origins of representative government.

Where democracy is snuffed out, where it is curtailed, there, too, the right to worship God in one's own way is circumscribed or abrogated. Shall we by our passiveness, by our silence, by assuming the attitude of the Levite who pulled his skirts together and passed by on the other side, lend encouragement to those who today persecute religion or deny it?

The answer to that is "no" today, just as in the days of the first Congress of the United States it was "no."...

Our fathers rightly believed that this government which they set up would seek as a whole to act as a whole for the good governing of the nation. It is in the same spirit that we are met here, today, 150 years later, to carry on their task. May God continue to guide our steps.

LETTER ACKNOWLEDGING THE AWARD OF THE AMERICAN HEBREW MEDAL MARCH 6, 1939

I LIKE ALSO to think that no matter how diverse and conflicting and mutually contradictory our views may be on any number of questions and policies - there remains one issue upon which we are in complete accord.

Embodied in the Federal Constitution and ingrained in our hearts and souls is the national conviction that every man has an inalienable right to worship God according to the dictates of his own conscience.

After all, the majority of Americans, whether they adhere to the ancient teaching of Israel or accept the tenets of the Christian religion, have a common source of inspiration in the Old Testament. In the spirit of brotherhood we should, therefore, seek to emphasize all those many essential things in which we find unity in our common Biblical heritage.

If we labor in that spirit may we not hope to attain the ideal put forth by the Prophet Micah: "And what doth the Lord require of thee, but to do justly, and to love mercy, and to walk humbly with thy God?"

MESSAGE TO ADOLF HITLER
AND BENITO MUSSOLINI
APRIL 14, 1939

HEADS OF GREAT Governments in this hour are literally responsible for the fate of humanity in the coming years. They cannot fail to hear the prayers of their peoples to be protected from the foreseeable chaos of war. History will hold them accountable for the lives and the happiness of all - even unto the least.

ADDRESS AT THE WHITE HOUSE CONFERENCE
ON CHILDREN IN A DEMOCRACY
APRIL 23, 1939

IN AN ADDRESS on Pan American Day, two weeks ago, I said "Men are not prisoners of fate, but only prisoners of their own minds. They have within themselves the power to become free at any moment."...

We are concerned about the children who are outside the reach of religious influences, and are denied help in attaining faith in an ordered universe and in the fatherhood of God...

I bid you, the members of the Conference, Godspeed in this, your high endeavor.

PROCLAMATION NO. 2331 ON EMPLOYMENT WEEK AND EMPLOYMENT SUNDAY APRIL 26, 1939

I, FRANKLIN D. ROOSEVELT, President of the United States of America, do hereby declare the week beginning April 30, 1939, as Employment Week, and do hereby declare Sunday, April 30, 1939, as Employment Sunday;

And urge all churches, civic organizations, Chambers of Commerce, veterans organizations, industry, labor, and the press, throughout the United States to observe that week and that Sunday as Employment Week and Employment Sunday to the end that interest in the welfare of the older workers may be stimulated and employment opportunity afforded them.

OPENING OF THE NEW YORK WORLD'S FAIR APRIL 30, 1939

ALL OF THE earlier Amendments may be accepted by us as a part of the original Constitution because that sacred Bill of Rights, which guaranteed and has maintained personal liberty through freedom of speech, freedom of the press, freedom of religion and freedom of assembly, was already popularly accepted by the inhabitants of thirteen states while the Constitution itself was in the process of ratification...

Often, I think, we Americans offer up a silent prayer that on the Continent of Europe, from which the American hemisphere was principally colonized, the years to come will break down many barriers to intercourse between nations.

PRESS CONFERENCE, HYDE PARK, NEW YORK
JULY 22, 1939

AS STEVE EARLY told you yesterday, about all we can do between now and January is to pray that there won't be another crisis, and pray awfully hard.

MESSAGE TO KING VICTOR EMMANUEL OF ITALY
ON THE POLAND CRISIS
AUGUST 24, 1939

THE GOVERNMENT OF Italy and the United States can today advance those ideals of Christianity which of late seem so often to have been obscured.

The unheard voices of countless millions of human beings ask that they shall not be vainly sacrificed again.

2ND LETTER TO ADOLF HITLER, CHANCELLOR
OF THE GERMAN REICH, BERLIN, GERMANY
AUGUST 25, 1939

COUNTLESS HUMAN LIVES can be yet saved and hope may still be restored that the nations of the modern world may even now construct a foundation for a peaceful and a happier relationship if you and the Government of the German Reich will agree to the pacific means of settlement accepted by the Government of Poland. All the world prays that Germany, too, will accept.

STATEMENT ON LABOR DAY
SEPTEMBER 3, 1939

SO LET US be thankful upon this Labor Day and the days to come for what we have accomplished in the great democracy which is the United States and let us pray that nothing may transpire to interrupt our progress toward the goal of peace, good will and national well-being, which we as a people always have had and, please God, always shall have as our objective in our own interest and that of the world at large.

FIRESIDE CHAT, WASHINGTON, D.C.
SEPTEMBER 3, 1939

UNTIL FOUR-THIRTY this morning I had hoped against hope that some miracle would prevent a devastating war in Europe and bring to an end the invasion of Poland by Germany...

In spite of spreading wars I think that we have every right and every reason to maintain as a national policy the fundamental moralities, the teachings of religion and the continuation of efforts to restore peace - for some day, though the time may be distant, we can be of even greater help to a crippled humanity...

Most of us in the United States believe in spiritual values. Most of us, regardless of what church we belong to, believe in the spirit of the New Testament - a great teaching which opposes itself to the use of force, of armed force, of marching armies and falling bombs. The overwhelming masses of our people seek peace - peace at home, and the kind of peace in other lands which will not jeopardize our peace at home...

We seek to keep war from our own firesides by keeping war from coming to the Americas.

For that we have historic precedent that goes back to the days of the Administration of President George Washington. It is serious enough and tragic enough to every American family in every State in the Union to live in a world that is torn by wars on other continents. Those wars today affect every American home. It is our national duty to use every effort to keep them out of the Americas.

PROCLAMATION 2348 PROCLAIMING THE NEUTRALITY OF THE UNITED STATES SEPTEMBER 5, 1939

ANY SHIP OF war...after the time this notification takes effect, be found in, or shall enter any port, harbor, roadstead, or waters subject to the jurisdiction of the United States, such vessel shall not be permitted to remain in such port, harbor, roadstead, or waters more than twenty-four hours...

Vessels used exclusively for scientific, religious, or philanthropic purposes are exempted from the foregoing provisions.

MESSAGE TO CONGRESS URGING REPEAL OF THE EMBARGO PROVISIONS OF THE NEUTRALITY LAW SEPTEMBER 21, 1939

THE UNITED STATES has constantly, consistently and conscientiously done all in its power to encourage peaceful settlements, to bring about reduction of armaments, and to avert threatened wars. We have done this not only because any war anywhere necessarily hurts American security and American prosperity, but because of the more important fact that any war anywhere retards the progress of morality and religion, and impairs the security of civilization itself...

Last January, also, I spoke to this Congress of the need for further warning of new threats of conquest, military and economic; of challenge to religion, to democracy and to international good faith. I said: "An ordering of society which relegates religion, democracy and good faith among nations to the background can find no place within it for the ideals of the Prince of Peace. The United States rejects such an ordering and retains its ancient faith..."

And I said:

"We know what might happen to us of the United States if the new philosophies of force were to encompass the other continents and invade our own. We, no more than other nations, can afford to be surrounded by the enemies of our faith and our humanity."...

In a period when it is sometimes said that free discussion is no longer compatible with national safety, may you by your deeds show the world that we of the United States are one people, of one mind, one spirit, one clear resolution, walking before God in the light of the living.

STATEMENT ON THE PRAYER FOR PEACE SEPTEMBER 29, 1939

IN THE LAST week the White House has received many hundreds of telegrams from churchmen, clergy, and, in general, from the religious homes of America asking the President to proclaim and set aside a Day of Prayer...

The President...hopes on this coming Sunday that the people of the United States will offer a prayer during the day for continued peace of the world. He would like the people throughout the country to join with him and his family in such a prayer.

LETTER ON PEACE IN THE RANKS OF LABOR, ADDRESSED TO THE HON. WILLIAM GREEN, PRESIDENT, AMERICAN FEDERATION OF LABOR, NETHERLAND-PLAZA HOTEL, CINCINNATI, OHIO SEPTEMBER 30, 1939

WHEN WE SEE Europe in a war which may cost many lives and imperil civilization itself, we may well offer thanks to God for the peace we have on this continent. It is the duty of each of us to leave nothing undone to promote the continuation of that peace for us, our children and our children's children. Peace, like charity, begins at home...

In the presence of these blessings and in the face of this world necessity we must adjourn our small grudges, our differences, and find the way to peace and good will within our borders in every department of life.

TRIBUTE TO THE LATE CARDINAL MUNDELEIN, ADDRESSED TO THE MOST REVEREND BERNARD J. SHEIL, CHICAGO, ILLINOIS OCTOBER 2, 1939

A CAREER OF great goodness and usefulness has been brought to an untimely close with the passing of Cardinal Mundelein. He served his day and generation with unfailing fidelity to the highest principles of Christianity.

As a citizen who gloried in our American democracy he was the advocate and exemplar of justice and righteousness whether in the relation of the individual to the state or in the field of international affairs. His influence was always potent for peace. My personal acquaintance with Cardinal Mundelein began when he was Bishop of Brooklyn and I mourn the loss of a true friend, a close friend for many years.

ADDRESS TO POSTMASTERS CONVENTION, WASHINGTON, D.C. OCTOBER 11, 1939

IT MATTERS NOT what the means of transportation of the mails may be - whether the mules and camels of the Old Testament which Job said made his days "swifter than a post" - or those modern annihilators of distance, the train, the automobile and the airplane.

ADDRESS TO INTERGOVERNMENTAL COMMITTEE OFFICERS ON POLITICAL REFUGEES OCTOBER 17, 1939

IN MARCH, 1938, it became clear to the world that a point had been reached where private agencies alone could no longer deal with the masses of unfortunate people who had been driven from their homes. These men, women and children were beating at the gate of any nation which seemed to offer them a haven.

Most of these fellow human beings belonged to the Jewish Race, though many thousands of them belonged to other races and other creeds. The flight from their countries of origin meant chaos for them and great difficulties for other nations which for other reasons - chiefly economic - had erected barriers against immigration. Many portions of the world which in earlier years provided areas for immigration had found it necessary to close their doors.

Therefore, a year and a half ago I took the initiative by asking thirty-two governments to cooperate with the

Government of the United States in seeking a long range solution of the refugee problem. Because the United States through more than three centuries has been built in great measure by people whose dreams in other lands had been thwarted, it seemed appropriate for us to make possible the meeting at Evian, which was attended by Mr. Myron C. Taylor as my personal representative.

That meeting made permanent the present Intergovernmental Committee, and since that time this Intergovernmental Committee has greatly helped in the settling of many refugees, in providing temporary refuge for thousands of others and in making important studies toward opening up new places of final settlement in many parts of the world...

Things were going well, although I must confess slowly, up to the outbreak of the war in Europe. Today we must recognize that the regular and planned course of refugee work has been of necessity seriously interrupted...

Nearly every great war leaves behind it vast numbers of human beings whose roots have been literally torn up. Inevitably there are great numbers of individuals who have lost all family ties - individuals who find no home to return to, no occupation to resume - individuals who for many different reasons must seek to rebuild their lives under new environments...

This problem involves no one race group - no one religious faith. It is the problem of all groups and all faiths...

Remembering the words written on the Statue of Liberty, let us lift a lamp beside new golden doors and built new refuges for the tired, for the poor, for the huddled masses yearning to be free.

THANKSGIVING DAY PROCLAMATION
OCTOBER 31, 1939

I, FRANKLIN D. ROOSEVELT, President of the United States o{ America, do hereby designate Thursday, the twenty-third of November, 1939, as a day of general thanksgiving.

More than. three centuries ago at the season of the gathering in of the harvest, the Pilgrims humbly paused in their work and gave thanks to God for the preservation of their community and for the abundant yield of the soil.

A century and a half later, after the new Nation had been formed, and the charter of government, the Constitution of the Republic, had received the assent of the States, President Washington and his successors invited the people of the Nation to lay down their tasks one day in the year and give thanks for the blessings that had been granted them by Divine Providence. It is fitting that we should continue this hallowed custom and select a day in 1939 to be dedicated to reverent thoughts of thanksgiving.

Our Nation has gone steadily forward in the application of democratic processes to economic and social problems. We have faced the specters of business depression, of unemployment, and of widespread agricultural distress, and our positive efforts to alleviate these conditions have met with heartening results.

We have also been permitted to see the fruition of measures which we have undertaken in the realms of health, social welfare, and the conservation of resources. As a Nation we are deeply grateful that in a world of turmoil we are at peace with all countries, and we especially rejoice in the strengthened bonds of our friendship with the other peoples of the Western Hemisphere.

Let us, on the day set aside for this purpose, give thanks to the Ruler of the Universe for the strength which He has vouchsafed us to carry on our daily labors and for the hope that lives within us of the coming of a day when peace and the productive activities of peace shall reign on every continent.

GREETING TO CONGRESS AT THE CLOSE OF THE EXTRAORDINARY SESSION, ADDRESSED TO THE VICE PRESIDENT OF THE UNITED STATES, UNITED STATES SENATE, WASHINGTON, D.C. NOVEMBER 3, 1939

I HOPE THAT world events will not make it necessary to have any other extraordinary session - and, therefore, in anticipation of seeing you all on the third of January next, I extend to you in the meantime my best wishes for a Happy Thanksgiving and a Merry Christmas.

May I add that I hope those Members from States whose Governors have set November thirtieth as Thanksgiving Day will celebrate both Thanksgivings - the twenty-third and the thirtieth.

ADDRESS ON THE 100TH ANNIVERSARY OF THE VIRGINIA MILITARY INSTITUTE, LEXINGTON, VIRGINIA, GREETING GENERAL KILBOURNE NOVEMBER 11, 1939

WE, AS A nation, like V.M.I., are determined to pursue our way within the Scriptural command not to "remove the ancient landmarks which thy fathers have set." And like our ancestors we work for peace, we pray for peace, and we arm for peace.

ADDRESS AT THE CORNERSTONE LAYING OF THE JEFFERSON MEMORIAL, WASHINGTON, D.C. NOVEMBER 15, 1939

WHEN IN THE year of 1939 America speaks of its Bill of Rights, we think of the author of the Statute for religious liberty in Virginia.

REMARKS AT THANKSGIVING DINNER, OLD WARM SPRINGS FOUNDATION, GEORGIA NOVEMBER 23, 1939

I AM VERY much in favor of the kind of war that we are conducting here at Warm Springs...the war against the crippling of men and women and, especially, of children.

It is a comparatively new fight. Even the older people here will be perhaps surprised a little when I tell them that fifty years ago, when some of us who are here tonight were alive, there was practically nothing being done in all of the United States to help crippled people to use their arms and legs again.

What did they do? Well, they were pushed off to the side; they were just unfortunate people.

It was just what they used to call "an act of God"; and there were a lot of very good religious people, people who belonged to churches, people who lived Christian lives, all over the United States who, when somebody in the family got infantile paralysis or something else in those days, would say that it was an act of God and they would do nothing more about it.

The child or the grownup would be regarded as an unfortunate victim of something about which no human being could do anything...

I think our attitude toward religion, toward helping our neighbors has changed. We believe that there are certain forms of human endeavor that may be called, very properly, war - war against things that we understand about, things that can be improved, ameliorated, bettered in every way because of human endeavor.

I do not have to tell all of you the tremendous strides that have been made in medicine and, incidentally, in the attitude of people in almost every community in this country toward certain types of human affliction. But it seems to me also that here at Warm Springs we have discovered something that has not yet been recognized as a fact all over the United States, and that is the fact of human relationships and their relation to science and medicine.

Way back there, fourteen or fifteen years ago, when some of the first people came down here because of a Sunday newspaper story and nothing else, there came into being a thing called "the Spirit of Warm Springs." Well, of course everybody likes to think in local terms, but gradually, over those years, that thing that we here call "the Spirit of Warm Springs" has, I think, developed into a major factor in medical science itself, something that is recognized by a great many doctors but not by all.

You and I can imagine and some of us have seen wonderful modern hospitals where there is everything that modern science can devise - the best of medical care, the best of nursing care - but somehow, when one has gone through a great modern institution of the kind I am talking about - and there are not many - he comes away feeling that it is all mechanized, it is all mechanical, it is all something that does not take into account human relationships.

Down here at Warm Springs in the last few years, principally of course because of the tremendous national support that we have had, we have built up a mechanically perfect place.

This new Infirmary, with all that modern science can possibly give, is all to the good - and yet I do hope to see Warm Springs go on in the position to give the spirit of Warm Springs, the human associations, the general feeling that we are all part of a family, that we are having a pretty good time out of it all, getting well not only in our legs and arms but also helping our minds in relationship to the minds of everybody around us, the other patients, the staff, the friends and the families, all of whom make up Warm Springs.

And so, now that our mechanical equipment is so good, now that we are up-to-date, I hope it is going to be our endeavor always in the years to come to keep up the old spirit of human relationships that has meant so much in the past...

Now I understand that we are going to have one of those old fashioned Warm Springs plays and then some songs from our Tuskegee friends.

CHRISTMAS GREETING TO THE FOREIGN SERVICE OF THE UNITED STATES DECEMBER 22, 1939

YOUR WILLINGNESS TO sacrifice yourselves, your stamina and the quality of the intelligence which you bring to the performance of your duties are being tested and will continue to be tested as they have never been tested before.

I do not send you a conventional holiday message at this time of anxiety and suffering for many millions throughout the world. Instead I wish to tell you of my faith in you and of my confidence that you will prove equal to the heavy burdens which you must carry.

LETTER TO THE POPE ON PEACE AND RELIEVING SUFFERING, ADDRESSED TO HIS HOLINESS PLUS XII, ROME, ITALY DECEMBER 23, 1939

BECAUSE, AT THIS Christmas time, the world is in sorrow, it is especially fitting that I send you a message of greeting and of faith.

The world has created for itself a civilization capable of giving to mankind security and peace firmly set in the foundations of religious teachings. Yet, though it has conquered the earth, the sea, and even the air, civilization today passes through war and travail.

I take heart in remembering that in a similar time, Isaiah first prophesied the birth of Christ, Then, several centuries before His coming, the condition of the world was not unlike that which we see today. Then, as now, a conflagration had been set; and nations walked dangerously in the light of the fires they had themselves kindled.

But in that very moment a spiritual rebirth was foreseen - a new day which was to loose the captives and to consume the conquerors in the fire of their own kindling; and those who had taken the sword were to perish by the sword. There was promised a new age wherein through renewed faith the upward progress of the human race would become more secure.

Again, during the several centuries which we refer to as the Dark Ages, the flame and sword of barbarians swept over Western civilization; and, again, through a rekindling of the inherent spiritual spark in mankind, another rebirth brought back order and culture and religion.

I believe that the travail of today is a new form of these old conflicts. Because the tempo of all worldly things has been so greatly accelerated in these modern days we can hope that the period of darkness and destruction will be vastly shorter than in the olden times.

In their hearts men decline to accept, for long, the law of destruction forced upon them by wielders of brute force. Always they seek, sometimes in silence, to find again the force without which the welfare of nations and the peace of the world cannot be rebuilt.

I have the rare privilege of reading the letters and confidences of thousands of humble people, living in scores of different nations. Their names are not known to history, but their daily work and courage carry on the life of the world.

I know that these, and uncounted numbers like them in every country, are looking for a guiding light. We remember that the Christmas Star was first seen by shepherds in the hills, long before the leaders knew of the Great Light which had entered the world.

I believe that while statesmen are considering a new order of things, the new order may well be at hand. I believe that it is even now being built, silently but inevitably, in the hearts of masses whose voices are not heard, but whose common faith will write the final history of our time.

They know that unless there is belief in some guiding principle and some trust in a divine plan, nations are without light, and peoples perish - They know that the civilization handed down to us by our fathers was built by men and women who knew in their hearts that all were brothers because they were children of God.

They believe that by His will enmities can be healed; that in His mercy the weak can find deliverance, and the strong can find grace in helping the weak.

In the grief and terror of the hour, these quiet voices, if they can be heard, may yet tell of the rebuilding of the world.

It is well that the world should think of this at Christmas.

Because the people of this nation have come to a realization that time and distance no longer exist in the older sense, they understand that that which harms one segment of humanity harms all the rest. They know that only by friendly association among the seekers of light and the seekers of peace everywhere can the forces of evil be overcome.

In these present moments, no spiritual leader, no civil leader, can move forward on a specific plan to terminate destruction and build anew. Yet the time for that will surely come.

It is, therefore, my thought that though no given action or given time may now be prophesied, it is well that we encourage a closer association between those in every part of the world - those in religion and those in government - who have a common purpose.

I am, therefore, suggesting to Your Holiness that it would give me great satisfaction to send to you my personal representative in order that our parallel endeavors for peace and the alleviation of suffering may be assisted.

When the time shall come for the reestablishment of world peace on a surer foundation, it is of the utmost importance to humanity and to religion that common ideals shall have united expression.

Furthermore, when that happy day shall dawn, great problems of practical import will face us all. Millions of people of all races, all nationalities and all religions may seek new lives by migration to other lands or by reestablishment of old homes. Here, too, common ideals call for parallel action.

I trust, therefore, that all of the churches of the world which believe in a common God will throw the great weight of their influence into this great cause.

To you, whom I have the privilege of calling a good friend and an old friend, I send my respectful greetings at this Christmas Season.

RADIO CHRISTMAS GREETING TO THE NATION DECEMBER 24, 1939

THE OLD YEAR draws to a close. It began with dread of evil things to come and it ends with the horror of another war adding its toll of anguish to a world already bowed under the burden of suffering laid upon it by man's inhumanity to man.

But, thank God for the interlude of Christmas. This night is a night of joy and hope and happiness and promise of better things to come. And so in the happiness of this Eve of the most blessed day in the year I give to all of my countrymen the old, old greeting - "Merry Christmas - Happy Christmas."

A Christmas rite for me is always to re-read that immortal little story by Charles Dickens, "A Christmas Carol." Reading between the lines and thinking as I always do of Bob Cratchit's humble home as a counterpart of millions of our own American homes, the story takes on a stirring significance to me.

Old Scrooge found that Christmas wasn't a humbug. He took to himself the spirit of neighborliness. But today neighborliness no longer can be confined to one's little neighborhood. Life has become too complex for that. In our country neighborliness has gradually spread its boundaries

- from town, to county, to State and now at last to the whole Nation.

For instance, who a generation ago would have thought that a week from tomorrow - January 1, 1940 - tens of thousands of elderly men and women in every State and every county and every city of the Nation would begin to receive checks every month for old age retirement insurance - and not only that but that there would be also insurance benefits for the wife, the widow, the orphan children and even dependent parents?

Who would have thought a generation ago that people who lost their jobs would, for an appreciable period, receive unemployment insurance - that the needy, the blind and the crippled children would receive some measure of protection which will reach down to the millions of Bob Cratchit's, the Marthas and the Tiny Tims of our own "four-room homes."

In these days of strife and sadness in many other lands, let us in the nations which still live at peace forbear to give thanks only for our good fortune in our peace.

Let us rather pray that we may be given strength to live for others - to live more closely to the words of the Sermon on the Mount and to pray that peoples in the nations which are at war may also read, learn and inwardly digest these deathless words.

May their import reach into the hearts of all men and of all nations.

I offer them as my Christmas message:

"Blessed are the poor in spirit: for theirs is the kingdom of heaven.

"Blessed are they that mourn: for they shall be comforted.

"Blessed are the meek: for they shall inherit the earth.

"Blessed are they which do hunger and thirst after righteousness: for they shall be filled.

"Blessed are the merciful: for they shall obtain mercy.

"Blessed are the pure in heart: for they shall see God.

"Blessed are the peacemakers: for they shall be called the children of God.

"Blessed are they which are persecuted for righteousness' sake: for theirs is the kingdom of heaven."

ANNUAL MESSAGE TO THE CONGRESS
JANUARY 3, 1940

YOU ARE WELL aware that dictatorships - and the philosophy of force that justifies and accompanies dictatorships - have originated in almost every case in the necessity for drastic action to improve internal conditions in places where democratic action for one reason or another has failed to respond to modern needs and modern demands.

It was with far-sighted wisdom that the framers of our Constitution brought together in one magnificent phrase three great concepts - "common defense," "general welfare" and "domestic tranquility."

More than a century and a half later we, who are here today, still believe with them that our best defense is the promotion of our general welfare and domestic tranquillity...

Already the crash of swiftly moving events over the earth has made us all think with a longer view. Fortunately, that thinking cannot be controlled by partisanship. The time is long past when any political party or any particular group can curry or capture public favor by labeling itself the "peace party" or the "peace bloc." That label belongs to the whole United States and to every right thinking man, woman and child within it...

We must look ahead and see the kind of lives our children would have to lead if a large part of the rest of the world were compelled to worship a god imposed by a military ruler, or were forbidden to worship God at all; if the rest of the world were forbidden to read and hear the facts - the daily news of their own and other nations - if they were deprived of the truth that makes men free.

We must look ahead and see the effect on our future generations if world trade is controlled by any nation or group of nations which sets up that control through military force.

It is, of course, true that the record of past centuries includes destruction of many small nations, the enslavement of peoples, and the building of empires on the foundation of force. But wholly apart from the greater international morality which we seek today, we recognize the practical fact that with modern weapons and modern conditions, modern man can no longer lead a civilized life if we are to go back to the practice of wars and conquests of the seventeenth and eighteenth centuries.

Summing up this need of looking ahead, and in words of common sense and good American citizenship. I hope that we shall have fewer American ostriches in our midst. It is not good for the ultimate health of ostriches to bury their heads in the sand...

The permanent security of America in the present crisis does not lie in armed force alone. What we face is a set of world-wide forces of disintegration - vicious, ruthless, destructive of all the moral, religious and political standards which mankind, after centuries of struggle, has come to cherish most.

In these moral values, in these forces which have made our nation great, we must actively and practically reassert our faith.

These words - "national unity" - must not be allowed to be come merely a high-sounding phrase, a vague generality, a pious hope, to which everyone can give lip-service. They must be made to have real meaning in terms of the daily thoughts and acts of every man, woman and child in our land during the coming year and during the years that lie ahead.

For national unity is, in a very real and a very deep sense, the fundamental safeguard of all democracy.

Doctrines that set group against group, faith against faith, race against race, class against class, fanning the fires of hatred in men too despondent, too desperate to think for themselves, were used as rabble-rousing slogans on which dictators could ride to power. And once in power they could saddle their tyrannies on whole nations and on their weaker neighbors...

ADDRESS AT JACKSON DAY DINNER
JANUARY 8, 1940

ONCE UPON A time there was a school teacher, who, after describing Heaven in alluring and golden terms, asked her class of small boys how many of them wanted to go to Heaven. With eyes that sparkled at the thought every small boy in the class held up his hand - except one.

Teacher said, "Why Charlie, Charlie McNary, you don't want to go to Heaven? Why not?" "Teacher," he said, "Sure I want to go to Heaven, but" pointing to the rest of the boys in the room "Not with that bunch."...

As the leader of the Democratic Party I felt no reluctance to give them good advice, for I was sure that they would not use it - they of little faith.

Seriously, the more I have studied American history and the more clearly I have seen what the problems are, I do believe that the common denominator of our great men in public life has not been mere allegiance to one political party, but the disinterested devotion with which they have tried to serve the whole country, and the relative unimportance that they have ascribed to politics, compared with the paramount importance of Government. By their motives may ye know them!

RADIO ADDRESS TO CONFERENCE ON CHILDREN IN A DEMOCRACY, WASHINGTON, D.C. JANUARY 19, 1940

SOON AFTER I was admitted to the Bar, I got to know another very great American, an old friend of yours and mine, Homer Folks. Probably Homer does not remember it himself, but in New York in those days we were just beginning to take up the problem of providing milk for babies and mothers, in all parts of that big city.

Wanting to do something in addition to learning a little law, I went in with an organization which has since been absorbed by greater organizations, the New York Milk Committee, and I worked for two or three years helping to place milk stations for babies on the East Side and West Side and up in the Bronx.

Homer Folks was one of the principal moving spirits behind that venture and it is rather interesting that the woman who was most responsible for helping to provide milk for dependent poor children in the great city of New

York was Mrs. Borden Harriman. I sent Mrs. Harriman as United States Minister to Norway two years ago.

Last April when this Conference first met in this room I asked you to consider two things: first, how a democracy can best serve its children; and, the corollary, how children can best be helped to grow into the kind of citizens who will know how to preserve and perfect our democracy...

This Conference report rightly calls on us to think of children as a whole. Each child is related not only to his own life but to the lives of his brothers and sisters, the life of his family and then, inevitably, to the life of his community, county, State and Nation...

Following that group of topics, the report discusses many other things that enter into the life of every American child; schools, religion, leisure time activities - mind you, these are all separate topics that we are trying to coordinate into one national picture - libraries, protection against child labor, youth and the needs of youth, the conserving of child health, the social services for children, children in minority groups...

I have read a book recently; it is called "Grapes of Wrath." There are 500,000 Americans that live in the covers of that book. I would like to see the Columbia Basin devoted to the care of the 500,000 people represented in "Grapes of Wrath."

Migratory families, children who have no homes, families who can put down no roots, cannot live in a community. That calls for special consideration...

We all recognize that the spirit within the home is the most important influence in the growth of the child. In family life the child should first learn confidence in his own powers, respect for the feelings and the rights of others, the feeling of security and mutual good will and faith in God...

Just as we cannot take care of the child apart from the family, so his welfare is bound up with a lot of other institutions that influence his development - the school, the church, the agencies that offer useful and happy activities and interests for leisure time. The work of all these institutions needs to be harmonized so as to give our children rounded growth with the least possible conflict and loss of effort...

Religion, religion especially, helps children to appreciate life in its wholeness, to develop a deep sense of the sacredness of human personality. In view of the estimate that perhaps one-half of the children of America are having no regular religious instruction, it seems to me important to consider how provision can best be made for some kind of religious training.

We can do it because we are capable of keeping in mind both the wisdom of maintaining the separation of Church and State and, at the same time, the great importance of religion in personal and social living.

I share with you the belief that fair opportunity for schooling ought to be available to every child in this country...

I believe with you that if anywhere in the country any child lacks opportunity for home life, for health protection, for education, for moral or spiritual development, the strength of the Nation and its ability to cherish and advance the principles of democracy are thereby weakened.

RADIO ADDRESS FOR THE BIRTHDAY BALL FOR CRIPPLED CHILDREN
JANUARY 30, 1940

THERE IS NOT any, has never been, the slightest attempt to play politics with the various efforts - the March of Dimes, the Birthday Balls - to raise money for a worthy national purpose...so the effect of this great celebration is to keep political discussion and partisan passion within the bounds of that neighborly good temper, which is still the chief quality that distinguishes the American electorate from the political masses of the Old World.

In sending a dime...and in dancing that others may walk, We the People are striking a powerful blow in defense of American freedom and human decency. For the answer to class hatred, race hatred, religious hatred, is not repression, criticism or opposition. The answer is the free expression of the love of our fellow men, which is the real thing we celebrate...

Today I think the nation as a whole is aware of and awake to the scourge of infantile paralysis. To minimize its effects, to drive it out entirely in the long run, is, as you know, our primary purpose today...

It is in that magnificent spirit and with the definite knowledge that we are making sure and steady progress that I say to each and every one of you tonight - "Thank you, and God bless you."

RADIO ADDRESS FOR THE THIRTIETH ANNIVERSARY OF THE BOY SCOUTS OF AMERICA FEBRUARY 8, 1940

I GREET YOU and the friends of scouting everywhere with especial pleasure on our thirtieth anniversary. For three decades in our American life, the record of the Boy Scouts has been one in which the people of the nation can take genuine, wholehearted satisfaction.

Through all these thirty years, millions of American boys have found stirring and worthwhile adventure in scouting. They have also found an opportunity to exemplify through practical service to the community the loyalty and patriotism which are obligatory upon them as faithful scouts and true Americans.

I am glad to learn through President Head's report that we have gained not in numbers alone but in the effectiveness of our program and in the scope of our achievements. The theme of Boy Scout Week, "Scouting - the American Way," seems to me to have a particular significance at this time.

Our Boy Scouts represent a cross-section of all American boys, from large cities and from villages and farms, from seaport towns and ranches, boys of all blood origins - all enrolled under the banner of scouting. Moreover, our movement embraces all sects and creeds and is above all class or sectional consciousness. It is, in a word, democratic and therefore truly American. God grant that it may ever remain so.

I like to think of Scouting as a kind of family group. This is as it should be, for the United States is a family nation. The family is the very base of our national life and the scouting movement does not take the individual away from it. Rather, it extends the spirit of the family into the activities of the boy outside the home.

Our twelfth scout law effectively expresses the spiritual ideals of scouting. It constitutes an excellent basis for citizenship. It affirms the importance of religion in the life of the individual and the life of the nation and emphasizes the necessity of respect for the convictions of other people.

Religious freedom is basic in Americanism. It is a tradition upon which our country is founded. A generation trained in the principles of the Scout oath and law cannot fail to be a generation trained in the responsibilities of good citizenship. The United States is looked on as a young nation, but in the spirit of social consciousness, which is the very essence of the Scout ideal, our country is fully grown up.

After all, I am inclined to think that the individual Scout himself, as he engages in the activities of his Troop and Patrol and as he acquires the skills that equip him for service, speaks to us all in a convincing manner of the importance of scouting in the life of the Nation today.

Now, as your Honorary President, I extend to you my hearty good wishes and my congratulations on your good record of the past year. For the years to come I wish you joy and happiness and deepening satisfaction in living up to the best traditions of scouting.

ADDRESS TO THE DELEGATES OF THE AMERICAN YOUTH CONGRESS, WASHINGTON, D.C. FEBRUARY 10, 1940

WE KNOW THAT the prosperity of the twenties can properly be compared to the prosperity of the Mississippi Bubble days before the bubble burst, when everybody was money-mad, when the money changers owned the temple, when the nation as a whole forgot the restraint of decent ethics and simple morals, and when the Government in Washington gave completely free rein to what they called individual liberty...

During those ten years you cannot find a single statute enacted for the restraint of excesses or for the betterment of the permanent security of the individual...

More than twenty years ago, while most of you were very young children, I had the utmost sympathy for the Russian people. In the early days of Communism, I recognized that many leaders in Russia were bringing education and better health and, above all, better opportunity to millions who had been kept in ignorance and serfdom under the imperial regime. I disliked the regimentation under Communism.

I abhorred the indiscriminate killings of thousands of innocent victims. I heartily deprecated the banishment of religion - though I knew that some day Russia would return to religion for the simple reason that four or five thousand years of recorded history have proven that mankind has always believed in God in spite of many abortive attempts to exile God.

I, with many of you, hoped that Russia would work out its own problems, and that its government would eventually become a peace-loving, popular government with a free ballot, which would not interfere with the integrity of its neighbors.

That hope is today either shattered or put away in storage against some better day. The Soviet Union, as everybody who has the courage to face the fact knows, is run by a dictatorship as absolute as any other dictatorship in the world. It has allied itself with another dictatorship, and it has invaded a neighbor so infinitesimally small that it could do no conceivable possible harm to the Soviet Union, a neighbor which seeks only to live at peace as a democracy, and a liberal, forward-looking democracy at that.

It has been said that some of you are Communists. That is a very unpopular term these days. As Americans you have a legal and constitutional right to call yourselves Communists, those of you who do.

You have a right peacefully and openly to advocate certain ideals of theoretical Communism; but as Americans you have not only a right but a sacred duty to confine your advocacy of changes in law to the methods prescribed by the Constitution of the United States - and you have no American right, by act or deed of any kind, to subvert the Government and the Constitution of this Nation.

LETTER ON THE STATUS OF MYRON TAYLOR AS THE PRESIDENT'S REPRESENTATIVE TO THE POPE, ADDRESSED TO THE REVEREND GEORGE A. BUTTRICK, D.D., PRESIDENT, FEDERAL COUNCIL OF THE CHURCHES OF CHRIST IN AMERICA MARCH 14, 1940

I HAVE RECEIVED your letter of February 27, 1940, concerning the status of Mr. Myron Taylor's mission to the Pope. I am sure that on further thought you will agree that no public statement is required, or indeed could be made, on the basis of a mere press report, which so far as I know has not emanated from a responsible source.

The status of Mr. Taylor's mission is exactly as Mr. Messersmith described it to you in his letter of January 25. Mr. Taylor is in Rome as my special representative. This appointment does not constitute the inauguration of formal diplomatic relations with the Vatican.

The President may determine the rank for social purposes of any special representative he may send; in this case the rank corresponding to Ambassador was obviously appropriate. The reason for and circumstances surrounding his designation were made clear in my Christmas letter to the Pope; and in the letter which I gave to Mr. Taylor for presentation to the Pope, which conforms to the Christmas message.

Mr. Taylor was sent to Rome to assist parallel endeavors for peace and the alleviation of suffering; and I am sure that all men of good-will must sympathize with this purpose.

There of course was not the slightest intention to raise any question relating to the union of the functions of Church and State, and it is difficult for me to believe that anyone could take seriously a contrary view, or that the action taken could interrupt in any way the necessary and healthy growth of interfaith comity.

RADIO ADDRESS FOR THE CHRISTIAN FOREIGN SERVICE CONVOCATION MARCH 16, 1940

BEFORE THE ADVENT of the Christian era, messengers and missionaries had traveled throughout the known world. They were commonly traders or soldiers seeking advantage for themselves, or agents of conquerors carrying notice of invasion to come.

When the Apostles and Disciples of Christ crossed into Macedonia and visited one after another the countries of the Western world, they wrote a new chapter in human relations - for they carried for the first time a message of brotherhood, of faith and good-will and peace among men.

Since those days the ideal of a peaceful world brotherhood has made glorious advances - for that ideal is not confined to the followers of the Christian faith but has been accepted as a part of the philosophy of other great religions - some of them older than Christianity and some more recent.

But the advance has not been in a straight line. It has met with serious reverses which have taken years and even centuries to offset. Nomad tribes from eastern Europe and western Asia required centuries of assimilation before they could understand the gospel of brotherhood.

The early feudal days set castle against castle in thousands of tiny wars and slaughters and slavery which ended only in the setting up of governments able to maintain peace within their borders.

Today we seem once more to be in a temporary era where organized force is seeking to divide men and nations from one another. That is why it is right and proper to call together the representatives of the great religious bodies which seek not to divide but to unite men and nations in the old message of brotherhood and good-will.

In dark days of the past that ideal has been saved in the long run by splendid efforts to maintain it in the minds and hearts of the average citizens in all nations.

Today we seek a moral basis for peace. It cannot be a real peace if it fails to recognize brotherhood. It cannot be a lasting peace if the fruit of it is oppression, or starvation, or cruelty, or human life dominated by armed camps. It cannot be a sound peace if small nations must live in fear of powerful neighbors.

It cannot be a moral peace if freedom from invasion is sold for tribute. It cannot be an intelligent peace if it denies free passage to that knowledge of those ideals which permit men to find common ground. It cannot be a righteous peace if worship of God is denied.

On these fundamentals the world did not have a true peace in those years between the ending of the World War and the beginning of present wars.

The band of missionaries whom you now meet to honor understood this well. They permitted no threat to the integrity or the institutions of the nations in which they worked. They sought to promote an international order based on human justice.

The active search for peace which the early Christians preached meant meeting and overcoming those forces in the world which had set themselves against the brotherhood of man and which denied the equality of souls before the throne of God. In those olden days they faced apparently unconquerable force - and yet were victorious.

I offer my greetings to you as a congregation of faith, in the certainty that you will help to keep alive that spirit of kindliness and faith which is the essence of civilization. I am confident of your ultimate triumph; for the ideals of justice, kindness, brotherhood and faith cannot die. These are the highest of human ideals. They will be defended and maintained. In their victory the whole world stands to gain; and the fruit of it is peace.

RADIO ADDRESS TO THE PAN AMERICAN GOVERNING BOARD APRIL 15, 1940

SELF-RESTRAINT AND the acceptance of the equal rights of our neighbors as an act of effective good will have given us the peace we have had, and will preserve that peace so long as we abide by this ultimate moral law...

The inter-American order was not built by hatred and terror. It has been paved by the endless and effective work of men of good will. We have built a foundation for the lives of hundreds of millions. We have unified these lives by a common devotion to a moral order...

At Panama we worked out means for keeping war away from our Hemisphere.

I pray God that we shall have to do no more than that; but should it be necessary, I am convinced that we should be wholly successful. For the inner strength of a group of free people is irresistible when they are prepared to act...

I affirm that that life must be based on positive and permanent values.

The value of love will always be stronger than the value of hate; since any nation or group of nations which employs hatred eventually is torn to pieces by hatred within itself...

GREETING TO AMERICAN NATIONAL RED CROSS CHAIRMAN NORMAN DAVIS, WASHINGTON, D.C. MAY 1, 1940

THE GREAT INTERNATIONAL Red Cross organization, founded seventy-six years ago to bring mercy to the battlefield...

I am confident that whatever may be the problems which intensification of warfare may bring, the American people will respond to any appeal for funds when the Red Cross deems it necessary to call upon them for additional aid. By such response we can aid in sustaining the spirit and morale of those in distress abroad until the happy day we all pray for, when hostilities shall cease.

RADIO ADDRESS TO THE 8TH PAN AMERICAN SCIENTIFIC CONGRESS, WASHINGTON, D.C. MAY 10, 1940

THE OVERWHELMINGLY GREATER part of the population of the world abhors conquest and war and bloodshed - prays that the hand of neighbor shall not be lifted against neighbor...

In contrast to that rather simple picture of our ideals, in other parts of the world, teachers and scholars are not permitted to search for truth, lest the truth, when made known, might not suit the designs of their masters. Too often they are not allowed to teach the truth as they see it, because truth might make men free.

They become objects of suspicion if they speak openly, if they show an interest in new truth, for their tongues and minds are supposed to be mobilized for other ends.

This has not happened in the New World. God willing, it shall not happen in the New World.

At the Pan American Conference at Buenos Aires, and again at Lima, we discussed a dim and unpleasant possibility. We feared that other Continents might become so involved in wars brought on by the school of destruction that the Americans might have to become the guardian of Western culture, the protector of Christian civilization.

In those days, not so long ago, it was merely a fear. Today the fear has become a fact...

The great achievements of science and even of art can be used in one way or another to destroy as well as to create; they are only instruments by which men try to do the things they most want to do. If death is desired, science can do that. If a full, rich, and useful life is sought, science can do that also.

Happily for us that question has been solved - for in the New World we live for each other and in the service of a Christian faith.

MESSAGE TO CONGRESS ON APPROPRIATIONS FOR NATIONAL DEFENSE
MAY 16, 1940

THE BRUTAL FORCE of modern offensive war has been loosed in all its horror. New powers of destruction, incredibly swift and deadly, have been developed; and those who wield them are ruthless and daring...

Motorized armies can now sweep through enemy territories at the rate of two hundred miles a day. Parachute troops are dropped from airplanes in large numbers behind enemy lines. Troops are landed from planes in open fields, on wide highways, and at local civil airports.

We have seen the treacherous use of the "fifth column" by which persons supposed to be peaceful visitors were actually a part of an enemy unit of occupation.

Lightning attacks, capable of destroying airplane factories and munition works hundreds of miles behind the lines, are a part of the new technique of modern war.

The element of surprise which has ever been an important tactic in warfare has become the more dangerous because of the amazing speed with which modern equipment can reach and attack the enemy's country...

I know that to cope with present dangers we must be strong in heart and mind; strong in our faith - strong in the faith in our way of living.

I, too, pray for peace - that the ways of aggression and force may be banished from the earth - but I am determined to face the fact realistically that this nation requires also a toughness of moral and physical fiber. Those qualities, I am convinced, the American people hold to a high degree...

These are the characteristics of a free people, a people devoted to the institutions they themselves have built, a people willing to defend a way of life that is precious to them all, a people who put their faith in God.

FIRESIDE CHAT
MAY 26, 1940

I THINK IT is right on this Sabbath evening that I should say a word in behalf of women and children and old men who need help - immediate help in their present distress - help from us across the seas, from us who are still free to give it.

Tonight over the once peaceful roads of Belgium and France millions are now moving, running from their homes to escape bombs and shells and fire and machine gunning, without shelter, and almost wholly without food. They stumble on, knowing not where the end of the road will be...

The American Red Cross, that represents each of us, is rushing food, clothing and medical supplies to these destitute civilian millions. Please - I beg you - please give according to your means to your nearest Red Cross chapter, give as generously as you can. I ask this in the name of our common humanity...

On this Sabbath evening, in our homes in the midst of our American families, let us calmly consider what we have done and what we must do.

There are several things we must continue to watch and safeguard, things which are just as important to the sound defense of a nation as physical armament itself. While our Navy and our airplanes and our guns and our ships may be our first lines of defense, it is still clear that way down at the bottom, underlying them all, giving them their strength, sustenance and power, are the spirit and morale of a free people...

Today's threat to our national security is not a matter of military weapons alone. We know of new methods of attack.

The Trojan Horse. The Fifth Column that betrays a nation unprepared for treachery.

Spies, saboteurs and traitors are the actors in this new strategy. With all of these we must and will deal vigorously...

It is the task of our generation, yours and mine. But we build and defend not for our generation alone. We defend the foundations laid down by our fathers. We build a life for generations yet unborn. We defend and we build a way of life, not for America alone, but for all mankind. Ours is a high duty, a noble task.

Day and night I pray for the restoration of peace in this mad world of ours. It is not necessary that I, the President, ask the American people to pray in behalf of such a cause - for I know you are praying with me.

I am certain that out of the heart of every man, woman and child in this land, in every waking minute, a supplication goes up to Almighty God; that all of us beg that suffering and starving, that death and destruction may end - and that peace may return to the world. In common affection for all mankind, your prayers join with mine - that God will heal the wounds and the hearts of humanity.

ADDRESS AT UNIVERSITY OF VIRGINIA, GREETING PRESIDENT NEWCOMB JUNE 10, 1940

ON THIS TENTH day of June, 1940, in this University founded by the first great American teacher of democracy, we send forth our prayers and our hopes to those beyond the seas who are maintaining with magnificent valor their battle for freedom.

PRESS CONFERENCE, HYDE PARK, NEW YORK JULY 5, 1940

NOW, I COME down to your questions. The first is - you might say there are certain freedoms. The first I would call "freedom of information," which is terribly important.

It is a much better phrase than "freedom of the press," because there are all kinds of information so that the inhabitants of a country can get news of what is going on in every part of the country and in every part of the world without censorship and through many forms of communication. That, I think, is one of the objectives of peace, because you will never have a completely stable world without freedom of knowledge, freedom of information.

The second, of course, is freedom of religion which, under democracies, has always - not always but almost all the time - been fairly well maintained. It is not maintained in those nations which have adopted other systems of Government.

MESSAGE TO CONGRESS ON APPROPRIATIONS FOR NATIONAL DEFENSE JULY 10, 1940

I SAID THEN that the storms from abroad directly challenged three institutions indispensable to Americans - religion, democracy and international good faith...

The people and their representatives in the Congress know that the threats to our liberties, the threats to our security, the threats against our way of life, the threats to our institutions of religion, of democracy, and of international good faith, have increased in number and gravity from month to month, from week to week, and almost from day to day...

Let no man in this country or anywhere else believe that because we in America still cherish freedom of religion, of speech, of assembly, of the press; that because we maintain our free democratic political institutions by which the nation after full discussion and debate chooses its representatives and leaders for itself-let no man here or elsewhere believe that we are weak.

RADIO ADDRESS TO DEMOCRATIC NATIONAL CONVENTION ACCEPTING THE NOMINATION JULY 19, 1940

ONLY THE PEOPLE themselves can draft a President. If such a draft should be made upon me, I say to you, in the utmost simplicity, I will, with God's help, continue to serve with the best of my ability and with the fullness of my strength...

The Government of the United States for the past seven years has had the courage openly to oppose by every peaceful means the spread of the dictator form of Government. If our Government should pass to other hands next January - untried hands, inexperienced hands - we can merely hope and pray that they will not substitute appeasement and compromise with those who seek to destroy all democracies everywhere, including here...

All that I have done to maintain the peace of this country and to prepare it morally, as well as physically, for whatever contingencies may be in store, I submit to the judgment of my countrymen.

We face one of the great choices of history...It is the continuance of civilization as we know it versus the ultimate destruction of all that we have held dear - religion against godlessness; the ideal of justice against the practice of force; moral decency versus the firing squad; courage to speak out, and to act, versus the false lullaby of appeasement...

The American people will sustain the progress of a representative democracy, asking the Divine Blessing as they face the future with courage and with faith.

PROCLAMATION 2418 FOR A DAY OF PRAYER
AUGUST 7, 1940

THE AMERICAN HERITAGE of individual freedom and of Government deriving its powers from the consent of the governed has from the time of the Fathers of our Republic been proudly transmitted to each succeeding generation, and to us of this generation has fallen the task of preserving it and transmitting it to the future. We are now engaged in a mighty effort to fortify that heritage.

Mindful of our duties in the family of nations we have endeavored to prevent the outbreak and the spread of war, and we have raised our voices against international injustice. As Americans and as lovers of freedom we are humbly sympathetic with those who are facing tribulation in lands across the seas.

When every succeeding day brings sad news of suffering and disaster abroad we are especially conscious of the Divine Power and of our dependence upon God's merciful guidance. With this consciousness in our hearts it is seemly that we should, at a time like this, pray to Almighty God for His blessing on our country and for the establishment of a just and permanent peace among all the nations of the world.

Now, therefore, I, Franklin D. Roosevelt, President of the United States of America, do hereby set aside Sunday, September 8, 1940, as a day of prayer; and I urge the people of the United States, of all creeds and denominations, to pray on that day, in their churches or at their homes, on the high seas or wherever they may be, beseeching the Ruler of the Universe to bless our Republic, to make us reverently grateful for our heritage and firm in its defense, and to grant to this land and to the troubled world a righteous, enduring peace.

ADDRESS AT DEDICATION OF GREAT SMOKY MOUNTAINS NATIONAL PARK, GREETING SECRETARY ICKES, GOVERNOR HOEY, GOVERNOR COOPER AND GOVERNOR MAYBANK SEPTEMBER 2, 1940

IF WE ARE to survive, we cannot be soft in a world in which there are dangers that threaten Americans - dangers far more deadly than were those that the frontiersmen had to face.

The earth has been so shrunk by the airplane and the radio that Europe is closer to America today than was one side of these mountains to the other side when the pioneers toiled through the primeval forest. The arrow, the tomahawk, and the scalping knife have been replaced by the airplane, the bomb, the tank, and the machine gun. Their threat is as close to us today as was the threat to the frontiersmen when hostile Indians were lurking on the other side of the gap.

Therefore, to meet the threat - to ward off these dangers - the Congress of the United States and the Chief Executive of the United States are establishing by law the obligation inherent in our citizenship to serve our forces for defense through training in many capacities.

It is not in every case easy or pleasant to ask men of the Nation to leave their homes, and women of the Nation to give their men to the service of the Nation. But the men and women of America have never held back even when it has meant personal sacrifice on their part if that sacrifice is for the common good.

We have come to realize the greatest attack that has ever been launched against freedom of the individual is nearer the Americas than ever before. To meet that attack we must prepare beforehand - for the simple reason that preparing later may and probably would be too late...

There is, moreover, another enemy at home.

That enemy is the mean and petty spirit that mocks at ideals, sneers at sacrifice and pretends that the American people can live by bread alone.

If the spirit of God is not in us, and if we will not prepare to give all that we have and all that we are to preserve Christian civilization in our land, we shall go to destruction.

It is good and right that we should conserve these mountain heights of the old frontier for the benefit of the American people. But in this hour we have to safeguard a greater thing: the right of the people of this country to live as free men. Our vital task of conservation is to preserve the freedom that our forefathers won in this land, and the liberties that were proclaimed in our Declaration of Independence and embodied in our Constitution...

That there is a danger from without is at last recognized by most of us Americans. That such a danger cannot longer be met with pitchforks and squirrel rifles...

What shall we be defending? The good earth of this land, our homes, our families - yes, and far more.

We shall be defending a way of life which has given more freedom to the soul and body of man than ever has been realized in the world before, a way of life that has let men scale whatever heights they could scale without hurting their fellows, a way of life that has let men hold up their heads and admit no master but God.

That way of life is menaced. We can meet the threat. We can meet it with the old frontier spirit. We can forge our weapons, train ourselves to shoot, meet fire with fire, and with the courage and the unity of the frontiersmen.

It is our pride that in our country men are free to differ with each other and with their Government and to follow their own thoughts and express them. We believe that the only whole man is a free man.

We believe that, in the face of danger, the old spirit of the frontiersmen that is in our blood will give us the courage and unity that we must have. We need that spirit in this hour. We need a conviction, felt deep in us all, that there are no divisions among us. We are all members of the same body. We are all Americans.

PRESS CONFERENCE ON BOARD PRESIDENT'S TRAIN EN ROUTE TO WASHINGTON, D.C. SEPTEMBER 3, 1940

THE PRESIDENT: I have something for you for your own information. It is a Washington story that will be out there in twenty-two minutes, so the story will come from Washington. I cannot add to it, but you ought to know about it because you will probably get all kinds of flashes, "For God's sake, get some news."...

In twenty minutes there is going to the Congress the following message, which I am going to read from the only copy I have, which is a rough copy, so there is no use taking it down...

TO THE CONGRESS OF THE UNITED STATES:

I transmit herewith for the information of the Congress notes exchanged between the British Ambassador at Washington and the Secretary of State on September 2, 1940: "This Government has acquired the right to lease naval and air bases in Newfoundland, and in the islands of Bermuda, the Bahamas, Jamaica, St. Lucia, Trindad, and Antigua, and in British Guiana. The right to bases in

Newfoundland and Bermuda are gifts - generously given and gladly received...It is an epochal and far-reaching act of preparation for continental defense in the face of grave danger.

Preparation for defense is an inalienable prerogative of a sovereign state...

In about...1803, Napoleon was at war with Great Britain. France was a belligerent, and we were scared pink because France had bought from Spain the whole of the Louisiana Territory, and especially the mouth of the Mississippi.

That was the important thing to our defense. France had a very weak army down there in Louisiana. I think they had one regiment, something like that, for the whole of the Territory.

We were scared to death that there might be, as an outcome of the Napoleonic wars, some threat or some danger of some power going in there and going up the valley to connect up with Canada, the back part of Canada, thereby confining the States practically to this side of the Mississippi.

There was an awful lot of discussion about it and everybody was yelling, "For God's sake protect us," all over the country, "by acquiring, if you can, this mouth of the Mississippi."

Of course in those days they, none of them, realized what they were getting with the Louisiana Purchase, that they were getting that tremendous back country that went clear up to Montana, but they saw it primarily from the standpoint of the mouth of the Mississippi and the control of the main stem of the Mississippi.

So Jefferson sent Monroe and Chancellor Robert R. Livingston over to Paris...He was my wife's great grandfather.

And they went to Paris and negotiated with Napoleon, who was a belligerent, fighting Great Britain at the time. In fact, he was fighting over most of Europe. They made this deal for the purchase of the whole thing from Napoleon for a price of - as I remember it - what was it, $15,000,000?

And Napoleon, at the same time, verbally agreed that a portion of that money would be spent over here in buying certain naval supplies and certain food supplies that he needed over there for the continuation of his wars.

The contract was signed over there in Paris, Monroe and, I think, Livingston hopped the first sail boat they could, and came back to Washington, and announced that the thing had been done. Thereupon there ensued a long session in the Cabinet and every other place, as to whether such a thing could be done. You see, there was nothing said about it in the Constitution...

He got the opinion of the Attorney General that he could do it without a treaty, do it for the national defense as Commander-in-Chief, and do it as President, as well, in an obvious emergency.

And, later on, he asked, not the Senate but he asked the Appropriations Committee of the House to please appropriate $15,000,000 to him as an item in an appropriation bill, which was done. There was never any treaty, there was never any two-thirds vote in the Senate, and today Louisiana is about one-third of the whole of the United States...

Some people will say, undoubtedly...it is not a good deal. And others will say, "My God, the old Dutchman and Scotchman in the White House has made a good trade."...

I have not finished the story...This is a restatement to the effect that the British Fleet, in case it is made too hot for them in home waters, is not going to be given to Germany or sunk...

Q: Would that mean moving the Fleet to Canada?

THE PRESIDENT: It might go to whatever place in the British Empire needed it for defense. That is the point. It might be Canada, it might be somewhere else. The Lord only knows.

ADDRESS AT TEAMSTERS UNION CONVENTION, WASHINGTON, D.C. SEPTEMBER 11, 1940

EVENTS ABROAD HAVE shown too late the result of the other kind of methods, promises of swift, revolutionary relief; seductive pictures of panaceas; short cuts to prosperity and plenty, pictured as simple and easy - all these have led, and I am talking recent history, to the same cruel disappointment.

For these promises people yielded up their liberties and all that made life dear. In exchange they have received only the rationing of their news, the rationing of their religion, the rationing of the clothes upon their backs and the rationing of the bread upon their tables...

All must stand a united people whose spiritual and moral strength has not been sapped through hunger or want or fear or insecurity. The morale of a people is an essential supplement to their guns and planes.

ADDRESS AT UNIVERSITY OF PENNSYLVANIA, GREETING PRESIDENT GATES AND CHIEF JUSTICE OF CANADA SEPTEMBER 20, 1940

EVEN THEN WE were in the midst of a strange period of relapse in the history of the civilization of the world - for in some lands it has become the custom to burn the books of scholars and to fix by Government decree the national forms of religion, morality, culture and education...

The very foundation of this University was concerned with freedom of religious teaching, and with free learning for the many who could not pay for higher education.

As I understand my history, this was originally proposed as a place where the good and Reverend Doctor George Whitefield who, incidentally, used to go to my little County of Dutchess on the Hudson River - might preach his religion without certain difficulties which the old conservatives of Philadelphia at that time threw in his path.

Indeed, it was desired to make it unnecessary for the good gentleman to preach in the sun and the rain of the open fields, when the doors of the established churches were closed against him. And it was the dream of the founders to make it a source of education to the children of the poor who otherwise might have gone untaught...

With the gaining of our political freedom you will remember that there came a conflict between the point of view of Alexander Hamilton, sincerely believing in the superiority of Government by a small group of public-spirited and usually wealthy citizens, and, on the other hand, the point of view of Thomas Jefferson, an advocate of Government by representatives chosen by all the people, an advocate of the universal right of free thought, free personal living, free religion, free expression of opinion and, above all, the right of free universal suffrage...

Benjamin Franklin, to whom this University owes so much, realized too that while basic principles of natural science, of morality and of the science of society were eternal and immutable, the application of these principles necessarily changes with the patterns of living conditions from generation to generation.

Eternal truths will be neither true nor eternal unless they have fresh meaning for every new social situation.

GREETING ON NAVY DAY
OCTOBER 2, 1940

I PRAY THAT it will continue to emphasize, by its strength, our determination to remain a free people, marching steadily along the open road that holds peace of the spirit as well as a full and worthy material life.

RADIO ADDRESS ON REGISTRATION DAY
OCTOBER 6, 1940

IN THE DAYS when our forefathers laid the foundation of our democracy, every American family had to have its gun and know how to use it. Today we live under threats, threats of aggression from abroad, which call again for the same readiness, the same vigilance.

Ours must once again be the spirit of those who were prepared to defend as they built, to defend as they worked, to defend as they worshipped.

The duty of this day has been imposed upon us from without. Those who have dared to threaten the whole world with war - those who have created the name and deed of total war - have imposed upon us and upon all free peoples the necessity of preparation for total defense...

To the sixteen million young men who register today, I say that democracy is your cause - the cause of youth...

We of today, with God's help, can bequeath to Americans of tomorrow a nation in which the ways of liberty and justice will survive and be secure. Such a nation must be devoted to the cause of peace. And it is for that cause that America arms itself.

ADDRESS ON HEMISPHERE DEFENSE, DAYTON, OHIO
OCTOBER 12, 1940

FOR MANY LONG years every ounce of energy I have had has been devoted to keeping this nation and the other Republics at peace with the rest of the world. That is what continues uppermost in my mind today-the objective for which I hope and work and pray.

RADIO ADDRESS FOR THE MOBILIZATION FOR HUMAN NEEDS, TO CHAIRMAN ADAMS
OCTOBER 13, 1940

IN THIS CRITICAL moment of our history, we must be more than ever conscious of the true meaning of the "community spirit" which it expresses. It is a spirit which comes from our community of interests, our community of faith in the democratic ideal, our community of devotion to God...

Even in the early days when our society centered in the village community, and when every neighbor knew all the neighbors, the care of the poor was in some measure a public undertaking. In colonial America money raised through taxation was often distributed by the churches among the poor...

As long as there is illness in the world, as long as there is poverty, as long as families are stricken with personal misfortune, it will be necessary for the good-hearted men and women of America to mobilize for human needs...

When we join together in serving our local community, we add strength to our national community, we help to fortify the structure of our whole Union. That form of fortification - that spiritual fortification is not to be dismissed lightly by those in other lands who believe that nations can live by force alone.

Human kindness has never weakened the stamina or softened the fiber of a free people. A nation does not have to be cruel in order to be tough. The vigorous expression of our American community spirit is truly important.

The ancient injunction to love thy neighbor as thyself is still the force that animates our faith - a faith that we are determined shall live and conquer in a world poisoned by hatred and ravaged by war.

I ask for your enlistment in the Mobilization for Human Needs, for your whole-hearted devotion to the American community spirit. I ask you to prove your good faith in good works.

STATEMENT ON SIGNING THE JOINT RESOLUTION FOR JUSTICE OLIVER WENDELL HOLMES OCTOBER 22, 1940

HE WAS, OF course, a man of superlative gifts, and his achievements in law and literature form an enduring part of the spiritual treasury of our country.

CAMPAIGN ADDRESS AT PHILADELPHIA, PA. OCTOBER 23, 1940

TONIGHT THERE IS one more false charge - one outrageously false charge - that has been made to strike terror into the hearts of our citizens. It is a charge that offends every political and religious conviction that I hold dear. It is the charge that this Administration wishes to lead this country into war.

That charge is contrary to every fact, every purpose of the past eight years. Throughout these years my every act and thought have been directed to the end of preserving the peace of the world, and more particularly, the peace of the United States - the peace of the Western Hemisphere.

CAMPAIGN ADDRESS AT MADISON SQUARE GARDEN, NEW YORK CITY, GREETING GOVERNOR LEHMAN OCTOBER 28, 1940

FOR ALMOST SEVEN years the Republican leaders in the Congress kept on saying that I was placing too much emphasis on national defense.

And now today these men of great vision have suddenly discovered that there is a war going on in Europe and another one in Asia. And so, now, always with their eyes on the good old ballot box, they are charging that we have placed too little emphasis on national defense...

In the Senate there was an amendment to permit the United States Government to prevent profiteering or unpatriotic obstruction by any corporation in defense work. It permitted the Government to take over, with reasonable compensation, any manufacturing plant which refused to cooperate in national defense...

The bill was adopted all right - by Democratic votes. But the opposing vote of those eight Republican leaders showed what would happen if the National Government were turned over to their control. For their vote said, in

effect, that they put money rights ahead of human lives -
to say nothing of national security.

You and I, and the overwhelming majority of
Americans, will never stand for that...

It is the same record of timidity, of weakness and of
shortsightedness that governed the policy of the confused,
reactionary governments in France and England before the
war.

That fact was discovered too late in France. It was
discovered just in time in England.

Pray God that, having discovered it, we won't forget
it either...

We have steadily sought to keep mobilized the
greatest force of all - religious faith, devotion to God.

Your Government is working at all times with
representatives of the Catholic, Protestant, and Jewish
faiths. Without these three, all three of them, without them
working with us toward that great end, things would not
be as clear or as easy.

Shadows, however, are still heavy over the faith and
the hope of mankind.

We - who walk in the ways of peace and freedom
and light have seen the tragedies enacted in one free land
after another.

We have not been blind to the causes or the
consequences of these tragedies.

We guard ourselves against all evils - spiritual as well
as material - which may beset us. We guard against the
forces of anti-Christian aggression, which may attack us
from without, and the forces of ignorance and fear which
may corrupt us from within.

We go forward with firm faith. And we shall continue
to go forward in peace.

THE FAITH OF FDR

RADIO ADDRESS FOR THE DRAWING UNDER THE SELECTIVE SERVICE ACT OF 1940, WASHINGTON, D.C. OCTOBER 29, 1940

MEMBERS OF YOUR Government are gathered here in this Federal Building in Washington to witness the drawing of numbers as provided for in the Selective Service Act of 1940.

This is a most solemn ceremony. It is accompanied by no fanfare - no blowing of bugles or beating of drums. There should be none.

We are mustering all our resources, manhood, and industry and wealth to make our nation strong in defense. For recent history proves all too clearly, I am sorry to say, that only the strong may continue to live in freedom and in peace...

The young men of America today have thought this thing through. They have not been stimulated by or misled by militarist propaganda. They fully understand the necessity for national defense and are ready, as all citizens of our country must be, to play their part in it.

They know simply that ours is a great country - great in perpetual devotion to the cause of liberty and justice, great in faith that always there can be and must be a will to a better future. They know that in the present world the survival of liberty and justice is dependent on strength to defend against attack...

I have here three letters from representatives of the three great faiths, Protestant, Jewish, and Catholic. They were written to me, in solemn recognition of this occasion, and I want to read you brief excerpts from them.

The first is from Dr. George A. Buttrick, President of the Federal Council of the Churches of Christ in America. He says:

"The twenty-two national communions...are united in a deep interest in the thousands of men called today to national service. We will give our best assistance in providing the ministries of the Christian faith. They shall be encompassed by friendship...We assure all men in the Army and Navy of our active comradeship and prayer. We are glad that the rights of sincere conscientious objectors have been recognized in the Selective Service Act."

The next letter is from Dr. Edward L. Israel, President of the Synagogue Council of America. He says:

"It is my supreme confidence that you, Mr. President, and the military officials of our nation will be ever mindful of the fact that this peacetime Selective Service System is an extraordinary measure in the interest of preserving democracy, and that the System will therefore be administered so as to deepen in the minds and hearts of our youth, a love and respect for democracy and our democratic institutions...And it must never be forgotten that democracies cannot indefinitely endure under a war system - and that the ultimate goal of a free people rallying to National Defense must ever be to help usher in that day when the prophetic ideal will be realized that 'nation shall not lift up sword against nation, neither shall they make war any more.'"

And finally a letter from the Bishop of the Catholics in the Army and Navy of the United States, His Excellency, The Most Reverend Francis J. Spellman. He says:

"I do believe: It is better to have protection and not need it than to need protection and not have it. I do believe that Americans want peace but that we must be prepared to demand it for other people have wanted peace and the peace they received was the peace of death.

"I do feel that our good will and the sincerity of our desire for peace have been demonstrated by our action in sinking many battleships and that no more sincere demonstration of a willingness to lead the way toward universal disarmament could have been given by any people.

"But we really cannot longer afford to be moles who cannot see, or ostriches who will not see. For some solemn agreements are no longer sacred, and vices have become virtues and truth a synonym of falsehood.

"We Americans want peace and we shall prepare for a peace, but not for a peace whose definition is slavery or death."

These three letters give eloquent testimony to the quality of the religious faith that inspires us today and forever.

To these spokesmen for the churches of America - to all my fellow countrymen of all races and creeds and ages - I give this solemn assurance:

Your Government is mindful of its profound responsibility to and for all the young men who will be called to train for our national service.

Your Government is aware that not only do these young men represent the future of our country: they are the future. They must profit as men by this one year of experience as soldiers. They must return to civilian life strong, and healthy, and self-respecting, and decent and free.

Your Government will devote its every thought, its every energy, to the cause that is common to all of us - the maintenance of the dignity, the prosperity and the peace of our country.

To the young men themselves I should like to speak as Commander-in-Chief of the United States Army:

You who will enter this peacetime army will be the inheritors of a proud history and an honorable tradition.

You will be members of any army which first came together to achieve independence and to establish certain fundamental rights for all men. Even since that first muster, our democratic army has existed for one purpose only: the defense of our freedom.

It is for that one purpose and that one purpose only that you will be asked to answer the call to training.

You have answered that call, as Americans always have, and as Americans always will, until the day when war is forever banished from this earth.

ADDRESS AT THE DEDICATION OF NATIONAL INSTITUTE OF HEALTH, BETHESDA, MARYLAND OCTOBER 31, 1940

I VOICE FOR America, and for the stricken world, our hopes, our prayers, our faith in the power of man's humanity to man.

CAMPAIGN ADDRESS AT BROOKLYN, NEW YORK NOVEMBER 1, 1940

THOSE FORCES HATE democracy and Christianity as two phases of the same civilization. They oppose democracy because it is Christian. They oppose Christianity because it preaches democracy.

Their objective is to prevent democracy from becoming strong and purposeful. We are strong and purposeful now and intend to remain so...

I am, as you know, a firm believer in private enterprise and in private property. I am a firm believer in the American opportunity of men and women to rise in private enterprise.

But, of course, if private opportunity is to remain safe, average men and women must be able to have it as a part of their own individual satisfaction in life and their own stake in democracy...

We are a nation of many nationalities, many races, many religions - bound together by a single unity, the unity of freedom and equality.

Whoever seeks to set one nationality against another, seeks to degrade all nationalities.

Whoever seeks to set one race against another seeks to enslave all races.

Whoever seeks to set one religion against another, seeks to destroy all religion.

So-called racial and religious voting blocs are the creation of designing politicians who profess to be able to deliver them on Election Day. But every American citizen - realizing how precious is his right to the sacred secret ballot - does scorn and will scorn such unpatriotic politicians. The vote of Americans will be American - and only American.

CAMPAIGN ADDRESS AT CLEVELAND, OHIO
NOVEMBER 2, 1940

THERE ARE CERTAIN forces within our own national community, composed of men who call themselves American but who would destroy America. They are the forces of dictatorship in our land - on one hand, the Communists, and on the other, the Girdlers.

It is their constant purpose in this as in other lands to weaken democracy, to destroy the free man's faith in his own cause...

You and I are proud of that opposition. It is positive proof that what we have built and strengthened in the past seven years is democracy!...

We in this Nation of many States have found the way by which men of many racial origins may live together in peace.

If the human race as a whole is to survive, the world must find the way by which men and nations can live together in peace. We cannot accept the doctrine that war must be forever a part of man's destiny...

But Americans will have none of that. They will never submit to domination or influence by Naziism or Communism...

Americans are determined to retain for themselves the right of free speech, free religion, free assembly and the right which lies at the basis of all of them - the right to choose the officers of their own Government in free elections...

But we have learned that freedom in itself is not enough.

Freedom of speech is of no use to a man who has nothing to say.

Freedom of worship is of no use to a man who has lost his God.

Democracy, to be dynamic, must provide for its citizens opportunity as well as freedom.

We of this generation have seen a rebirth of dynamic democracy in America in these past few years...

Of course we intend to preserve and build up the land of this country - its soil, its forests and its rivers - all the resources with which God has endowed the people of the United States.

Of course we intend to continue to build up the bodies and the minds of the men, women and children of the Nation - through democratic education and a democratic program for health...

Of course we intend to continue our efforts to protect our system of private enterprise and private property, but to protect it from monopoly of financial control on the one hand and from Communistic wrecking on the other.

Of course we shall continue our efforts to prevent economic dictatorship as well as political dictatorship.

Of course we intend to continue to build up the morale of this country, not as blind obedience to some leader, but as the expression of confidence in the deeply ethical principles upon which this Nation and its democracy were founded.

For there lies the road to democracy that is strong...

And all the forces of evil shall not prevail against it.

For so it is written in the Book, and so it is written in the moral law, and so it is written in the promise of a great era of world peace...

It is the destiny of this American generation to point the road to the future for all the world to see. It is our prayer that all lovers of freedom may join us - the anguished common people of this earth for whom we seek to light the path...

I see an America devoted to our freedom - unified by tolerance and by religious faith - a people consecrated to peace, a people confident in strength because their body and their spirit are secure and unafraid...

The spirit of the common man is the spirit of peace and good will. It is the spirit of God. And in His faith is the strength of all America.

RADIO CAMPAIGN ADDRESS, HYDE PARK, N.Y.
NOVEMBER 4, 1940

AS I SIT here tonight with my own family, I think of all the other American families - millions of families all through the land - sitting in their own homes. They have eaten their supper in peace, they will be able to sleep in their homes tonight in peace. Tomorrow they will be free to go out to live their ordinary lives in peace - free to say and do what they wish, free to worship as they please. Tomorrow, of all days, they will be free to choose their own leaders who, when that choice has been made, become in turn only the instruments to carry out the will of all the people.

And I cannot help but think of the families in other lands - millions of families - living in homes like ours. On some of these homes, bombs of destruction may be dropping even as I speak to you.

Across the seas life has gone underground. I think I speak the minds of all of you when I say that we thank God that we live in the sunlight and in the starlight of peace, that we are not in war and that we propose and expect to continue to live our lives in peace - under the peaceful light of Heaven.

In this town, as in every other community in our nation, friends and neighbors will gather together around the polling place.

They will discuss the state of the Nation, the weather, and the prospect for their favorite football team. They will discuss the present political campaign. Some will wear buttons proclaiming their allegiance to one candidate or another. And, I suppose, there will be a few warm arguments.

But when you and I step into the voting booth, we can proudly say: "I am an American, and this vote I am casting is the exercise of my highest privilege and my most solemn duty to my country."

We vote as free men, impelled only by the urgings of our own wisdom and our own conscience.

In our polling places are no storm troopers or secret police to look over our shoulders as we mark our ballots...

Dictators have forgotten - or perhaps they never knew - the basis upon which democratic Government is founded: that the opinion of all the people, freely formed and freely expressed, without fear or coercion, is wiser than the opinion of any one man or any small group of men...

The service of democracy must be something much more than mere lip-service.

It is a living thing - a human thing - compounded of brains and muscles and heart and soul. The service of democracy is the birthright of every citizen, the white and the colored; the Protestant, the Catholic, the Jew; the sons and daughters of every country in the world, who make up the people of this land. Democracy is every man and woman who loves freedom and serves the cause of freedom.

Last Saturday night, I said that freedom of speech is of no use to the man who has nothing to say and that freedom of worship is of no use to the man who has lost his God. And tonight I should like to add that a free election is of no use to the man who is too indifferent to vote...

We people of America know that man cannot live by bread alone.

We know that we have a reservoir of religious strength which can withstand attacks from abroad and corruption from within.

We people of America will always cherish and preserve that strength. We will always cling to our religion, our devotion to God - to the faith which gives us comfort and the strength to face evil.

On this election eve, we all have in our hearts and minds a prayer for the dignity, the integrity and the peace of our beloved country.

Therefore, in this last hour before midnight, I believe that you will find it fitting that I read to you an old prayer which asks the guidance of God for our nation:

Almighty God, who hast given us this good land for our heritage; We humbly beseech Thee that we may always prove ourselves a people mindful of Thy favor and glad to do Thy will. Bless our land with honourable industry, sound learning, and pure manners. Save us from violence, discord, and confusion; from pride and arrogancy, and from every evil way.

Defend our liberties, and fashion into one united people the multitudes brought hither out of many kindreds and tongues. Endue with the spirit of wisdom those to whom in Thy Name we entrust the authority of government, that there may be justice and peace at home, and that, through obedience to Thy law, we may show forth Thy praise among the nations of the earth.

In the time of prosperity, fill our hearts with thankfulness, and in the day of trouble, suffer not our trust in Thee to fail; Amen.

THANKSGIVING DAY PROCLAMATION
NOVEMBER 9, 1940

I, FRANKLIN D. ROOSEVELT, President of the United States of America, do hereby designate Thursday, the twenty-first day of November, 1940, to be observed nationally as a day of thanksgiving.

In a year which has seen calamity and sorrow fall upon many peoples elsewhere in the world may we give thanks for our preservation.

On the same day, in the same hour, let us pray:

Almighty God, who hast given us this good land for our heritage; We humbly beseech Thee that we may always prove ourselves a people mindful of Thy favor and glad to do Thy will. Bless our land with honourable industry, sound learning, and pure manners. Save us from violence, discord, and confusion; from pride and arrogancy, and from every evil way.

Defend our liberties, and fashion into one united people the multitudes brought hither out of many kindreds and tongues. Endue with the spirit of wisdom those to whom in Thy Name we entrust the authority of government, that there may be justice and peace at home, and that, through obedience to Thy law, we may show forth Thy praise among the nations of the earth.

In the time of prosperity, fill our hearts with thankfulness, and in the day of trouble, suffer not our trust in Thee to fail; Amen.

ADDRESS ON ARMISTICE DAY, ARLINGTON NATIONAL CEMETERY NOVEMBER 11, 1940

VETERANS OF THE Army and Navy of the United States:

On this day which commemorates the end of fighting between human beings in a World War, it is, I think, permissible for me to search far back in the history of civilization in order to visualize important trends.

On the Great Seal of the United States which, for a century and a half, has reposed in the loving care of a long line of Secretaries of State of the United States, there appear these words: "NOVUS ORDO SECLORUM" which means: "A new order of the ages."

In almost every century since the day that recorded history began, people have thought, quite naturally, that they were creating or establishing some kind of "new order of the ages."

But in the scheme of civilization from which ours descends I suppose that we can recognize that in approximately 2,500 years there have been only a very few "new orders" in the development of human living under a thing called Government.

Without question, the philosophy of orderly Government in which the governed had some form of voice in a civilized society goes back to the days of ancient Greece. We must remember, however, that while the philosophy of democracy was there first expressed in words and on paper, the practice of it was by no means consistent, and was confined to a relatively small number of human beings and to a relatively small geographical area.

We came to the age of Rome - an age of a strange admixture of elections and laws and military conquest and personal dictatorship. It was an age which extended the civilization of the period to the greater part of the then known world. It was an age which forced its own conception of laws and ways of life on millions of less civilized people who previously had lived under tribal custom or centralized direction. Definitely, Rome was an age.

With Rome's collapse and with the overrunning of Europe by vast population movements from farther east, orderly progress deteriorated for a number of centuries, and the sword drove learning into hiding. That dark period could hardly be called an age because it was essentially an interim between ages.

Then, with the reawakening of a thousand years ago, with the Crusades, the Feudal System, the Guilds, the Kings and the Renaissance, that age which immediately preceded our own was born and grew and flourished. It was an era of enormous distinction - arts and literature and education and exploration - marching armies, barons and empires. Human security was still non-existent - democracy was not permitted.

But toward the close of that great age, the appearance of tiny movements in tiny places, led by tiny people forecast the next vast step forward - what we like to think of as the era of 1776, the age in which, thank God, we still live.

It is true that those small beginnings originated in the old world among the philosophers, among the seekers of many kinds of freedom that were forbidden by those who governed.

Those beginnings found their freest development in the colonies that were organized along the seaboard of North America. There, by the processes of trial and error, democracy as it has since been accepted in so many lands, had its birth and its training.

There came into being the first far-flung Government in all the world whose cardinal principle was democracy - the United States of America.

We must accept that as fact because, truly and fundamentally, it was a new order. Nothing like it had ever been seen before. We must accept it because the new order spread into almost every part of the civilized world.

It spread in many forms, and over the next century almost all peoples had acquired some form of popular expression of opinion, some form of election, some form of franchise, some form of the right to be heard. The Americas, all of the Americas in that century, and the British Isles, England and Scotland and Ireland and Wales, led the world in spreading the gospel of democracy among peoples, great and small.

And the world as a whole felt with much right that by that time it had discarded feudalism and conquest and dictatorship.

People felt that way, within the memory of many of us who are here today, until 1914, when a definite effort was made in a part of the world to destroy this existing settled "new order of the ages" - to destroy it after its relatively short trial, and to substitute for it the doctrine that might makes right. That attempt failed with our help twenty-two years ago.

You and I who served in the period of the World War have faced in later years unpatriotic efforts by some of our own countrymen to make us believe that the sacrifices made by our own nation were wholly in vain.

A hundred years from now, historians will brand such efforts as puny and false.

A hundred years from now, historians will say rightly that the World War preserved the new order of the ages for at least a generation - a full twenty years - and that if the axis of 1918 had been successful in military victory over the associated nations, resistance on behalf of democracy in 1940 would have been wholly impossible.

And so America is proud of its share in maintaining the era of democracy in that war in which we took part. America is proud of you who served - and ever will be proud.

I, for one, do not believe that the era of democracy in human affairs can or ever will be snuffed out in our lifetime. I, for one, do not believe that mere force will be successful in sterilizing the seeds which had taken such firm root as a harbinger of better lives for mankind.

I, for one, do not believe that the world will revert either to a modern form of ancient slavery or to controls vested in modern feudalism or modern emperors or modern dictators or modern oligarchs in these days. I, for one, do believe that the very people under their iron heels will, themselves, rebel.

What are a few months or even a few years in the lifetime of any of us? We, alive today, live and think in terms of our grandparents, and our own parents, and ourselves, and our children - yes, and our grandchildren. We, alive today, not in the existent democracies alone, but also among the populations of the smaller nations already overrun, are thinking in the larger terms of the maintenance of the new order to which we have been accustomed and in which we intend to continue.

Time has marched on. We recognize certain facts of 1940 which did not exist in 1918: a need for the elimination of aggressive armaments, a need for the breaking down of barriers in a more closely knitted world, a need for restoring honor in the written and spoken word. We recognize that the processes of democracies must be greatly improved in order that we may attain those purposes.

But over and above the present, over and above this moment, we recognize and salute the eternal verities that lie with us in the future of mankind.

You, young men of 1917 and 1918, helped to preserve those truths of democracy for our generation.

We still unite, we still strive mightily to preserve intact that new order of the ages founded by the Fathers of America.

GREETING TO AMERICAN FEDERATION OF LABOR, ADDRESSED TO WILLIAM GREEN, PRESIDENT, NEW ORLEANS, LOUISIANA NOVEMBER 13, 1940

SACRIFICE MAY BE necessary in the future for everyone. Responsible action and self-discipline, physical and moral fitness are now required of all of us as our part in the defense of our country and democracy...

We as a people today have the common determination to put our country above all else. Please God we may always keep it so as to preserve our priceless heritage of the world's greatest democracy which came from the Fathers of the Republic.

GREETING TO THE ECONOMICS CLUB OF NEW YORK DECEMBER 2, 1940

THE FREE AND frank discussion of national problems in open meeting, as in the public forum of the Economics Club of New York, helps to create an enlightened public opinion. It invokes the spiritual strength of a free people...

In the totalitarian scheme such a discussion has no place. There can be no real unity where the people have no voice.

LETTER ON RELIGION IN DEMOCRACY TO HON. SAMUEL I. ROSENMAN, PRESIDENT, JEWISH EDUCATION COMMITTEE, NEW YORK, N. Y. DECEMBER 16, 1940

PLEASE CONVEY MY best wishes to your co-workers in the Jewish Education Committee of New York, at the annual Hanukkah Dinner. Please tell them for me how much I believe in the value of their endeavors to extend and improve religious education among the children and youth of the Jewish faith in your city.

Our modern democratic way of life has its deepest roots in our great common religious tradition, which for ages past has taught to civilized mankind the dignity of the human being, his equality before God, and his responsibility in the making of a better and fairer world.

Everywhere in the world there are men of stout heart and firm faith now engaged in a great spiritual struggle to test whether that ancient wisdom is to endure, or whether it must give way to the older, discarded doctrine that some few men shall dominate multitudes of others and dictate to them their thinking, their religion, their living.

This conflict has found its most terrible expression in a war which has now engulfed a large portion of humanity. In its more peaceful aspects, the same struggle also pervades all efforts of men of good will who are seeking through democracy the way to the world to come.

In teaching this democratic faith to American children, we need the sustaining, buttressing aid of those great ethical religious teachings which are the heritage of our modern civilization. For "not upon strength nor upon power, but upon the spirit of God" shall our democracy be founded.

I hope that your Committee and all American citizens will continue to strive to bring a new, fresh vigor into the teaching and lessons of religion for the children of our beloved land.

CHRISTMAS GREETING TO THE NATION
DECEMBER 24, 1940

AT THIS CHRISTMASTIDE of 1940 it is well for all humanity to remind itself that while this is in its name a Christian celebration, it is participated in reverently and happily by hundreds of millions of people who are members of other religions, or belong actively to no church at all.

The reason is not far to seek. It is because the spirit of unselfish service personified by the life and the teachings of Christ makes appeal to the inner conscience and hope of every man and every woman in every part of the earth. It transcends in the ultimate all lines of race, of habitat, of nation. It lives in the midst of war, of slavery, of conquest. It survives prohibitions and decrees and force. It is an unquenchable Spring of Promise to humanity.

Sometimes we who have lived through the strifes and the hates of a quarter century wonder if this old world of ours has abandoned the ideals of the Brotherhood of Man. Sometimes we ask if contention and anger in our own midst in America are a portent of disunion and disaster. Sometimes we fear that the selfishness of the individual is more and more controlling in our lives.

When we are in those moods it is hard for us to keep from putting our tongues in our cheeks when we say "Merry Christmas" - for we think in thoughts of futility and not of hope. A few people are cynics all of the time; some people are cynics part of the time; but most people keep their faith most of the time.

That is why we must keep on striving for a better and a more happy world.

It is unintelligent to be defeatist. Crisis may beget crisis but the progress underneath does not wholly halt - it does go forward.

In a century we have gained much. Aside from great areas stricken by actual warfare in the present moment, the lives of human beings are safer than they were in the olden days. Great and spreading plagues take smaller toll; starvation of millions is less; the forces of nature are better controlled.

There is in the civilization we recognize a greater security for the young, for the worker, for the aged. Charity in the narrower sense of the word helps the needy more usefully.

Compared with the days when Charles Dickens wrote the Christmas Carol, we see a definite betterment. We do not claim attainment, and we recognize that there is much - oh, so much - to do.

Most of all we ask a chance to do it - yes, a peaceful chance to do it.

We want to do it the voluntary way - and most human beings in all the world want to do it the voluntary way. We do not want to have the way imposed on the world by the conquest of the world by the sword.

That would not follow in the footsteps of Christ. That would not make for happier Christmases in the future of any nation. Mankind is all one - and what happens in distant lands tomorrow will leave its mark on the happiness of our Christmases to come.

Let us make this Christmas a merry one for the little children in our midst. For us of maturer years it cannot be merry.

But for most of us it can be a Happy Christmas if by happiness we mean that we have done with doubts, that we have set our hearts against fear, that we still believe in the Golden Rule for all mankind, that we intend to live more purely in the spirit of Christ, and that by our works, as well as our words, we will strive forward in Faith and in Hope and in Love.

In that spirit I wish a Happy Christmas to all, and happier Christmases yet to come.

FIRESIDE CHAT BROADCAST FROM THE WHITE HOUSE, WASHINGTON, D.C. DECEMBER 29, 1940

WE FACE THIS new crisis - this new threat to the security of our nation - with the same courage and realism.

Never before since Jamestown and Plymouth Rock has our American civilization been in such danger as now.

For, on September 27, 1940, by an agreement signed in Berlin, three powerful nations, two in Europe and one in Asia, joined themselves together in the threat that if the United States of America interfered with or blocked the expansion program of these three nations - a program aimed at world control - they would unite in ultimate action against the United States.

The Nazi masters of Germany have made it clear that they intend not only to dominate all life and thought in their own country, but also to enslave the whole of Europe, and then to use the resources of Europe to dominate the rest of the world.

It was only three weeks ago their leader stated this: "There are two worlds that stand opposed to each other." And then in defiant reply to his opponents, he said this: "Others are correct when they say: With this world we cannot ever reconcile ourselves...I can beat any other power in the world." So said the leader of the Nazis.

In other words, the Axis not merely admits but proclaims that there can be no ultimate peace between their philosophy of government and our philosophy of government...

If Great Britain goes down, the Axis powers will control the continents of Europe, Asia, Africa, Australasia, and the high seas - and they will be in a position to bring enormous military and naval resources against this hemisphere. It is no exaggeration to say that all of us, in all the Americas, would be living at the point of a gun - a gun loaded with explosive bullets, economic as well as military.

We should enter upon a new and terrible era in which the whole world, our hemisphere included, would be run by threats of brute force. To survive in such a world, we would have to convert ourselves permanently into a militaristic power on the basis of war economy...

During the past week many people in all parts of the nation have told me what they wanted me to say tonight. Almost all of them expressed a courageous desire to hear the plain truth about the gravity of the situation.

One telegram, however, expressed the attitude of the small minority who want to see no evil and hear no evil, even though they know in their hearts that evil exists. That telegram begged me not to tell again of the ease with which our American cities could be bombed by any hostile power which had gained bases in this Western Hemisphere. The gist of that telegram was: "Please, Mr. President, don't frighten us by telling us the facts."

Frankly and definitely there is danger ahead - danger against which we must prepare. But we well know that we cannot escape danger, or the fear of danger, by crawling into bed and pulling the covers over our heads...

There are those who say that the Axis powers would never have any desire to attack the Western Hemisphere.

That is the same dangerous form of wishful thinking which has destroyed the powers of resistance of so many conquered peoples.

The plain facts are that the Nazis have proclaimed, time and again, that all other races are their inferiors and therefore subject to their orders. And most important of all, the vast resources and wealth of this American Hemisphere constitute the most tempting loot in all the round world...

Their secret emissaries are active in our own and in neighboring countries. They seek to stir up suspicion and dissension to cause internal strife. They try to turn capital against labor, and vice versa. They try to reawaken long slumbering racial and religious enmities which should have no place in this country.

They are active in every group that promotes intolerance. They exploit for their own ends our natural abhorrence of war. These trouble-breeders have but one purpose. It is to divide our people into hostile groups and to destroy our unity and shatter our will to defend ourselves.

There are also American citizens, many of them in high places, who, unwittingly in most cases, are aiding and abetting the work of these agents. I do not charge these American citizens with being foreign agents. But I do charge them with doing exactly the kind of work that the dictators want done in the United States.

These people not only believe that we can save our own skins by shutting our eyes to the fate of other nations. Some of them go much further than that. They say that we can and should become the friends and even the partners of the Axis powers. Some of them even suggest that we should imitate the methods of the dictatorships. Americans never can and never will do that.

The experience of the past two years has proven beyond doubt that no nation can appease the Nazis. No man can tame a tiger into a kitten by stroking it. There can be no appeasement with ruthlessness. There can be no reasoning with an incendiary bomb. We know now that a nation can have peace with the Nazis only at the price of total surrender...

Even the people of Italy have been forced to become accomplices of the Nazis; but at this moment they do not know how soon they will be embraced to death by their allies.

The American appeasers ignore the warning to be found in the fate of Austria, Czechoslovakia, Poland, Norway, Belgium, the Netherlands, Denmark, and France. They tell you that the Axis powers are going to win anyway; that all this bloodshed in the world could be saved; that the United States might just as well throw its influence into the scale of a dictated peace, and get the best out of it that we can.

They call it a "negotiated peace." Nonsense! Is it a negotiated peace if a gang of outlaws surrounds your community and on threat of extermination makes you pay tribute to save your own skins?

Such a dictated peace would be no peace at all. It would be only another armistice, leading to the most gigantic armament race and the most devastating trade wars in all history. And in these contests the Americas would offer the only real resistance to the Axis powers.

With all their vaunted efficiency, with all their parade of pious purpose in this war, there are still in their background the concentration camp and the servants of God in chains.

The history of recent years proves that shootings and chains and concentration camps are not simply the transient tools but the very altars of modern dictatorships. They may talk of a "new order" in the world, but what they have in mind is only a revival of the oldest and the worst tyranny. In that there is no liberty, no religion, no hope.

The proposed "new order" is the very opposite of a United States of Europe or a United States of Asia. It is not a Government based upon the consent of the governed. It is not a union of ordinary, self-respecting men and women to protect themselves and their freedom and their dignity from oppression. It is an unholy alliance of power and pelf to dominate and enslave the human race.

The British people and their allies today are conducting an active war against this unholy alliance. Our own future security is greatly dependent on the outcome of that fight. Our ability to "keep out of war" is going to be affected by that outcome.

Thinking in terms of today and tomorrow, I make the direct statement to the American people that there is far less chance of the United States getting into war, if we do all we can now to support the nations defending themselves against attack by the Axis than if we acquiesce in their defeat, submit tamely to an Axis victory, and wait our turn to be the object of attack in another war later on.

If we are to be completely honest with ourselves, we must admit that there is risk in any course we may take. But I deeply believe that the great majority of our people agree that the course that I advocate involves the least risk now and the greatest hope for world peace in the future.

The people of Europe who are defending themselves do not ask us to do their fighting. They ask us for the implements of war, the planes, the tanks, the guns, the freighters which will enable them to fight for their liberty and for our security. Emphatically we must get these weapons to them in sufficient volume and quickly enough, so that we and our children will be saved the agony and suffering of war which others have had to endure.

Let not the defeatists tell us that it is too late. It will never be earlier. Tomorrow will be later than today. Certain facts are self-evident.

In a military sense Great Britain and the British Empire are today the spearhead of resistance to world conquest. They are putting up a fight which will live forever in the story of human gallantry.

There is no demand for sending an American Expeditionary Force outside our own borders. There is no intention by any member of your Government to send such a force. You can, therefore, nail any talk about sending armies to Europe as deliberate untruth.

Our national policy is not directed toward war. Its sole purpose is to keep war away from our country and our people. Democracy's fight against world conquest is being greatly aided, and must be more greatly aided, by the rearmament of the United States and by sending every ounce and every ton of munitions and supplies that we can possibly spare to help the defenders who are in the front lines.

It is no more unneutral for us to do that than it is for Sweden, Russia and other nations near Germany, to send steel and ore and oil and other war materials into Germany every day in the week.

We are planning our own defense with the utmost urgency; and in its vast scale we must integrate the war needs of Britain and the other free nations which are resisting aggression.

This is not a matter of sentiment or of controversial personal opinion. It is a matter of realistic, practical military policy, based on the advice of our military experts who are in close touch with existing warfare. These military and naval experts and the members of the Congress and the Administration have a single-minded purpose - the defense of the United States.

This nation is making a great effort to produce everything that is necessary in this emergency - and with all possible speed. This great effort requires great sacrifice.

I would ask no one to defend a democracy which in turn would not defend everyone in the nation against want and privation. The strength of this nation shall not be diluted by the failure of the Government to protect the economic well-being of its citizens.

If our capacity to produce is limited by machines, it must ever be remembered that these machines are operated by the skill and the stamina of the workers. As the Government is determined to protect the rights of the workers, so the nation has a right to expect that the men who man the machines will discharge their full responsibilities to the urgent needs of defense.

The worker possesses the same human dignity and is entitled to the same security of position as the engineer or the manager or the owner. For the workers provide the human power that turns out the destroyers, the airplanes and the tanks.

The nation expects our defense industries to continue operation without interruption by strikes or lock-outs. It expects and insists that management and workers will reconcile their differences by voluntary or legal means, to continue to produce the supplies that are so sorely needed.

And on the economic side of our great defense program, we are, as you know, bending every effort to maintain stability of prices and with that the stability of the cost of living.

Nine days ago I announced the setting up of a more effective organization to direct our gigantic efforts to increase the production of munitions. The appropriation of vast sums of money and a well coordinated executive direction of our defense efforts are not in themselves enough.

Guns, planes, ships and many other things have to be built in the factories and arsenals of America. They have to be produced by workers and managers and engineers with the aid of machines which in turn have to be built by hundreds of thousands of workers throughout the land....

Our defense efforts must not be blocked by those who fear the future consequences of surplus plant capacity. The possible consequences of failure of our defense efforts now are much more to be feared...

No pessimistic policy about the future of America shall delay the immediate expansion of those industries essential to defense. We need them.

I want to make it clear that it is the purpose of the nation to build now with all possible speed every machine, every arsenal, every factory that we need to manufacture our defense material. We have the men - the skill - the wealth - and above all, the will.

I am confident that if and when production of consumer or luxury goods in certain industries requires the use of machines and raw materials that are essential for defense purposes, then such production must yield, and will gladly yield, to our primary and compelling purpose.

I appeal to the owners of plants - to the managers - to the workers - to our own Government employees - to put every ounce of effort into producing these munitions swiftly and without stint. With this appeal I give you the pledge that all of us who are officers of your Government will devote ourselves to the same whole-hearted extent to the great task that lies ahead.

As planes and ships and guns and shells are produced, your Government, with its defense experts, can then determine how best to use them to defend this hemisphere. The decision as to how much shall be sent abroad and how much shall remain at home must be made on the basis of our over-all military necessities.

We must be the great arsenal of democracy. For us this is an emergency as serious as war itself. We must apply ourselves to our task with the same resolution, the same sense of urgency, the same spirit of patriotism and sacrifice as we would show were we at war.

We have furnished the British great material support and we will furnish far more in the future.

There will be no "bottlenecks" in our determination to aid Great Britain. No dictator, no combination of dictators, will weaken that determination by threats of how they will construe that determination.

The British have received invaluable military support from the heroic Greek army, and from the forces of all the governments in exile. Their strength is growing. It is the strength of men and women who value their freedom more highly than they value their lives.

I believe that the Axis powers are not going to win this war. I base that belief on the latest and best information.

We have no excuse for defeatism. We have every good reason for hope - hope for peace, hope for the defense of our civilization and for the building of a better civilization in the future.

I have the profound conviction that the American people are now determined to put forth a mightier effort than they have ever yet made to increase our production of all the implements of defense, to meet the threat to our democratic faith.

ANNUAL MESSAGE TO CONGRESS
JANUARY 6, 1941

IN TIMES LIKE these it is immature - and incidentally, untrue - for anybody to brag that an unprepared America, single-handed, and with one hand tied behind its back, can hold off the whole world.

No realistic American can expect from a dictator's peace international generosity, or return of true independence, or world disarmament, or freedom of expression, or freedom of religion - or even good business.

Such a peace would bring no security for us or for our neighbors. "Those, who would give up essential liberty to purchase a little temporary safety, deserve neither liberty nor safety."

As a nation, we may take pride in the fact that we are softhearted; but we cannot afford to be soft-headed.

We must always be wary of those who with sounding brass and a tinkling cymbal preach the "ism" of appeasement...

Just as our national policy in internal affairs has been based upon a decent respect for the rights and the dignity of all our fellow men within our gates, so our national policy in foreign affairs has been based on a decent respect for the rights and dignity of all nations, large and small. And the justice of morality must and will win in the end...

The Nation takes great satisfaction and much strength from the things which have been done to make its people conscious of their individual stake in the preservation of democratic life in America. Those things have toughened the fiber of our people, have renewed their faith and strengthened their devotion to the institutions we make ready to protect...

In the future days, which we seek to make secure, we look forward to a world founded upon four essential human freedoms.

The first is freedom of speech and expression - everywhere in the world.

The second is freedom of every person to worship God in his own way - everywhere in the world.

The third is freedom from want - which, translated into world terms, means economic understandings which will secure to every nation a healthy peacetime life for its inhabitants - everywhere in the world.

The fourth is freedom from fear - which, translated into world terms, means a world-wide reduction of armaments to such a point and in such a thorough fashion that no nation will be in a position to commit an act of physical aggression against any neighbor - anywhere in the world.

That is no vision of a distant millennium. It is a definite basis for a kind of world attainable in our own time and generation. That kind of world is the very antithesis of the so-called new order of tyranny which the dictators seek to create with the crash of a bomb.

To that new order we oppose the greater conception - the moral order. A good society is able to face schemes of world domination and foreign revolutions alike without fear...

This nation has placed its destiny in the hands and heads and hearts of its millions of free men and women; and its faith in freedom under the guidance of God.

THE FAITH OF FDR

THIRD TERM
JANUARY 20, 1941-JANUARY 19, 1945

THIRD INAUGURAL ADDRESS
JANUARY 20, 1941

LIVES OF NATIONS are determined not by the count of years, but by the lifetime of the human spirit. The life of a man is threescore years and ten: a little more, a little less. The life of a Nation is the fullness of the measure of its will to live...

And yet, we all understand what it is - the spirit - the faith of America. It is the product of centuries. It was born in the multitudes of those who came from many lands - some of high degree, but mostly plain people - who sought here, early and late, to find freedom more freely.

The democratic aspiration is no mere recent phase in human history. It is human history. It permeated the ancient life of early peoples. It blazed anew in the Middle Ages. It was written in Magna Charta.

In the Americas its impact has been irresistible. America has been the New World in all tongues, and to all peoples, not because this continent was a new-found land, but because all those who came here believed they could create upon this continent a new life - a life that should be new in freedom.

Its vitality was written into our own Mayflower Compact, into the Declaration of Independence, into the Constitution of the United States, into the Gettysburg Address...

But it is not enough to achieve these purposes alone. It is not enough to clothe and feed the BODY of this Nation, to instruct, and inform its MIND. For there is also the SPIRIT. And of the three, the greatest is the spirit.

Without the body and the mind, as all men know, the Nation could not live.

But if the spirit of America were killed, even though the Nation's body and mind, constricted in an alien world, lived on, the America we know would have perished.

That spirit - that faith - speaks to us in our daily lives in ways often unnoticed, because they seem so obvious...

The destiny of America was proclaimed in words of prophecy spoken by our first President in his first Inaugural in 1789 - words almost directed, it would seem, to this year of 1941: "The preservation of the sacred fire of liberty and the destiny of the republican model of government are justly considered...deeply...finally, staked on the experiment intrusted to the hands of the American people."

If you and I in this later day lose that sacred fire - if we let it be smothered with doubt and fear - then we shall reject the destiny which Washington strove so valiantly and so triumphantly to establish. The preservation of the spirit and faith of the Nation does, and will, furnish the highest justification for every sacrifice that we may make in the cause of national defense.

In the face of great perils never before encountered, our strong purpose is to protect and to perpetuate the integrity of democracy.

For this we muster the spirit of America, and the faith of America.

We do not retreat. We are not content to stand still. As Americans, we go forward, in the service of our country, by the will of God.

FOREWORD TO A SPECIAL MILITARY EDITION OF THE NEW TESTAMENT AND BOOK OF PSALMS, PUBLISHED BY THE GIDEON'S INTERNATIONAL, 201 SOUTH STATE STREET, CHICAGO, ILLINOIS JANUARY 25, 1941

The White House, Washington
To the Armed Forces:

AS COMMANDER-IN-CHIEF I take pleasure in commending the reading of the Bible to all who serve in the armed forces of the United States. Throughout the centuries men of many faiths and diverse origins have found in the Sacred Book words of wisdom, counsel and inspiration. It is a fountain of strength and now, as always, an aid in attaining the highest aspirations of the human soul.

Very sincerely yours,
Franklin D. Roosevelt

Attention: By special request of the U.S. Military and Naval Authorities you are instructed to place your NAME ONLY on the fly leaf, nothing more. On no account name your organization, post, ship or station at any place in this book. To do so might afford valuable information to the enemy.

Look up your chaplain at the first opportunity. Your welfare is his first concern, and you will find him friendly and helpful at all times. His counsel and advice will guide you in avoiding or overcoming difficulties. In many ways you can help him in his services for others. A close friendship between a chaplain and his men preserves and promotes a fine spirit in any service unit. - The Gideons

PRESS CONFERENCE
FEBRUARY 21, 1941

Q. MR. PRESIDENT, GENERAL MARSHALL was quoted as having said that we were strengthening our armed forces in Hawaii and perhaps some of the islands we possess south of Hawaii; is that correct?

THE PRESIDENT: Who quoted him?

Q. Various members of Congress, I believe.

THE PRESIDENT: Who was supposed to have said this?

Q. General Marshall.

THE PRESIDENT: In what kind of meeting?

Q. In a secret meeting.

THE PRESIDENT: Oh, I don't know why this should be anything more than background; I don't think it needs to be off the record. I read the papers this morning.

Now mind you, it is not important for the people to know whether my left eyebrow is raised or whether my tone of voice is angry - you better cut that out. I am not the least bit angry - I am interested; I am really interested in a problem of ethics that I think the American people ought to be interested in. It does present a problem, and it is interesting, in times of world upheaval.

I will try to put this - what shall I say? - logically; there are certain things in regard to the defense of the United States that it is advisable, for the defense of the United States, should be kept confidential; and that is why, occasionally, before certain committees on the Hill, these matters - which for national safety it is believed ought to be kept confidential - are spoken of by the experts along those lines - are spoken of only in secret or executive sessions of a committee.

There is not very much new in this; I mean, it has been going on, I think, since 1776. It still lives, this problem does; and this morning, when I started my breakfast, I read front page stories in all the papers about the Chief of Staff of the Army who was said to have given certain information to the Senate Committee on Military Affairs; and the stories then went on to say exactly what this Nation was supposed to have done.

Well, you raise two questions, both of which concern ethics, morals, and patriotism in exactly the same way.

The first question is, frankly, as to whether members of that committee, ethically, morally, or patriotically ought to disclose to anybody on the outside what was said. I am simply raising this as an interesting problem.

No. 2: If they do disclose what went on in the secret meeting, it is perfectly obvious that any reporter who is worth his salt will try to find out - perfectly all right. If the story is disclosed to him by a member of the committee, either under seal of secrecy or without any seal of secrecy - it is perfectly all right for the reporter to take that story to his office, because that is part of a reporter's business.

So I don't think there is any blame attaching to any reporter who carried those stories to his office; but the printing of the story or putting it on the wires by press associations or newspaper offices in Washington presents another very different, very difficult problem:

Is or isn't the owner or the manager or the managing editor or the head of the Washington office under the same moral or ethical or patriotic duty not to print a story which has come out through a violation of confidence, out of a secret session of a Senate committee?

That is a nice question - something that ought to be thought about; and, as I say, I don't attach any blame to any of the newspapermen who got these stories - that is a part of your job, obviously - but I do raise the question in regard to newspapers printing a story of that kind.

And, finally, just to close the thing up, I have got in my hand here from the Chief of Staff a story of what he said, that size It is completely different from any of the stories which actually did appear, second or third-hand, in any of the papers this morning.

Q. Mr. President...isn't there a difference between what might be published in peacetime and what might be published in wartime? High officials do give some testimony affecting the welfare of the American people; don't you think it is the function of the press to keep the public informed?

THE PRESIDENT: Do you mean to say that it is the duty of the press to publish what are considered to be military secrets involving the safety of the country?

Q. No, sir, I made that clear... Can you tell us, in the interests of accuracy, what the facts are?

THE PRESIDENT: Certainly not! That would be what you might call compounding a felony.

Q. Would you consider, sir, that the publication this morning has injured American defense in any way?

THE PRESIDENT: Yes, I do.

Q. The reason I ask that is because you threw a doubt in my mind as to its accuracy.

THE PRESIDENT: It is not correct, in the first place, but a lot of people are going to think it is...

Q. Mr. President, what does constitute a national defense secret?

THE PRESIDENT: Well, I don't think we have ever had any trouble about that before. There has been mighty little that has been kept secret, and I don't think it has hurt anybody. They are things that have been kept secret on the advice or recommendation of the people who are responsible - primarily responsible - for American defense, the Army and Navy.

Q. Mr. President, if the attitude is taken that any testimony given on the Hill in executive session remains secret, isn't the final test what the Government wants to give out and what it doesn't want to give out?

THE PRESIDENT: No, only if the Government didn't give out or held secret things that there was no reason for holding secret.

Q. Then what is the test?

THE PRESIDENT: The test is what the Commander-in-Chief of the Army and Navy thinks would be harmful to the defense of this country to give out.

Q. He is not required to give that to a Congressional committee which leaks.

THE PRESIDENT: No.

Q. Then that would be the safest way - not to give it to a Congressional committee.

THE PRESIDENT: It might be the safest way; but of course, naturally, one doesn't like to withhold information from committees of Congress. The best way would be to have no disclosures by members of the committee and no disclosures by publishers.

Q. If there is a conflict?

THE PRESIDENT: Then the second is essential.

Q. The second is a reporter taking it to his office.

THE PRESIDENT: No, the printing of it, I am talking about.

Q. You would not have the second if the first did not arise.

THE PRESIDENT: No.

Q. In your criticism of the press-

THE PRESIDENT: (interposing) I am not criticizing the press - haven't been.

Q. May we suggest that you include the radio also?

THE PRESIDENT: Yes, quite right. It does raise an interesting question of ethics, morals, and patriotism.

Q. Assuming that these reports endanger the country, do you think we ought to be thinking about the possibility of censorship, without a declaration of war?

THE PRESIDENT: Of course not; that is why I am putting it up to the people of the country.

Q. You think it ought to be done voluntarily?

THE PRESIDENT: There is no question of censorship.

Q. You want the papers to figure on some method of their own?

THE PRESIDENT: Yes.

Q. You have taken it up with the press; do you intend to raise the problem before the members of Congress?

THE PRESIDENT: Let's have a little discussion and see what the Congress does.

TRIBUTE TO MR. JUSTICE OLIVER WENDELL HOLMES, JR., ON THE ONE HUNDREDTH ANNIVERSARY OF HIS BIRTH. MARCH 8, 1941

OLIVER WENDELL HOLMES's life was devoted to those ultimate purposes of civilization to which the Founders dedicated this Nation. He believed passionately in the moral worth of the individual regardless of race or religion or the accident of antecedents. He therefore believed in the unfettered spirit without which man cannot live a civilized life.

ADDRESS AT THE ANNUAL DINNER OF WHITE HOUSE CORRESPONDENTS' ASSOCIATION MARCH 15, 1941

HISTORY CANNOT BE rewritten by wishful thinking. We, the American people, are writing new history today...

These modern tyrants find it necessary to. their plans to eliminate all democracies - eliminate them one by one...

A few weeks ago I spoke of four freedoms - freedom of speech and expression, freedom of every person to worship God in his own way, freedom from want, freedom from fear. They are the ultimate stake.

They may not be immediately attainable throughout the world but humanity does move toward those glorious ideals through democratic processes. And if we fail - if democracy is superseded by slavery - then those four freedoms, or even the mention of them, will become forbidden things. Centuries will pass before they can be revived.

By winning now, we strengthen the meaning of those freedoms, we increase the stature of mankind, we establish the dignity of human life...

China likewise expresses the magnificent will of millions of plain people to resist the dismemberment of their historic Nation. China, through the Generalissimo, Chiang Kai-shek, asks our help. America has said that China shall have our help.

And so our country is going to be what our people have proclaimed it must be - the arsenal of democracy. Our country is going to play its full part.

And when - no, I didn't say if, I said when - dictatorships disintegrate - and pray God that will be sooner than any of us now dares to hope - then our country must continue to play its great part in the period of world reconstruction for the good of humanity...

Never, in all our history, have Americans faced a job so well worth while. May it be said of us in the days to come that our children and our children's children rise up and call us blessed.

PRESS CONFERENCE
APRIL 8, 1941

THE UNITED SERVICE Organizations for National Defense - Yesterday they announced their program of service to soldiers, sailors, and defense workers.

This worK...is essentially around the various camps, navy yards, and new plants, and provides for the recreation, welfare, and spiritual needs of the young men and women who have answered, and will answer, the call to the national defense...

This duty - of maintaining morale on the home front - is one in which every American shares...

The national private organizations which have incorporated the United Service Organizations as an over-all planning body are: The Y.M.C.A.; Y.W.C.A.; Catholic Community Service; Jewish Welfare Board; Salvation Army; and the Travelers Aid Society.

PRESS CONFERENCE
APRIL 15, 1941

IN THE CASE of Danish possessions, there were principally two of them; one was what used to be called the Danish West Indies, colonized in large part by Danes, and the other was Greenland, which again had been colonized in large part by Scandinavians. They had a civilization up there, as you know, which started at the time of Leif Ericson. They had a Christian people up there. They had a cathedral.

REMARKS AT THE DEDICATION OF WOODROW WILSON'S BIRTHPLACE, STAUNTON, VIRGINIA MAY 4, 1941

I CAN THINK of no more fitting place in all the land for Americans to pledge anew their faith in the democratic way of life than at the birthplace of Woodrow Wilson. In this quiet Presbyterian manse first saw the light of day one whose whole active life was dedicated to the cause of freedom, to the conquest of fear, and to the liberation of the eternal spirit of man from every thralldom imposed by fear.

Woodrow Wilson was fortunate in his birthplace. He was favored in his parentage and his environment. I like the old phrase that this was a home of plain living and high thinking and wherever the family moved in the migrations incident to the religious calling of the father, they carried with them ideals which put faith in spiritual values above every material consideration.

In the tragic conflict which the world witnesses today and which threatens everything that we have most loved as a free people, we see more clearly than ever before the unyielding strength of things of the spirit. All of recorded history bears witness that the human race has made true advancement only as it has appreciated spiritual values. Those unhappy peoples who have placed their sole reliance on the sword have inevitably perished by the sword in the end.

No, physical strength can never permanently withstand the impact of spiritual force.

And Woodrow Wilson's whole career was a triumph of the spiritual over the sordid forces of brute strength. Under his leadership this country made, as we know, very great spiritual progress...

RADIO ADDRESS ANNOUNCING AN UNLIMITED NATIONAL EMERGENCY MAY 27, 1941

WHAT STARTED AS a European war has developed, as the Nazis always intended it should develop, into a world war for world domination.

Adolf Hitler never considered the domination of Europe as an end in itself. European conquest was but a step toward ultimate goals in all the other continents. It is unmistakably apparent to all of us that, unless the advance of Hitlerism is forcibly checked now, the Western Hemisphere will be within range of the Nazi weapons of destruction...

Yes, even our right of worship would be threatened. The Nazi world does not recognize any God except Hitler; for the Nazis are as ruthless as the Communists in the denial of God. What place has religion which preaches the dignity of the human being, the majesty of the human soul, in a world where moral standards are measured by treachery and bribery and fifth columnists? Will our children, too, wander off, goose-stepping in search of new gods?...

To them I say this: never in the history of the world has a Nation lost its democracy by a successful struggle to defend its democracy. We must not be defeated by the fear of the very danger which we are preparing to resist. Our freedom has shown its ability to survive war, but our freedom would never survive surrender. "The only thing we have to fear is fear itself."

There is, of course, a small group of sincere, patriotic men and women whose real passion for peace has shut their eyes to the ugly realities of international banditry and to the need to resist it at all costs. I am sure they are embarrassed by the sinister support they are receiving from the enemies of democracy in our midst the Bundists, the Fascists, and Communists, and every group devoted to bigotry and racial and religious intolerance...

Today the whole world is divided between human slavery and human freedom - between pagan brutality and the Christian ideal.

We choose human freedom - which is the Christian ideal.

No one of us can waver for a moment in his courage or his faith.

We will not accept a Hitler-dominated world. And we will not accept a world, like the postwar world of the 1920's, in which the seeds of Hitlerism can again be planted and allowed to grow.

We will accept only a world consecrated to freedom of speech and expression - freedom of every person to worship God in his own way - freedom from want - and freedom from terror...

We reassert our abiding faith in the vitality of our constitutional Republic as a perpetual home of freedom, of tolerance, and of devotion to the word of God...

I repeat the words of the signers of the Declaration of Independence - that little band of patriots, fighting long ago against overwhelming odds, but certain, as we are now, of ultimate victory: "With a firm reliance on the protection of Divine Providence, we mutually pledge to each other our lives, our fortunes, and our sacred honor."

MEMORANDUM CONDEMNING DISCRIMINATION IN DEFENSE WORK, ADDRESSED TO HONORABLE WILLIAM S. KNUDSEN AND HONORABLE SIDNEY HILLMAN JUNE 12, 1941

COMPLAINTS HAVE REPEATEDLY been brought to my attention that available and much-needed workers are being barred from defense production solely because of race, religion, or national origin...

Even more important is it for us to strengthen our unity and morale by refuting at home the very theories which we are fighting abroad...

Industry must take the initiative in opening the doors of employment to all loyal and qualified workers regardless of race, national origin, religion, or color.

MESSAGE TO THE SPECIAL CONVOCATION OF THE UNIVERSITY OF OXFORD JUNE 19, 1941

IT IS RIGHT that this unfettered search for truth "is universal and knows no restriction of place or race or creed." There have been other symbols throughout the years and in the present. The American Ambassador in Britain gave recognition to this recently when he said:

"Only this week in London in the early morning hours of the Sabbath Day, enemy bombs destroyed the House of Commons room of the Parliament and smashed the altar of Westminster Abbey. These two hits seemed to me to symbolize the objectives of the dictator and the pagan. Across the street from the wreckage of these two great historic buildings of State and Church, Saint-Gaudens' statue of Abraham Lincoln was still standing.

"As I looked at the bowed figure of the Great Emancipator and thought of his life, I could not help but remember that he loved God, that he had defined and represented democratic government, and that he hated slavery. And as an American I was proud that he was there in all that wreckage as a friend and sentinel of gallant days that have gone by, and a reminder that in this great battle for freedom he waited quietly for support for those things for which he lived and died."

PRESS CONFERENCE ON THE U.S.S POTOMAC AUGUST 16, 1941

Q: COULD YOU TELL us where this conference with Mr. Churchill was held?

THE PRESIDENT: I suppose it has been published. The Prime Minister was there on the Prince of Wales and I was there on the Augusta, but outside of that, nothing about ships, nothing about times, dates, and nothing about locations. All those things for perfectly obvious reasons, which I don't have to explain.

Things of that kind cause trouble, if you make known the exact location on the high seas of the President and the Prime Minister. However, it was foggy between North Haven and Rockland, and while it's open season out there, no submarine fired a torpedo at us as far as we could see, and we are here safely.

You want to know certain things, I suppose. The easiest thing to do is to give you what we might call the impressions that stand out. I think the first thing in the minds of all of us was a very remarkable religious service on the quarterdeck of the Prince of Wales last Sunday morning. There was their own ship's complement, with three or four hundred bluejackets and marines from American ships, on the quarterdeck, completely intermingled, first one uniform and then another uniform.

The service was conducted by two chaplains, one English and one American, and, as usual, the lesson was read by the captain of the British ship. They had three hymns that everybody took part in, and a little ship's altar was decked with the American flag and the British flag. The officers were all intermingled on the fantail, and I think the pictures of it have been released. The point is, I think everybody there, officers and enlisted men, felt that it was one of the great historic services. I know I did.

PRESS CONFERENCE
AUGUST 19, 1941

I SORT OF felt that I was perhaps squaring myself with the Good Lord by building those two buildings during my Administration, and being able to take down the present Navy Building and Munitions Building in the park.

MESSAGE TO CONGRESS ON THE ATLANTIC
MEETING WITH PRIME MINISTER CHURCHILL
AUGUST 21, 1941

IT IS ALSO unnecessary for me to point out that the declaration of principles includes of necessity the world need for freedom of religion and freedom of information.

No society of the world organized under the announced principles could survive without these freedoms which are a part of the whole freedom for which we strive.

LABOR DAY RADIO ADDRESS
SEPTEMBER 1, 1941

ON THIS DAY - this American holiday - we are celebrating the rights of free laboring men and women.

The preservation of these rights is vitally important now, not only to us who enjoy them - but to the whole future of Christian civilization.

American labor now bears a tremendous responsibility in the winning of this most brutal, most terrible of all wars...

In times of national emergency, one fact is brought home to us, clearly and decisively - the fact that all of our rights are interdependent.

The right of freedom of worship would mean nothing without freedom of speech. And the rights of free labor as we know them today could not survive without the rights of free enterprise...

That is what unites us - men and women of all sections, of all races, of all faiths, of all occupations, of all political beliefs. That is why we have been able to defy and frustrate the enemies who believed that they could divide us and conquer us from within...

The present position of labor in the United States as an interdependent unit in the life of the Nation has not come about by chance. It has been an evolutionary process of a healthy democracy at work.

Hitler has not worked that way. He will not - he cannot work that way. Just as he denies all rights to individuals, he must deny all rights to groups - groups of labor, of business - groups of learning, of the church. He has abolished trade unions as ruthlessly as he has persecuted religion...

The task of defeating Hitler may be long and arduous. There are a few appeasers and Nazi sympathizers who say it cannot be done. They even ask me to negotiate with Hitler - to pray for crumbs from his victorious table. They do, in fact, ask me to become the modern Benedict Arnold and betray all that I hold dear - my devotion to our freedom - to our churches - to our country. This course I have rejected...

American workers, American farmers, American businessmen, American church people - all of us together - have the great responsibility and the great privilege of laboring to build a democratic world on enduring foundations.

FIRESIDE CHAT
SEPTEMBER 11, 1941

BECAUSE OF THE clear, repeated proof that the present Government of Germany has no respect for treaties or for international law, that it has no decent attitude toward neutral Nations or human life - we Americans are now face to face not with abstract theories but with cruel, relentless facts...

This was one determined step toward creating a permanent world system based on force, on terror, and on murder...

The Nazi danger to our Western world has long ceased to be a mere possibility. The danger is here now - not only from a military enemy but from an enemy of all law, all liberty, all morality, all religion.

There has now come a time when you and I must see the cold, inexorable necessity of saying to these inhuman, unrestrained seekers of world conquest and permanent world domination by the sword: "You seek to throw our children and our children's children into your form of terrorism and slavery. You have now attacked our own safety. You shall go no further."...

I have no illusions about the gravity of this step. I have not taken it hurriedly or lightly. It is the result of months and months of constant thought and anxiety and prayer. In the protection of your Nation and mine it cannot be avoided...

The times call for clear heads and fearless hearts. And with that inner strength that comes to a free people conscious of their duty, and conscious of the righteousness of what they do, they will - with Divine help and guidance - stand their ground against this latest assault upon their democracy, their sovereignty, and their freedom.

ADDRESS FOR LIBERTY FLEET DAY
SEPTEMBER 26, 1941

THE PATRICK HENRY, as one of the Liberty ships launched today, renews that great patriot's stirring demand: "Give me liberty or give me death."

There shall be no death for America, for democracy, for freedom! There must be liberty, world-wide and eternal. That is our prayer - our pledge to all mankind.

PRESS CONFERENCE
SEPTEMBER 30, 1941

Q. MR. PRESIDENT, THE State Department got out a letter from the Polish Ambassador today showing that the Russians are going to allow the Poles to have their own churches.

THE PRESIDENT: I have just got the mimeographed State Department letter, but I also got it from another source this morning.

Q. Would you care to make any comment on it?

THE PRESIDENT: No. It speaks for itself. As I think I suggested a week or two ago, some of you might find it useful to read Article 124 of the Constitution of Russia.

Q. What does that say, Mr. President?

THE PRESIDENT: Well, I haven't learned it by heart sufficiently to quote - I might be off a little bit, but anyway: Freedom of conscience, freedom of religion. Freedom equally to use propaganda against religion, which is essentially what is the rule in this country, only we don't put it quite the same way.

For instance, you might go out tomorrow to the corner of Pennsylvania Avenue, down below the Press Club, and stand on a soapbox and preach Christianity, and nobody would stop you. And then, if it got into your head, perhaps the next day preach against religion of all kinds, and nobody would stop you. . . .

RADIO ADDRESS ON COMMUNITY MOBILIZATION FOR HUMAN NEEDS OCTOBER 3, 1941

ONCE MORE I am making a straightforward, simple appeal to the people of our country to support a great annual event - the Community Mobilization for Human Needs. Many of you do not recognize this name but it represents the tying together of hundreds of local community efforts...These represent consolidations of many thousands of local charities run by churches, social welfare organizations, health associations, and many others...

It would be a calamity for the Nation and for its future if private charity did not exist and grow. That is why I am asking each and every person in every town and village and on every farm to contribute something, large or small, toward this great and proven service. You will be helping to build a stronger and a better America. When I have said that, I have said all that is necessary for it is a spiritual as well as a practical appeal to the better natures of my fellow citizens.

MESSAGE TO CONGRESS ON THE ARMING OF MERCHANT SHIPS OCTOBER 9, 1941

IN THESE PAST two tragic years - war has spread from continent to continent; very many Nations have been conquered and enslaved; great cities have been laid in ruins; millions of human beings have been killed, soldiers and sailors and civilians alike. Never before has such widespread devastation been visited upon God's earth and God's children...

Hitler has offered a challenge which we as Americans cannot and will not tolerate.

We will not let Hitler prescribe the waters of the world on which our ships may travel. The American flag is not going to be driven from the seas either by his submarines, his airplanes, or his threats.

We cannot permit the affirmative defense of our rights to be annulled and diluted by sections of the Neutrality Act which have no realism in the light of unscrupulous ambition of mad-men.

PRESS CONFERENCE OCTOBER 24, 1941

Q. MR. PRESIDENT, WE have a story that one or two papers issued, about a seaman in Honolulu who said he passed through the Red Sea. His ship, he said, was subjected to a very severe Nazi bombing. He said that they couldn't hit a bull with a bass fiddle, but indicated that there is a great deal of that in that area. Are you aware of that, or have you had anything on that line?

THE PRESIDENT: No. The only thing I heard on that was that Hitler had been going to one of the few prominent Jews left in Germany, and told him that he could stay, if he would explain to him how Moses managed to get the waters to stand aside and let the Children of Israel across.

STATEMENT DENOUNCING THE NAZI MURDER OF FRENCH HOSTAGES OCTOBER 25, 1941

THE NAZI MIGHT have learned from the last war the impossibility of breaking men's spirit by terrorism. Instead they develop their "lebensraum" and "new order" by depths of frightfulness which even they have never approached before. These are the acts of desperate men who know in their hearts that they cannot win. Frightfulness can never bring peace to Europe.

ADDRESS FOR NAVY AND TOTAL DEFENSE DAY OCTOBER 27, 1941

FIVE MONTHS AGO tonight I proclaimed to the American people the existence of a state of unlimited national emergency...

Hitler has attacked shipping in areas close to the Americas in the North and South Atlantic...

For example, I have in my possession a secret map made in Germany by Hitler's Government - by the planners of the new world order. It is a map of South America and a part of Central America, as Hitler proposes to reorganize it.

Today in this area there are fourteen separate countries. But the geographical experts of Berlin have ruthlessly obliterated all existing boundary lines; they have divided South America into five vassal states, bringing the whole continent under their domination. And they have also so arranged it that the territory of one of these new puppet states includes the Republic of Panama and our great life line - the Panama Canal.

That is his plan. It will never go into effect.

This map, my friends, makes clear the Nazi design not only against South America but against the United States as well.

Your Government has in its possession another document, made in Germany by Hitler's Government. It is a detailed plan, which, for obvious reasons, the Nazis did not wish and do not wish to publicize just yet, but which they are ready to impose, a little later, on a dominated world - if Hitler wins.

It is a plan to abolish all existing religions - Catholic, Protestant, Mohammedan, Hindu, Buddhist, and Jewish alike. The property of all churches will be seized by the Reich and its puppets. The cross and all other symbols of religion are to be forbidden. The clergy are to be forever liquidated, silenced under penalty of the concentration camps, where even now so many fearless men are being tortured because they have placed God above Hitler.

In the place of the churches of our civilization, there is to be set up an International Nazi Church - a church which will be served by orators sent out by the Nazi Government. And in the place of the Bible, the words of Mein Kampf will be imposed and enforced as Holy Writ. And in the place of the cross of Christ will be put two symbols - the swastika and the naked sword.

The god of Blood and Iron will take the place of the God of Love and Mercy. Let us well ponder that statement which I have made tonight...

And when we have helped to end the curse of Hitlerism we shall help to establish a new peace which will give to decent people everywhere a better chance to live and prosper in security and in freedom and in faith...

It has not been easy for us Americans to adjust ourselves to the shocking realities of a world in which the principles of common humanity and common decency are being mowed down by the firing squads of the Gestapo.

We have enjoyed many of God's blessings. We have lived in a broad and abundant land, and by our industry and productivity we have made it flourish.

There are those who say that our great good fortune has betrayed us - that we are now no match for the regimented masses who have been trained in the Spartan ways of ruthless brutality. They say that we have grown fat, and flabby, and lazy - and that we are doomed.

But those who say that know nothing of America...

Today in the face of this newest and greatest challenge of them all, we Americans have cleared our decks and taken our battle stations. We stand ready in the defense of our Nation and in the faith of our fathers to do what God has given us the power to see as our full duty.

ADDRESS TO INTERNATIONAL LABOR ORGANIZATION NOVEMBER 6, 1941

TO BE SURE, there are still some misguided - unenlightened that is putting it politely - some people of that kind among us - thank God they are but few - both industrialists and leaders of labor, who place personal advantage above the welfare of their Nation. There are still a few who place their little victories over one another above triumph against Hitlerism.

THANKSGIVING DAY PROCLAMATION
NOVEMBER 8, 1941

I, FRANKLIN D. ROOSEVELT, President of the United States of America, do hereby designate and set aside Thursday, the twentieth day of November, 1941, as a day to be observed in giving thanks to the Heavenly Source of our earthly blessings.

Our beloved country is free and strong. Our moral and physical defenses against the forces of threatened aggression are mounting daily in magnitude and effectiveness.

In the interest of our own future, we are sending succor at increasing pace to those peoples abroad who are bravely defending their homes and their precious liberties against annihilation.

We have not lost our faith in the spiritual dignity of man, our proud belief in the right of all people to live out their lives in freedom and with equal treatment. The love of democracy still burns brightly in our hearts.

We are grateful to the Father of us all for the innumerable daily manifestations of His beneficent mercy in affairs both public and private, for the bounties of the harvest, for opportunities to labor and to serve, and for the continuance of those homely joys and satisfactions which enrich our lives.

Let us ask the Divine Blessing on our decision and determination to protect our way of life against the forces of evil and slavery which seek in these days to encompass us.

On the day appointed for this purpose, let us reflect at our homes or places of worship on the goodness of God and, in giving thanks, let us pray for a speedy end to strife and the establishment on earth of freedom, brotherhood, and justice for enduring time.

PROCLAMATION 2524 ON BILL OF RIGHTS DAY NOVEMBER 27, 1941

I, FRANKLIN D. ROOSEVELT, President of the United States of America, do hereby designate December 15, 1941, as Bill of Rights Day. And I call upon the officials of the Government, and upon the people of the United States, to observe the day by displaying the flag of the United States on public buildings and by meeting together for such prayers and such ceremonies as may seem to them appropriate.

The first ten amendments, the great American charter of personal liberty and human dignity, became a part of the Constitution of the United States on the fifteenth day of December, 1791.

It is fitting that the anniversary of its adoption should be remembered by the Nation which, for one hundred and fifty years, has enjoyed the immeasurable privileges which that charter guaranteed: the privileges of freedom of religion, freedom of speech, freedom of the press, freedom of assembly, and the free right to petition the Government for redress of grievances.

It is especially fitting that this anniversary should be remembered and observed by those institutions of a democratic people which owe their very existence to the guarantees of the Bill of Rights: the free schools, the free churches, the labor unions, the religious and educational and civic organizations of all kinds which, without the guarantee of the Bill of Rights, could never have existed.

PRESS CONFERENCE
NOVEMBER 28, 1941

WE SHOULD THINK not only of our own selfish purposes for this country of ours, but also think a little bit about other people, people in countries which have been overrun, people in countries which have been attacked, and, yes, people in those countries which are doing the attacking.

I think we can offer up a little silent prayer and I think lots of us do this without anybody knowing it.

REMARKS BIRTHDAY BALL COMMITTEE
CHAIRMEN
DECEMBER 2, 1941

THE PUBLIC, I think, is coming to realize the importance of what we are doing. We have pretty well got rid of certain scourges that existed in the past. The scourge of TB (Tuberculosis) is so much better than it was in our grandparents' day. There is absolutely no comparison.

We can go back to any family Bible and read about the death of young people from - they didn't call it TB in those days - they called it "they went into a decline, and died." We are getting on top of certain things. There are other diseases that we don't know nearly so many things about.

ADDRESS TO CONGRESS REQUESTING A
DECLARATION OF WAR WITH JAPAN
DECEMBER 8, 1941

MR. VICE PRESIDENT, and Mr. Speaker, and Members of the Senate and House of Representatives:

Yesterday, December 7, 1941 - a date which will live in infamy - the United States of America was suddenly and deliberately attacked by naval and air forces of the Empire of Japan.

The United States was at peace with that Nation and, at the solicitation of Japan, was still in conversation with its Government and its Emperor looking toward the maintenance of peace in the Pacific.

Indeed, one hour after Japanese air squadrons had commenced bombing in the American Island of Oahu, the Japanese Ambassador to the United States and his colleague delivered to our Secretary of State a formal reply to a recent American message. And while this reply stated that it seemed useless to continue the existing diplomatic negotiations, it contained no threat or hint of war or of armed attack.

It will be recorded that the distance of Hawaii from Japan makes it obvious that the attack was deliberately planned many days or even weeks ago. During the intervening time the Japanese Government has deliberately sought to deceive the United States by false statements and expressions of hope for continued peace.

The attack yesterday on the Hawaiian Islands has caused severe damage to American naval and military forces. I regret to tell you that very many American lives have been lost. In addition American ships have been reported torpedoed on the high seas between San Francisco and Honolulu.

Yesterday the Japanese Government also launched an attack against Malaya.

Last night Japanese forces attacked Hong Kong.

Last night Japanese forces attacked Guam.

Last night Japanese forces attacked the Philippine Islands.

Last night the Japanese attacked Wake Island. And this morning the Japanese attacked Midway Island.

Japan has, therefore, undertaken a surprise offensive extending throughout the Pacific area. The facts of yesterday and today speak for themselves. The people of the United States have already formed their opinions and well understand the implications to the very life and safety of our Nation.

As Commander in Chief of the Army and Navy I have directed that all measures be taken for our defense.

But always will our whole Nation remember the character of the onslaught against us.

No matter how long it may take us to overcome this premeditated invasion, the American people in their righteous might will win through to absolute victory. I believe that I interpret the will of the Congress and of the people when I assert that we will not only defend ourselves to the uttermost but will make it very certain that this form of treachery shall never again endanger us.

Hostilities exist. There is no blinking at the fact that our people, our territory, and our interests are in grave danger.

With confidence in our armed forces - with the unbounding determination of our people - we will gain the inevitable triumph - so help us God.

I ask that the Congress declare that since the unprovoked and dastardly attack by Japan on Sunday, December 7, 1941, a state of war has existed between the United States and the Japanese Empire.

FIRESIDE CHAT
DECEMBER 9, 1941

THE SUDDEN CRIMINAL attacks perpetrated by the Japanese in the Pacific provide the climax of a decade of international immorality.

Powerful and resourceful gangsters have banded together to make war upon the whole human race. Their challenge has now been flung at the United States of America. The Japanese have treacherously violated the long-standing peace between us. Many American soldiers and sailors have been killed by enemy action. American ships have been sunk; American airplanes have been destroyed.

The Congress and the people of the United States have accepted that challenge.

Together with other free peoples, we are now fighting to maintain our right to live among our world neighbors in freedom and in common decency, without fear of assault.

I have prepared the full record of our past relations with Japan, and it will be submitted to the Congress. It begins with the visit of Commodore Perry to Japan 88 years ago. It ends with the visit of two Japanese emissaries to the Secretary of State last Sunday, an hour after Japanese forces had loosed their bombs and machine guns against our flag, our forces, and our citizens.

I can say with utmost confidence that no Americans, today or a thousand years hence, need feel anything but pride in our patience and in our efforts through all the years toward achieving a peace in the Pacific which would be fair and honorable to every Nation, large or small.

And no honest person, today or a thousand years hence, will be able to suppress a sense of indignation and horror at the treachery committed by the military dictators of Japan, under the very shadow of the flag of peace borne by their special envoys in our midst.

The course that Japan has followed for the past ten years in Asia has paralleled the course of Hitler and Mussolini in Europe and in Africa. Today, it has become far more than a parallel. It is actual collaboration so well calculated that all the continents of the world, and all the oceans, are now considered by the Axis strategists as one gigantic battlefield.

In 1931, ten years ago, Japan invaded Manchukuo - without warning.

In 1935, Italy invaded Ethiopia - without warning.

In 1938, Hitler occupied Austria - without warning.

In 1939, Hitler invaded Czechoslovakia - without warning.

Later in 1939, Hitler invaded Poland - without warning.

In 1940, Hitler invaded Norway, Denmark, the Netherlands, Belgium, and Luxembourg - without warning.

In 1940, Italy attacked France and later Greece - without warning.

And this year, in 1941, the Axis powers attacked Yugoslavia and Greece and they dominated the Balkans - without warning. In 1941, also, Hitler invaded Russia - without warning.

And now Japan has attacked Malaya and Thailand - and the United States - without warning.

It is all of one pattern.

We are now in this war. We are all in it - all the way. Every single man, woman, and child is a partner in the most tremendous undertaking of our American history. We must share together the bad news and the good news, the defeats and the victories - the changing fortunes of war.

So far, the news has been all bad. We have suffered a serious set-back in Hawaii. Our forces in the Philippines, which include the brave people of that Commonwealth, are taking punishment, but are defending themselves vigorously. The reports from Guam and Wake and Midway islands are still confused, but we must be prepared for the announcement that all these three outposts have been seized.

The casualty lists of these first few days will undoubtedly be large. I deeply feel the anxiety of all of the families of the men in our armed forces and the relatives of people in cities which have been bombed. I can only give them my solemn promise that they will get news just as quickly as possible.

This Government will put its trust in the stamina of the American people, and will give the facts to the public just as soon as two conditions have been fulfilled: first, that the information has been definitely and officially confirmed; and, second, that the release of the information at the time it is received will not prove valuable to the enemy directly or indirectly.

Most earnestly I urge my countrymen to reject all rumors. These ugly little hints of complete disaster fly thick and fast in wartime. They have to be examined and appraised.

As an example, I can tell you frankly that until further surveys are made, I have not sufficient information to state the exact damage which has been done to our naval vessels at Pearl Harbor. Admittedly the damage is serious. But no one can say how serious, until we know how much of this damage can be repaired and how quickly the necessary repairs can be made.

I cite as another example a statement made on Sunday night that a Japanese carrier had been located and sunk off the Canal Zone. And when you hear statements that are attributed to what they call "an authoritative source," you can be reasonably sure from now on that under these war circumstances the "authoritative source" is not any person in authority.

Many rumors and reports which we now hear originate with enemy sources. For instance, today the Japanese are claiming that as a result of their one action against Hawaii they have gained naval supremacy in the Pacific.

This is an old trick of propaganda which has been used innumerable times by the Nazis. The purposes of such fantastic claims are, of course, to spread fear and confusion among us, and to goad us into revealing military information which our enemies are desperately anxious to obtain.

Our Government will not be caught in this obvious trap - and neither will the people of the United States.

It must be remembered by each and every one of us that our free and rapid communication these days must be greatly restricted in wartime. It is not possible to receive full, speedy, accurate reports from distant areas of combat.

This is particularly true where naval operations are concerned. For in these days of the marvels of radio it is often impossible for the commanders of various units to report their activities by radio at all, for the very simple reason that this information would become available to the enemy, and would disclose their position and their plan of defense or attack.

Of necessity there will be delays in officially confirming or denying reports of operations but we will not hide facts from the country if we know the facts and if the enemy will not be aided by their disclosure.

To all newspapers and radio stations - all those who reach the eyes and ears of the American people - I say this: You have a most grave responsibility to the Nation now and for the duration of this war.

If you feel that your Government is not disclosing enough of the truth, you have every right to say so. But - in the absence of all the facts, as revealed by official sources - you have no right in the ethics of patriotism to deal out unconfirmed reports in such a way as to make people believe that they are gospel truth.

Every citizen, in every walk of life, shares this same responsibility. The lives of our soldiers and sailors - the whole future of this Nation - depend upon the manner in which each and every one of us fulfills his obligation to our country.

Now a word about the recent past - and the future. A year and a half has elapsed since the fall of France, when the whole world first realized the mechanized might which the Axis Nations had been building for so many years. America has used that year and a half to great advantage. Knowing that the attack might reach us in all too short a time, we immediately began greatly to increase our industrial strength and our capacity to meet the demands of modern warfare.

Precious months were gained by sending vast quantities of our war material to the Nations of the world still able to resist Axis aggression. Our policy rested on the fundamental truth that the defense of any country resisting Hitler or Japan was in the long run the defense of our own country. That policy has been justified. It has given us time, invaluable time, to build our American assembly lines of production.

Assembly lines are now in operation. Others are being rushed to completion. A steady stream of tanks and planes, of guns and ships, and shells and equipment - that is what these eighteen months have given us.

But it is all only a beginning of what still has to be done. We must be set to face a long war against crafty and powerful bandits. The attack at Pearl Harbor can be repeated at any one of many points, points in both oceans and along both our coast lines and against all the rest of the hemisphere.

It will not only be a long war, it will be a hard war. That is the basis on which we now lay all our plans. That is the yardstick by which we measure what we shall need and demand; money, materials, doubled and quadrupled production - ever-increasing. The production must be not only for our own Army and Navy and Air Forces. It must reinforce the other armies and navies and air forces fighting the Nazis and the war lords of Japan throughout the Americas and throughout the world.

I have been working today on the subject of production. Your Government has decided on two broad policies.

The first is to speed up all existing production by working on a seven-day-week basis in every war industry, including the production of essential raw materials.

The second policy, now being put into form, is to rush additions to the capacity of production by building more new plants, by adding to old plants, and by using the many smaller plants for war needs.

Over the hard road of the past months, we have at times met obstacles and difficulties, divisions and disputes, indifference and callousness. That is now all past - and, I am sure, forgotten.

The fact is that the country now has an organization in Washington built around men and women who are recognized experts in their own fields. I think the country knows that the people who are actually responsible in each and every one of these many fields are pulling together with a teamwork that has never before been excelled.

On the road ahead there lies hard work - grueling workday and night, every hour and every minute.

I was about to add that ahead there lies sacrifice for all of us.

But it is not correct to use that word. The United States does not consider it a sacrifice to do all one can, to give one's best to our Nation, when the Nation is fighting for its existence and its future life.

It is not a sacrifice for any man, old or young, to be in the Army or the Navy of the United States. Rather is it a privilege.

It is not a sacrifice for the industrialist or the wage earner, the farmer or the shopkeeper, the trainman or the doctor, to pay more taxes, to buy more bonds, to forego extra profits, to work longer or harder at the task for which he is best fitted. Rather is it a privilege.

It is not a sacrifice to do without many things to which we are accustomed if the national defense calls for doing without.

A review this morning leads me to the conclusion that at present we shall not have to curtail the normal use of articles of food. There is enough food today for all of us and enough left over to send to those who are fighting on the same side with us.

But there will be a clear and definite shortage of metals of many kinds for civilian use, for the very good reason that in our increased program we shall need for war purposes more than half of that portion of the principal metals which during the past year have gone into articles for civilian use. Yes, we shall have to give up many things entirely.

And I am sure that the people in every part of the Nation are prepared in their individual living to win this war. I am sure that they will cheerfully help to pay a large part of its financial cost while it goes on. I am sure they will cheerfully give up those material things that they are asked to give up.

And I am sure that they will retain all those great spiritual things without which we cannot win through.

I repeat that the United States can accept no result save victory, final and complete. Not only must the shame of Japanese treachery be wiped out, but the sources of international brutality, wherever they exist, must be absolutely and finally broken.

In my message to the Congress yesterday I said that we "will make it very certain that this form of treachery shall never again endanger us." In order to achieve that certainty, we must begin the great task that is before us by abandoning once and for all the illusion that we can ever again isolate ourselves from the rest of humanity.

In these past few years - and, most violently, in the past three days - we have learned a terrible lesson.

It is our obligation to our dead - it is our sacred obligation to their children and to our children - that we must never forget what we have learned.

And what we all have learned is this:

There is no such thing as security for any Nation - or any individual - in a world ruled by the principles of gangsterism.

There is no such thing as impregnable defense against powerful aggressors who sneak up in the dark and strike without warning.

We have learned that our ocean-girt hemisphere is not immune from severe attack - that we cannot measure our safety in terms of miles on any map any more.

We may acknowledge that our enemies have performed a brilliant feat of deception, perfectly timed and executed with great skill. It was a thoroughly dishonorable deed, but we must face the fact that modern warfare as conducted in the Nazi manner is a dirty business. We don't like it - we didn't want to get in it - but we are in it and we're going to fight it with everything we've got.

I do not think any American has any doubt of our ability to administer proper punishment to the perpetrators of these crimes.

Your Government knows that for weeks Germany has been telling Japan that if Japan did not attack the United States, Japan would not share in dividing the spoils with Germany when peace came. She was promised by Germany that if she came in she would receive the complete and perpetual control of the whole of the Pacific area - and that means not only the Far East, but also all of the islands in the Pacific, and also a stranglehold on the west coast of North, Central, and South America.

We know also that Germany and Japan are conducting their military and naval operations in accordance with a joint plan. That plan considers all peoples and Nations which are not helping the Axis powers as common enemies of each and every one of the Axis powers.

That is their simple and obvious grand strategy. And that is why the American people must realize that it can be matched only with similar grand strategy.

We must realize for example that Japanese successes against the United States in the Pacific are helpful to German operations in Libya; that any German success against the Caucasus is inevitably an assistance to Japan in her operations against the Dutch East Indies; that a German attack against Algiers or Morocco opens the way to a German attack against South America, and the Canal.

On the other side of the picture, we must learn also to know that guerrilla warfare against the Germans in, let us say, Serbia or Norway helps us; that a successful Russian offensive against the Germans helps us; and that British successes on land or sea in any part of the world strengthen our hands.

Remember always that Germany and Italy, regardless of any formal declaration of war, consider themselves at war with the United States at this moment just as much as they consider themselves at war with Britain or Russia. And Germany puts all the other Republics of the Americas into the same category of enemies. The people of our sister Republics of this hemisphere can be honored by that fact.

The true goal we seek is far above and beyond the ugly field of battle. When we resort to force, as now we must, we are determined that this force shall be directed toward ultimate good as well as against immediate evil. We Americans are not destroyers - we are builders.

We are now in the midst of a war, not for conquest, not for vengeance, but for a world in which this Nation, and all that this Nation represents, will be safe for our children. We expect to eliminate the danger from Japan, but it would serve us ill if we accomplished that and found that the rest of the world was dominated by Hitler and Mussolini.

We are going to win the war and we are going to win the peace that follows.

And in the difficult hours of this day - through dark days that may be yet to come - we will know that the vast majority of the members of the human race are on our side. Many of them are fighting with us. All of them are praying for us. For in representing our cause, we represent theirs as well - our hope and their hope for liberty under God.

MESSAGE TO CONGRESS ON HISTORY OF RELATIONS BETWEEN UNITED STATES AND JAPAN DECEMBER 15, 1941

THE GERMAN THESIS that seventy or eighty million Germans were by race, training, ability, and might superior in every way to any other race in Europe - superior to about four hundred million other human beings in that area.

And Japan, following suit, announced that the seventy or eighty million Japanese people were also superior to the seven or eight hundred million other inhabitants of the Orient - nearly all of whom were infinitely older and more developed in culture and civilization than themselves. Their conceit would make them masters of a region containing almost one-half the population of the earth...

The military operations which followed in China flagrantly disregarded American rights. Japanese armed forces killed Americans. They wounded or abused American men, women, and children. They sank American vessels - including a naval vessel, the Panay. They bombed American hospitals, churches, schools, and missions.

RADIO ADDRESS ON THE 150TH ANNIVERSARY OF THE RATIFICATION OF THE BILL OF RIGHTS DECEMBER 15, 1941

FREE AMERICANS:

No date in the long history of freedom means more to liberty loving men in all liberty-loving countries than the fifteenth day of December, 1791. On that day, 150 years ago, a new Nation, through an elected Congress, adopted a declaration of human rights which has influenced the thinking of all mankind from one end of the world to the other.

There is not a single Republic of this hemisphere which has not adopted in its fundamental law the basic principles of freedom of man and freedom of mind enacted in the American Bill of Rights.

There is not a country, large or small, on this continent and in this world which has not felt the influence of that document, directly or indirectly.

Indeed, prior to the year 1933, the essential validity of the American Bill of Rights was accepted everywhere at least in principle. Even today, with the exception of Germany, Italy, and Japan, the peoples of the whole world - in all probability four-fifths of them - support its principles, its teachings, and its glorious results.

But, in the year 1933, there came to power in Germany a political clique which did not accept the declarations of the American bill of human rights as valid: a small clique of ambitious and unscrupulous politicians whose announced and admitted platform was precisely the destruction of the rights that instrument declared.

Indeed the entire program and goal of these political and moral tigers was nothing more than the overthrow, throughout the earth, of the great revolution of human liberty of which our American Bill of Rights is the mother charter.

The truths which were self-evident to Thomas Jefferson which have been self-evident to the six generations of Americans who followed him - were to these men hateful. The rights to life, liberty, and the pursuit of happiness which seemed to the Founders of the Republic, and which seem to us, inalienable, were, to Hitler and his fellows, empty words which they proposed to cancel forever.

The propositions they advanced to take the place of Jefferson's inalienable rights were these:

That the individual human being has no rights whatsoever in himself and by virtue of his humanity;

That the individual human being has no right to a soul of his own, or a mind of his own, or a tongue of his own, or a trade of his own; or even to live where he pleases or to marry the woman he loves;

That his only duty is the duty of obedience, not to his God, not to his conscience, but to Adolf Hitler; and that his only value is his value, not as a man, but as a unit of the Nazi state.

To Hitler the ideal of the people, as we conceive it - the free, self-governing, and responsible people - is incomprehensible. The people, to Hitler, are "the masses" and the highest human idealism is, in his own words, that a man should wish to become "a dust particle" of the order "of force" which is to shape the universe.

To Hitler, the government, as we conceive it, is an impossible conception. The government to him is not the servant and the instrument of the people but their absolute master and the dictator of their every act.

To Hitler the church, as we conceive it, is a monstrosity to be destroyed by every means at his command. The Nazi church is to be the "National Church," a pagan church, "absolutely and exclusively in the service of but one doctrine, one race, one Nation."

To Hitler, the freedom of men to think as they please and speak as they please and worship as they please is, of all things imaginable, most hateful and most desperately to be feared.

The issue of our time, the issue of the war in which we are engaged, is the issue forced upon the decent, self-respecting peoples of the earth by the aggressive dogmas of this attempted revival of barbarism; this proposed return to tyranny; this effort to impose again upon the peoples of the world doctrines of absolute obedience, of dictatorial rule, of the suppression of truth, of the oppression of conscience, which the free Nations of the earth have long ago rejected.

What we face is nothing more nor less than an attempt to overthrow and to cancel out the great upsurge of human liberty of which the American Bill of Rights is the fundamental document: to force the peoples of the earth, and among them the peoples of this continent and this Nation, to accept again the absolute authority and despotic rule from which the courage and the resolution and the sacrifices of their ancestors liberated them many, many years ago.

It is an attempt which could succeed only if those who have inherited the gift of liberty had lost the manhood to preserve it. But we Americans know that the determination of this generation of our people to preserve liberty is as fixed and certain as the determination of that early generation of Americans to win it.

We will not, under any threat, or in the face of any danger, surrender the guarantees of liberty our forefathers framed for us in our Bill of Rights.

We hold with all the passion of our hearts and minds to those commitments of the human spirit.

We are solemnly determined that no power or combination of powers of this earth shall shake our hold upon them.

We covenant with each other before all the world, that having taken up arms in the defense of liberty, we will not lay them down before liberty is once again secure in the world we live in. For that security we pray; for that security we act - now and evermore.

REMARKS TO MANAGEMENT-LABOR CONFERENCE
DECEMBER 17, 1941

AND SO I was just thinking of an old idea of self-discipline an old Chinese proverb - of a Chinese Christian. He prayed every day - he had been told to pray to our kind of God - and his prayer was: "Lord, reform Thy world, beginning with me." It is rather a nice line for us all to keep in the back of our heads...

I hope very much, in fact I am very confident, you will realize the spiritual side of this war emergency. We want our type of civilization to go on. It is threatened. We want our freedoms. We want freedom to express our own opinions. We want freedom of religion and the others as well. They are threatened.

I think very much the country is looking to you gentlemen to give us, just as fast as you possibly can - by tomorrow or the next day - some kind of an agreement so that we all can shake hands. After this war is won, let's go back if we want to, if we have to, to old Kilkenny. And you know what a Kilkenny fight is. But that is something that we can put aside until that date comes.

The country is looking to you. I am looking at you. The Congress is looking at you. All I can say is, Godspeed your efforts.

CHRISTMAS EVE MESSAGE TO THE NATION
DECEMBER 24, 1941

FELLOW WORKERS FOR freedom:

There are many men and women in America - sincere and faithful men and women - who are asking themselves this Christmas:

How can we light our trees? How can we give our gifts?

How can we meet and worship with love and with uplifted spirit and heart in a world at war, a world of fighting and suffering and death?

How can we pause, even for a day, even for Christmas Day, in our urgent labor of arming a decent humanity against the enemies which beset it?

How can we put the world aside, as men and women put the world aside in peaceful years, to rejoice in the birth of Christ?

These are natural - inevitable - questions in every part of the world which is resisting the evil thing.

And even as we ask these questions, we know the answer. There is another preparation demanded of this Nation beyond and beside the preparation of weapons and materials of war. There is demanded also of us the preparation of our hearts; the arming of our hearts. And when we make ready our hearts for the labor and the suffering and the ultimate victory which lie ahead, then we observe Christmas Day - with all of its memories and all of its meanings - as we should.

Looking into the days to come, I have set aside a day of prayer, and in that Proclamation I have said:

"The year 1941 has brought upon our Nation a war of aggression by powers dominated by arrogant rulers whose selfish purpose is to destroy free institutions. They would thereby take from the freedom-loving peoples of the earth the hard-won liberties gained over many centuries.

"The new year of 1942 calls for the courage and the resolution of old and young to help to win a world struggle in order that we may preserve all we hold dear.

"We are confident in our devotion to country, in our love of freedom, in our inheritance of courage. But our strength, as the strength of all men everywhere, is of greater avail as God upholds us.

"Therefore, I... do hereby appoint the first day of the year 1942 as a day of prayer, of asking forgiveness for our shortcomings of the past, of consecration to the tasks of the present, of asking God's help in days to come.

"We need His guidance that this people may be humble in spirit but strong in the conviction of the right; steadfast to endure sacrifice, and brave to achieve a victory of liberty and peace."

Our strongest weapon in this war is that conviction of the dignity and brotherhood of man which Christmas Day signifies - more than any other day or any other symbol.

Against enemies who preach the principles of hate and practice them, we set our faith in human love and in God's care for us and all men everywhere.

It is in that spirit, and with particular thoughtfulness of those, our sons and brothers, who serve in our armed forces on land and sea, near and far - those who serve for us and endure for us that we light our Christmas candles now across the continent from one coast to the other on this Christmas Eve.

We have joined with many other Nations and peoples in a very great cause. Millions of them have been engaged in the task of defending good with their life-blood for months and for years.

One of their great leaders stands beside me. He and his people in many parts of the world are having their Christmas trees with their little children around them, just as we do here. He and his people have pointed the way in courage and in sacrifice for the sake of little children everywhere.

And so I am asking my associate, my old and good friend, to say a word to the people of America, old and young, tonight Winston Churchill, Prime Minister of Great Britain.

STATEMENT AGAINST DISCHARGING LOYAL ALIENS FROM JOBS JANUARY 2, 1942

REMEMBER THE NAZI technique: "Pit race against race, religion against religion, prejudice against prejudice. Divide and conquer!"

STATE OF THE UNION ADDRESS JANUARY 6, 1942

EXACTLY ONE YEAR ago today I said to this Congress: "When the dictators...are ready to make war upon us, they will not wait for an act of war on our part...They - not we - will choose the time and the place and the method of their attack."

We now know their choice of the time: a peaceful Sunday morning - December 7, 1941.

We know their choice of the place: an American outpost in the Pacific.

We know their choice of the method: the method of Hitler himself.

Japan's scheme of conquest goes back half a century. It was not merely a policy of seeking living room: it was a plan which included the subjugation of all the peoples in the Far East and in the islands of the Pacific, and the domination of that ocean by Japanese military and naval control of the western coasts of North, Central, and South America.

The development of this ambitious conspiracy was marked by the war against China in 1894; the subsequent occupation of Korea; the war against Russia in 1904; the illegal fortification of the mandated Pacific islands following 1920; the seizure of Manchuria in 1931; and the invasion of China in 1937.

A similar policy of criminal conquest was adopted by Italy. The Fascists first revealed their imperial designs in Libya and Tripoli. In 1935 they seized Abyssinia. Their goal was the domination of all North Africa, Egypt, parts of France, and the entire Mediterranean world.

But the dreams of empire of the Japanese and Fascist leaders were modest in comparison with the gargantuan aspirations of Hitler and his Nazis. Even before they came to power in 1933, their plans for that conquest had been drawn. Those plans provided for ultimate domination, not of any one section of the world, but of the whole earth and all the oceans on it...

We shall not fight isolated wars - each Nation going its own way. These 26 Nations are united - not in spirit and determination alone, but in the broad conduct of the war in all its phases...

They know that victory for us means victory for freedom.

They know that victory for us means victory for the institution of democracy - the ideal of the family, the simple principles of common decency and humanity.

They know that victory for us means victory for religion. And they could not tolerate that. The world is too small to provide adequate "living room" for both Hitler and God. In proof of that, the Nazis have now announced their plan for enforcing their new German, pagan religion all over the world - a plan by which the Holy Bible and the Cross of Mercy would be displaced by Mein Kampf and the swastika and the naked sword.

Our own objectives are clear; the objective of smashing the militarism imposed by war lords upon their enslaved peoples the objective of liberating the subjugated Nations - the objective of establishing and securing freedom of speech, freedom of religion, freedom from want, and freedom from fear everywhere in the world...

I have just sent a letter of directive to the appropriate departments and agencies of our Government, ordering that immediate steps be taken:

First, to increase our production rate of airplanes...Second, to increase our production rate of tanks...Third, to increase our production rate of anti-aircraft guns...And fourth, to increase our production rate of merchant ships.

These figures and similar figures for a multitude of other implements of war will give the Japanese and the Nazis a little idea of just what they accomplished in the attack at Pearl Harbor...

We must, on the other hand, guard against defeatism. That has been one of the chief weapons of Hitler's propaganda machine - used time and again with deadly results. It will not be used successfully on the American people.

We must guard against divisions among ourselves and among all the other United Nations. We must be particularly vigilant against racial discrimination in any of its ugly forms. Hitler will try again to breed mistrust and suspicion between one individual and another, one group and another, one race and another, one Government and another...

There were only some 400 United States Marines who in the heroic and historic defense of Wake Island inflicted such great losses on the enemy. Some of those men were killed in action; and others are now prisoners of war. When the survivors of that great fight are liberated and restored to their homes, they will learn that a hundred and thirty million of their fellow citizens have been inspired to render their own full share of service and sacrifice...

We are fighting today for security, for progress, and for peace, not only for ourselves but for all men, not only for one generation but for all generations. We are fighting to cleanse the world of ancient evils, ancient ills.

Our enemies are guided by brutal cynicism, by unholy contempt for the human race. We are inspired by a faith that goes back through all the years to the first chapter of the Book of Genesis: "God created man in His own image."

We on our side are striving to be true to that divine heritage. We are fighting, as our fathers have fought, to uphold the doctrine that all men are equal in the sight of God. Those on the other side are striving to destroy this deep belief and to create a world in their own image - a world of tyranny and cruelty and serfdom...

No compromise can end that conflict. There never has been - there never can be - successful compromise between good and evil. Only total victory can reward the champions of tolerance, and decency, and freedom, and faith.

RADIO ADDRESS ON PRESIDENT'S
60TH BIRTHDAY
JANUARY 30, 1942

IN THE MIDST of world tragedy - in the midst of sorrow, suffering, destruction, and death - it is natural for most of us to say even on a birthday or a feast day: "Isn't the word 'happy' a bit out of place just now?"

That was perhaps my own predominant thought this morning. Yet the day itself and the evening have brought with them a great reassurance that comes from the deep knowledge that most of this world is still ruled by the spirit of Faith, and Hope, and Charity.

Even in time of war those Nations which still hold to the old ideals of Christianity and democracy are carrying on services to humanity which have little or no relationship to torpedoes or guns or bombs.

That means very definitely that we have an abiding faith in the future - a definite expectancy that we are going to win through to a peace that will bring with it continuing progress and substantial success in our efforts for the security and not for the destruction of humanity.

Our enemies must at this moment be wondering - if they are permitted to know what goes on - how we are finding the time during the grim business of war to work for the cause of little children. For, under the enemies' kind of government, there is no time for or interest in such things - no time for ideals; no time for decency; no interest in the weak and the afflicted to whom we in this country have dedicated this day.

It would not be strictly true to say that our enemies pay no attention to health or the relief of need. But the difference is this: with them it all comes from the top. It is done only on order from the Ruler. It is carried out by uniformed servants of the Ruler. It is based, in great part, on direction, compulsion, and fear. And the Rulers are concerned not with human beings as human beings but as mere slaves of the state - or as cannon fodder...

The fight against the disease of infantile paralysis has proven beyond doubt that the way democracy works - the voluntary way - is efficient and is successful. It is only ten years ago that this country undertook, through wholly private contributions, to organize every locality to carry on this great effort, not for a year or two, but for all the future years - so long as the fight can help humanity.

PRESS CONFERENCE
JANUARY 30, 1942

I DO KNOW we have sent quite a lot of food to the children of France, on the assumption that it would be delivered through non-governmental sources like the Quakers, and the Red Cross.

FIRESIDE CHAT
FEBRUARY 23, 1942

WE OF THE United Nations are agreed on certain broad principles in the kind of peace we seek. The Atlantic Charter applies not only to the parts of the world that border the Atlantic but to the whole world; disarmament of aggressors, self-determination of Nations and peoples, and the four freedoms - freedom of speech, freedom of religion, freedom from want, and freedom from fear.

LETTER TO THE ECONOMIC CLUB OF NEW YORK
MARCH 12, 1942

WE ARE UNITED against those who willfully and deliberately, and with every weapon of force, propaganda, and terror, are aiming to destroy man's right "to think as he will and to say what he thinks."

We are united to maintain man's religious heritage against those who would destroy the great spiritual resources of resistance to injustice.

We are united against those who would enslave humanity by substituting terror for law, treachery for statecraft, and force for justice. We are united against the tyranny that has created untold want, privation, and suffering in a large part of the world.

These are the pledges inherent in the four freedoms which are the essence of the Atlantic Charter: Freedom of speech, freedom of religion, freedom from fear, and freedom from want.

PROCLAMATION 2542 ARMY DAY
MARCH 20, 1942

I HAVE PROCLAIMED April 6 Army Day. That day means more than ever to us this year. We are fighting an all-out war in defense of our rights and liberties.

Army Day becomes, therefore, in fact a total-war day. It becomes a day when all of our citizens in civil pursuits can rally to the support of our armed forces, for only in the united effort of all of our forces - Army, Navy, and civilians - can we find the strength to defeat our enemies.

Never before in the one hundred and sixty-six years of our history as a free Republic under God have our armed forces had so much meaning for us all. We are engaged in our greatest war, a war that will leave none of our lives wholly untouched.

We shall win that war as we have won every war we have fought. We are fighting it with a combined force of free men that is, in Lincoln's words, of the people, by the people, for the people of the United States of America.

Our Army is a mighty arm of the tree of liberty. It is a living part of the American tradition, a tradition that goes back to Israel Putnam, who left his plow in a New England furrow to take up a gun and fight at Bunker Hill. In this tradition American men of many ages have always left the pacific round of their usual occupations to fight in causes that were worth their lives - from Lexington to the Argonne.

In times of peace we do not maintain a vast standing Army that might terrorize our neighbors and oppress our people. We do not like to rehearse interminably the cruel art of war. But whenever a tyrant from across the seas has threatened our liberties, our citizens have been ready to forge and use the weapons necessary for their defense.

FIRESIDE CHAT
APRIL 28, 1942

THE NEWS IN Burma tonight is not good. The Japanese may cut the Burma Road; but I want to say to the gallant people of China that no matter what advances the Japanese may make, ways will be found to deliver airplanes and munitions of war to the armies of Generalissimo Chiang Kai-shek...

Although the treacherous attack on Pearl Harbor was the immediate cause of our entry into the war, that event found the American people spiritually prepared for war on a world-wide scale...

The price for civilization must be paid in hard work and sorrow and blood. The price is not too high. If you doubt it, ask those millions who live today under the tyranny of Hitlerisms...

This great war effort must be carried through to its victorious conclusion by the indomitable will and determination of the people as one great whole.

It must not be impeded by the faint of heart...

And, above all, it shall not be imperiled by the handful of noisy traitors - betrayers of America, betrayers of Christianity itself - would-be dictators who in their hearts and souls have yielded to Hitlerism and would have this Republic do likewise...

I should like to tell you one or two stories about the men we have in our armed forces:

There is, for example, Dr. Corydon M. Wassell. He was a missionary, well known for his good works in China. He is a simple, modest, retiring man, nearly sixty years old, but he entered the service of his country and was commissioned a Lieutenant Commander in the Navy.

Dr. Wassell was assigned to duty in Java caring for wounded officers and men of the cruisers Houston and Marblehead which had been in heavy action in the Java seas.

When the Japanese advanced across the island, it was decided to evacuate as many as possible of the wounded to Australia. But about twelve of the men were so badly wounded that they could not be moved.

Dr. Wassell remained with these men, knowing that he would be captured by the enemy. But he decided to make a last desperate attempt to get the men out of Java. He asked each of them if he wished to take the chance, and every one agreed.

He first had to get the twelve men to the seacoast - fifty miles away. To do this, he had to improvise stretchers for the hazardous journey. The men were suffering severely, but Dr. Wassell kept them alive by his skill, and inspired them by his own courage.

And as the official report said, Dr. Wassell was "almost like a Christ-like shepherd devoted to his flock."

On the seacoast, he embarked the men on a little Dutch ship. They were bombed, they were machine-gunned by waves of Japanese planes. Dr. Wassell took virtual command of the ship, and by great skill avoided destruction, hiding in little bays and little inlets.

A few days later, Dr. Wassell and his small flock of wounded men reached Australia safely.

And today Dr. Wassell wears the Navy Cross.

One more story that I heard only this morning:

This is a story of one of our Army Flying Fortresses operating in the western Pacific. The pilot of this plane is a modest young man, proud of his crew for one of the toughest fights a bomber has yet experienced.

The bomber departed from its base, as part of a flight of five bombers, to attack Japanese transports that were landing troops against us in the Philippines. When they had gone about halfway to their destination, one of the motors of this bomber went out of commission. The young pilot lost contact with the other bombers. The crew, however, got the motor working again and the plane proceeded on its mission alone.

By the time it arrived at its target the other four Flying Fortresses had already passed over, had dropped their bombs, and had stirred up the hornets' nest of Japanese "Zero" planes. Eighteen of these "Zero" fighters attacked our one Flying Fortress. Despite this mass attack, our plane proceeded on its mission, and dropped all of its bombs on six Japanese transports which were lined up along the docks.

As it turned back on its homeward journey a running fight between the bomber and the eighteen Japanese pursuit planes continued for 75 miles. Four pursuit planes of the Japs attacked simultaneously at each side. Four were shot down with the side guns. During this fight, the bomber's radio operator was killed, the engineer's right hand was shot off, and one gunner was crippled, leaving only one man available to operate both side guns.

Although wounded in one hand, this gunner alternately manned both side guns, bringing down three more Japanese "Zero" planes. While this was going on, one engine on the American bomber was shot out, one gas tank was hit, the radio was shot off, and the oxygen system was entirely destroyed. Out of eleven control cables all but four were shot away. The rear landing wheel was blown off entirely, and the two front wheels were both shot flat.

The fight continued until the remaining Japanese pursuit ships exhausted their ammunition and turned back. With two engines gone and the plane practically out of control, the American bomber returned to its base after dark and made an emergency landing. The mission had been accomplished.

The name of that pilot is Captain Hewitt T. Wheless, of the United States Army. He comes from a place called Menard, Texas - with a population of 2,375. He has been awarded the Distinguished Service Cross. And I hope that he is listening.

GREETING TO YANK MAGAZINE ON THE PUBLICATION OF ITS FIRST ISSUE MAY 28, 1942

UPON YOU AND upon your comrades in arms of all the United Nations depend the lives and liberties of all the human race. You bear with you the hopes of all the millions who have suffered under the oppression of the war lords of Germany and Japan. You bear with you the highest aspirations of mankind for a life of peace and decency under God.

All of you well know your own personal stakes in this war: your homes, your families, your free churches, the thousand and one simple, homely little virtues which Americans fought to establish, and which Americans have fought to protect, and which Americans today are fighting to extend and perpetuate throughout this earth.

LETTER ACCEPTING AWARD FROM DR. GUY EMERY SHIPLER, EDITOR OF THE CHURCHMAN JUNE 8, 1942

THE SPIRITUAL LIBERTIES of mankind are in jeopardy. Their religious freedom is at stake. The road ahead is dark and perilous. Yet we and our associates in the great alliance of the United Nations are determined to establish a new age of freedom on this earth. We are dedicating all that we have and are to that end. We are fighting in that cause at the side of valiant forces, representing every race and every creed. And with the united help of all free men and of all the great institutions of freedom, of which the churches of the free stand first, we shall create a new world in which there is freedom of worship and utterance, freedom from want and from fear, for all peoples everywhere in the world.

PRESS CONFERENCE JUNE 9, 1942

Q. MR. PRESIDENT, WILL the scrap rubber go to civilian use, or will the Army take it?

THE PRESIDENT: The Government will take it...

Q. Mr. President, how soon do you think this "Pick-Up-the-Rubber" campaign might get under way?

THE PRESIDENT: I don't know. Pretty soon, I think. I think it is a pretty good idea to strike while the iron's hot, and the Lord knows it's hot now.

RADIO ADDRESS ON UNITED FLAG DAY
JUNE 14, 1942

THE BELIEF IN the four freedoms of common humanity - the belief in man, created free, in the image of God - is the crucial difference between ourselves and the enemies we face today. In it lies the absolute unity of our alliance, opposed to the oneness of the evil we hate. Here is our strength, the source and promise of victory.

We of the United Nations know that our faith cannot be broken by any man or any force. And we know that there are other millions who in their silent captivity share our belief.

We ask the German people, still dominated by their Nazi whipmasters, whether they would rather have the mechanized hell of Hitler's "New" Order or - in place of that, freedom of speech and religion, freedom from want and from fear.

We ask the Japanese people, trampled by their savage lords of slaughter, whether they would rather continue slavery and blood or - in place of them, freedom of speech and religion, freedom from want and from fear.

We ask the brave, unconquered people of the Nations the Axis invaders have dishonored and despoiled whether they would rather yield to conquerors or - have freedom of speech and religion, freedom from want and from fear.

We know the answer. They know the answer. We know that man, born to freedom in the image of God, will not forever suffer the oppressors' sword. The peoples of the United Nations are taking that sword from the oppressors' hands. With it they will destroy those tyrants. The brazen tyrannies pass. Man marches forward toward the light.

I am going to close by reading you a prayer that has been written for the United Nations on this Day:

"God of the free, we pledge our hearts and lives today to the cause of all free mankind.

"Grant us victory over the tyrants who would enslave all free men and Nations. Grant us faith and understanding to cherish all those who fight for freedom as if they were our brothers. Grant us brotherhood in hope and union, not only for the space of this bitter war, but for the days to come which shall and must unite all the children of earth.

"Our earth is but a small star in the great universe. Yet of it we can make, if we choose, a planet unvexed by war, untroubled by hunger or fear, undivided by senseless distinctions of race, color, or theory. Grant us that courage and foreseeing to begin this task today that our children and our children's children may be proud of the name of man.

"The spirit of man has awakened and the soul of man has gone forth. Grant us the wisdom and the vision to comprehend the greatness of man's spirit, that suffers and endures so hugely for a goal beyond his own brief span. Grant us honor for our dead who died in the faith, honor for our living who work and strive for the faith, redemption and security for all captive lands and peoples. Grant us patience with the deluded and pity for the betrayed. And grant us the skill and the valor that shall cleanse the world of oppression and the old base doctrine that the strong must eat the weak because they are strong.

"Yet most of all grant us brotherhood, not only for this day but for all our years - a brotherhood not of words but of acts and deeds. We are all of us children of earth -

grant us that simple knowledge. If our brothers are oppressed, then we are oppressed. If they hunger, we hunger. If their freedom is taken away, our freedom is not secure. Grant us a common faith that man shall know bread and peace - that he shall know justice and righteousness, freedom and security, an equal opportunity and an equal chance to do his best, not only in our own lands, but throughout the world. And in that faith let us march, toward the clean world our hands can make. Amen."

LETTER ON NATIONAL PHYSICAL & MORAL FITNESS
JUNE 17, 1942

FROM RELIGIOUS LEADERS and responsible citizens come to me, almost daily, expressions of their concern, which they are translating into active local cooperation for total effectiveness...

I, therefore, call for the united efforts of Government- Federal, State, and local - of business and industry, of the medical profession, of the schools and of the churches; in short, of all citizens, for the establishment of total physical and moral fitness.

MESSAGE TO PRIME MINISTER CHURCHILL ON THE ANNIVERSARY OF THE ATLANTIC CHARTER
AUGUST 14, 1942

NOW, THESE NATIONS and groups of Nations in all the continents of the earth have united. They have formed a great union of humanity, dedicated to the realization of that common program of purposes and principles set forth in the Atlantic Charter, through world-wide victory over their common enemies. Their faith in life, liberty, independence and religious freedom, and in the preservation of human rights and justice in their own lands as well as in other lands, has been given form and substance and power through a great gathering of peoples now known as the United Nations.

CABLE TO PRESIDENT VARGAS ON BRAZIL'S DECLARATION OF WAR AUGUST 22, 1942

I HAVE BEEN informed that the United States of Brazil has today recognized that a state of war exists between Brazil, on one hand, and Germany and Italy on the other hand.

On behalf of the Government and people of the United States I express to Your Excellency the profound emotion with which this courageous action has been received in this country. This solemn decision more firmly aligns the people of Brazil with the free peoples of the world in a relentless struggle against the lawless and predatory Axis powers.

It adds power and strength, moral and material, to the armies of liberty. As brothers in arms, our soldiers and sailors will write a new page in the history of friendship, confidence, and cooperation which has marked since the earliest days of independence relations between your country and mine.

The action taken today by your Government has hastened the coming of the inevitable victory of freedom over oppression, of Christian religion over the forces of evil and darkness.

ADDRESS AT THE DEDICATION OF THE NAVAL MEDICAL CENTER, BETHESDA, MARYLAND AUGUST 31, 1942

LET THIS HOSPITAL then stand, for all men to see throughout all the years, as a monument to our determination to work and to fight until the time comes when the human race shall have that true health in body and mind and spirit which can be realized only in a climate of equity and faith.

ADDRESS TO INTERNATIONAL STUDENT ASSEMBLY SEPTEMBER 3, 1942

A RADIO IN Tokyo says that I am admitting to you at this moment that my people in the United States are decadent weaklings - playboys - spoiled by jazz music and Hollywood pictures...

For many years they have made their hypocritical appeal to youth - they have tried, with all their blatant publicity, to represent themselves as the champions of youth.

But now the world knows that the Nazis, the Fascists, and the militarists of Japan have nothing to offer to youth - except death...

Other young people in the democracies listened to gospels of despair. They took refuge in cynicism, and in bitterness...

You young Americans today are conducting yourselves in a manner that is worthy of the highest, proudest traditions of our Nation.

No pilgrims who landed on the uncharted New England coast, no pioneers who forced their way through the trackless wilderness, showed greater fortitude, greater determination, than you are showing now...

You know why you are fighting. You know that the road that has led you to the Solomon Islands, or to the Red Sea, or to the coast of France, is in fact an extension of Main Street, and that when you fight, anywhere along that road, you are fighting in the defense of your own homes, your own free schools, your own churches, your own ideals.

We must be sure that when you have won victory, you will not have to tell your children that you fought in vain - that you were betrayed. We must be sure that in your homes there will not be want - that in your schools only the living truth will be taught - that in your churches there may be preached without fear a faith in which men may deeply believe...

But we do believe that, with divine guidance, we can make in this dark world of today, and in the new postwar world of tomorrow - a steady progress toward the highest goals that men have ever imagined...

We must maintain the offensive against evil in all its forms. We must work, and we must fight to insure that our children shall have and shall enjoy in peace their inalienable rights to freedom of speech, freedom of religion, freedom from want, and freedom from fear.

STATEMENT ON LABOR DAY
SEPTEMBER 5, 1942

THIS IS INDEED labor's grave hour as it is the grave hour of the farmer, the industrialist, the teacher and preacher, the aproned housewife, the smallest child in the cradle. All these are the beneficiaries and heirs of the democratic system, and it is democracy itself that the evil men of West and East hate and seek to destroy.

STATEMENT ON THE PLAN TO TRY
NAZI WAR CRIMINALS
OCTOBER 7, 1942

ON AUGUST TWENTY-FIRST I said that this Government was constantly receiving information concerning the barbaric crimes being committed by the enemy against civilian populations in occupied countries, particularly on the continent of Europe. I said it was the purpose of this Government, as I knew it to be the purpose of the other United Nations, to see that when victory is won the perpetrators of these crimes shall answer for them before courts of law...

The number of persons eventually found guilty will undoubtedly be extremely small compared to the total enemy populations. It is not the intention of this Government or of the Governments associated with us to resort to mass reprisals. It is our intention that just and sure punishment shall be meted out to the ringleaders responsible for the organized murder of thousands of innocent persons and the commission of atrocities which have violated every tenet of the Christian faith.

STATEMENT ON COLUMBUS DAY
OCTOBER 12, 1942

IT IS 450 years since Christopher Columbus first saw the new western world off his bow.

He and his followers found a great expanse where new beginnings could be made, where men could steer their courses free of the fetters of tyranny and the encompassment of outworn institutions. In the wake of his courageous and unprecedented voyage there came to the

Americas the seeking people of many countries - people who sought liberty, democracy, religious tolerance, the fuller life.

This was the American experiment, a bold experiment and successful. Our immigrant ancestors, yours and mine, made it successful.

But now the free Nations we created on two continents, the very liberties we made law, are endangered by destructive forces from without. We are in the midst of mankind's greatest war, a war to determine whether the march of progress shall proceed or be halted by the totality of conquest.

Our cause is not only liberty for ourselves but liberation for others. An American victory will be a United Nations victory and a victory for oppressed and enslaved people everywhere. I like to remember on this significant anniversary the words of a contemporary poet:

"Columbus found a world and had no chart, save one that faith deciphered in the skies."

We have faith; deeds will implement it.

FIRESIDE CHAT
OCTOBER 12, 1942

ONE OF THE principal weapons of our enemies in the past has been their use of what is called the "War of Nerves." They have spread falsehood and terror; they have started fifth columns everywhere; they have duped the innocent; they have fomented suspicion and hate between neighbors; they have aided and abetted those people in other Nations - including our own - whose words and deeds are advertised from Berlin and Tokyo as proof of our disunity.

The greatest defense against all such propaganda, of course, is the common sense of the common people - and that defense is prevailing.

The "War of Nerves" against the United Nations is now turning into a boomerang. For the first time, the Nazi propaganda machine is on the defensive...

I want every father and every mother who has a son in the service to know - again, from what I have seen with my own eyes - that the men in the Army, Navy, and Marine Corps are receiving today the best possible training, equipment, and medical care. And we will never fail to provide for the spiritual needs of our officers and men under the Chaplains of our armed services...

One of the greatest of American soldiers, Robert E. Lee, once remarked on the tragic fact that in the war of his day all of the best generals were apparently working on newspapers instead of in the Army. And that seems to be true in all wars...

We, therefore, fight for the restoration and perpetuation of faith and hope and peace throughout the world.

The objective of today is clear and realistic. It is to destroy completely the military power of Germany, Italy, and Japan to such good purpose that their threat against us and all the other United Nations cannot be revived a generation hence. We are united in seeking the kind of victory that will guarantee that our grandchildren can grow and, under God, may live their lives, free from the constant threat of invasion, destruction, slavery, and violent death.

RADIO ADDRESS TO THE FRENCH PEOPLE ON THE NORTH AFRICAN INVASION NOVEMBER 7, 1942

WE COME AMONG you to repulse the cruel invaders who would remove forever your rights of self-government, your rights to religious freedom, and your rights to live your own lives in peace and security.

GREETINGS TO JEWISH THEOLOGICAL SEMINARY ON ITS 55TH ANNIVERSARY, ADDRESSED TO RABBI LOUIS FINKELSTEIN, NEW YORK CITY NOVEMBER 11, 1942

THE FIFTY-FIFTH anniversary of the Jewish Theological Seminary of America is an occasion for congratulation not only to the members of your faculty, board of directors, alumni, and others associated with the institution, but the community. Of special importance today is the emphasis which your teachers and graduates place on the intimate relationship between religious traditions deriving from the prophets of Scripture and the democratic ideals for which we are struggling in the present world conflict.

If the world to emerge from the war after a victory of the United Nations is to be a world of enduring peace and of freedom, that peace and that freedom must be founded on renewed loyalty to the spiritual values inherent in the great religious traditions which have saved mankind from degradation in the past and which offer the greatest promise for civilization in the future.

The enemies of mankind who are arrayed in battle against us realized this, and therefore began their effort to subdue the world with an assault on religious institutions. It has become an attack upon all monotheistic religions and the principles which they have taught mankind - the dignity and worth of human personality, the value of reason and truth, the blessedness of mercy and justice.

The seminary has made impressive efforts to study the problems of relationships among men of different faiths. Never has it been more important for the lovers of freedom to work harmoniously together in mutual understanding.

The Institute for Religious Studies, established at the seminary and conducted in cooperation with Catholic, Jewish, and Protestant scholars, is an important symbol of national solidarity. It will in time, I trust, become an increasingly powerful instrument for enlightening men of all faiths regarding the basic values of each other's doctrine and practice and their common responsibility for the development of democratic civilization.

In the difficult days before us all, I hope that the seminary and those within the wide circle of its influence will continue to carry on their work for our country and for religious faith.

ARMISTICE DAY ADDRESS
NOVEMBER 11, 1942

IN ARLINGTON WE are in the presence of the honored dead.

We are accountable to them - and accountable to the generations yet unborn for whom they gave their lives.

Today, as on all Armistice Days since 1918, our thoughts go back to the first World War; and we remember with gratitude the bravery of the men who fought and helped to win that fight against German militarism.

But this year our thoughts are also very much of the living present, and of the future which we begin to see opening before us - a picture illumined by a new light of hope.

Today, Americans and their British brothers-in-arms are again fighting on French soil. They are again fighting against a German militarism which transcends a hundred-fold the brutality and the barbarism of 1918.

The Nazis of today and their appropriate associates, the Japanese - have attempted to drive history into reverse, to use all the mechanics of modern civilization to drive humanity back to conditions of prehistoric savagery.

They sought to conquer the world, and for a time they seemed to be successful in realizing their boundless ambition. They overran great territories. They enslaved - they killed.

But, today, we know and they know that they have conquered nothing. Today, they face inevitable, final defeat.

Yes, the forces of liberation are advancing.

Britain, Russia, China, and the United States grow rapidly to full strength. The opponents of decency and justice have passed their peak.

And - as the result of recent events - very recent - the United States' and the United Nations' forces are being joined by large numbers of the fighting men of our traditional ally, France. On this day, of all days, it is heartening for us to know that soldiers of France go forward with the United Nations.

The American Unknown Soldier who lies here did not give his life on the fields of France merely to defend his American home for the moment that was passing. He gave it that his family, his neighbors, and all his fellow Americans might live in peace in the days to come. His hope was not fulfilled.

American soldiers are giving their lives today in all the continents and on all the seas in order that the dream of the Unknown Soldier may at last come true. All the heroism, all the unconquerable devotion that free men and women are showing in this war shall make certain the survival and the advancement of civilization. That is why on this day of remembrance we do not cease from our work. We are going about our tasks in behalf of our fighting men everywhere. Our thoughts turn in gratitude to those who have saved our Nation in days gone by.

We stand in the presence of the honored dead.

We stand accountable to them, and to the generations yet unborn for whom they gave their lives.

God, the Father of all living, watches over these hallowed graves and blesses the souls of those who rest here. May He keep us strong in the courage that will win the war, and may He impart to us the wisdom and the vision that we shall need for true victory in the peace which is to come.

RADIO ADDRESS ON THE 7TH ANNIVERSARY OF PHILIPPINES COMMONWEALTH GOVERNMENT NOVEMBER 15, 1942

IT IS A pattern of what men of good will look forward to in the future - a pattern of a global civilization which recognizes no limitations of religion, or of creed, or of race.

ADDRESS TO NEW YORK HERALD-TRIBUNE NOVEMBER 17, 1942

THERE ARE NO citations, no medals, which carry with them such high honor as that accorded to fighting men by the respect of their comrades-in-arms.

The Commanding General of the marines on Guadalcanal, General Vandegrift, yesterday sent a message to the Commander of the Fleet, Admiral Halsey, saying, "We lift our battered helmets in admiration for those who fought magnificently against overwhelming odds and drove the enemy back to crushing defeat."

Let us thank God for such men as these. May our Nation continue to be worthy of them, throughout this war, and forever.

PRESS CONFERENCE
NOVEMBER 17, 1942

Q. MR. PRESIDENT, IS any effort being made to change or modify the anti-Jewish laws and regulations now in effect in North Africa?

THE PRESIDENT: Yes. That is included in this statement which I have for you...

"I have requested the liberation of all persons in North Africa who have been imprisoned because they opposed the efforts of the Nazis to dominate the world; and I have asked for the abrogation of all laws and decrees inspired by Nazi Governments or Nazi ideologists.

Reports indicate the French of North Africa are subordinating all political questions to the formation of a common front against the common enemy."

PROCLAMATION 2571 ON THANKSGIVING DAY
NOVEMBER 26, 1942

"IT IS A good thing to give thanks unto the Lord." Across the uncertain ways of space and time our hearts echo those words, for the days are with us again when, at the gathering of the harvest, we solemnly express our dependence upon Almighty God.

The final months of this year, now almost spent, find our Republic and the Nations joined with it waging a battle on many fronts for the preservation of liberty.

In giving thanks for the greatest harvest in the history of our Nation, we who plant and reap can well resolve that in the year to come we will do all in our power to pass that milestone; for by our labors in the fields we can share some part of the sacrifice with our brothers and sons who wear the uniform of the United States.

It is fitting that we recall now the reverent words of George Washington, "Almighty God, we make our earnest prayer that Thou wilt keep the United States in Thy holy Protection," and that every American in his own way lift his voice to heaven.

I recommend that all of us bear in mind this great Psalm: "The Lord is my shepherd; I shall not want.

"He maketh me to lie down in green pastures: he leadeth me beside the still waters.

"He restoreth my soul; he leadeth me in the paths of righteousness for his name's sake.

"Yea, though I walk through the valley of the shadow of death, I will fear no evil: for thou art with me; thy rod and thy staff they comfort me.

"Thou preparest a table before me in the presence of mine enemies: thou anointest my head with oil; my cup runneth over.

"Surely goodness and mercy shall follow me all the days of my life: and I will dwell in the house of the Lord for ever."

Inspired with faith and courage by these words, let us turn again to the work that confronts us in this time of national emergency: in the armed services and the merchant marine; in factories and offices; on farms and in the mines; on highways, railways, and airways; in other places of public service to the Nation; and in our homes.

Now, therefore, I, Franklin D. Roosevelt, President of the United States of America, do hereby invite the attention of the people to the joint resolution of Congress approved December 26, 1941, which designates the fourth Thursday in November of each year as Thanksgiving Day; and I request that both Thanksgiving Day, November 26, 1942, and New Year's Day, January 1, 1943, be observed in prayer, publicly and privately.

TOAST AT STATE DINNER FOR CUBAN PRESIDENT
DECEMBER 8, 1942

WELL, THAT WAS the beginning. I think the Bible says, "By their fruits shall ye know them."

MESSAGE ON CHRISTMAS EVE
DECEMBER 24, 1942

THIS YEAR I am speaking on Christmas Eve not to this gathering at the White House only but to all of the citizens of our Nation, to the men and women serving in our American armed forces and also to those who wear the uniforms of the other United Nations.

I give you a message of cheer. I cannot say "Merry Christmas" - for I think constantly of those thousands of soldiers and sailors who are in actual combat throughout the world - but I can express to you my thought that this is a happier Christmas than last year in the sense that the forces of darkness stand against us with less confidence in the success of their evil ways.

To you who toil in industry for the common cause of helping to win the war, I send a message of cheer - that you can well continue to sacrifice without recrimination and with a look of Christmas cheer - a kindly spirit toward your fellow men.

To you who serve in uniform I also send a message of cheer that you are in the thoughts of your families and friends at home, and that Christmas prayers follow you wherever you may be.

To all Americans I say that loving our neighbor as we love ourselves is not enough - that we as a Nation and as individuals will please God best by showing regard for the laws of God. There is no better way of fostering good will toward man than by first fostering good will toward God. If we love Him we will keep His Commandments.

In sending Christmas greetings to the armed forces and merchant sailors of the United Nations we include therein our pride in their bravery on the fighting fronts and on all the seas. But we remember in our greetings and in our pride those other men who guard remote islands and bases and will, in all probability, never come into active combat with the common enemy.

They are stationed in distant places far from home. They have few contacts with the outside world, and I want them to know that their work is essential to the conduct of the war - essential to the ultimate victory - and that we have not forgotten them.

It is significant that tomorrow - Christmas Day - our plants and factories will be stilled. That is not true of the other holidays we have long been accustomed to celebrate. On all other holidays work goes on - gladly - for the winning of the war. So Christmas becomes the only holiday in all the year.

I like to think that this is so because Christmas is a holy day. May all it stands for live and grow throughout the years.

STATEMENT ON WAR AND PEACE
JANUARY 1, 1943

ONE YEAR AGO, twenty-six Nations signed at Washington the Declaration by United Nations...They thus created the mightiest coalition in history, mighty not only for its overwhelming material force but still more for its eternal spiritual values...Our task on this New Year's Day is...to cooperate to the end that mankind may enjoy in peace and in freedom the unprecedented blessings which Divine Providence through the progress of civilization has put within our reach.

STATE OF THE UNION ADDRESS
JANUARY 7, 1943

WHAT MATTERS MOST in war is results. And the one pertinent fact is that after only a few years of preparation and only one year of warfare, we are able to engage, spiritually as well as physically, in the total waging of a total war...

Two years ago I spoke in my Annual Message of four freedoms. The blessings of two of them - freedom of speech and freedom of religion - are an essential part of the very life of this Nation; and we hope that these blessings will be granted to all men everywhere...

Every normal American prays that neither he nor his sons nor his grandsons will be compelled to go through this horror again...

Today the United Nations are the mightiest military coalition in all history. They represent an overwhelming majority of the population of the world. Bound together in solemn agreement that they themselves will not commit acts of aggression or conquest against any of their neighbors, the United Nations can and must remain united for the maintenance of peace by preventing any attempt to rearm in Germany, in Japan, in Italy, or in any other Nation which seeks to violate the Tenth Commandment - "Thou shalt not covet."...

But, as we face that continuing task, we may know that the state of this Nation is good - the heart of this Nation is sound - the spirit of this Nation is strong - the faith of this Nation is eternal.

GREETING TO THE BOY SCOUTS
FEBRUARY 7, 1943

CERTAINLY THOSE WHO help to make boys physically strong, mentally awake, and morally straight in these times deserve the appreciation of all who are leaders in America.

ADDRESS TO WHITE HOUSE CORRESPONDENTS' ASSOCIATION
FEBRUARY 12, 1943

TWO YEARS AGO - many months before Pearl Harbor - I spoke to you of the thought that was then uppermost in our minds - of the determination of America to become the arsenal of democracy. Almost all Americans had by that time determined to play their full part in helping to save civilization from the barbarians. Even then, we were in the midst of the historic job of production - a job which the American people have been performing with zest and skill and, above all, with success.

Tonight, as I speak to you, we are in the war, and another thought is uppermost in our minds. That is our determination to fight this war through to the finish - to the day when United Nations forces march in triumph through the streets of Berlin, and Rome, and Tokyo....

Our men in the field are worthy of the great faith, the high hopes that we have placed in them. That applies as well to the men of our Navy, without whom no American expeditionary force could land safely on foreign shores. And it applies equally to the men of our merchant marine who carry the essential munitions and supplies, without which neither the United States nor our allies could continue the battle....

In every battalion, and in every ship's crew, you will find every kind of American citizen representing every occupation, every section, every origin, every religion, and every political viewpoint.

Ask them what they are fighting for, and every one of them will say, "I am fighting for my country." Ask them what they really mean by that, and you will get what on the surface may seem to be a wide variety of answers.

One will say that he is fighting for the right to say what he pleases, and to read and listen to what he likes.

Another will say he is fighting because he never wants to see the Nazi swastika flying over the old First Baptist Church on Elm Street.

Another soldier will say that he is fighting for the right to work, and to earn three square meals a day for himself and his folks.

And another one will say that he is fighting in this world war so that his children and his grandchildren will not have to go back to Europe, or Africa, or Asia, or the Solomon Islands, to do this ugly job all over again.

But all these answers really add up to the same thing; every American is fighting for freedom. And today the personal freedom of every American and his family depends, and in the future will increasingly depend, upon the freedom of his neighbors in other lands...

The people as a whole in the United States are in this war to see it through with heart and body and soul; and that our population is willing and glad to give up some of their shoes, and their sugar, and coffee, and automobile riding - and privileges and profits - for the sake of the common cause...

In the years of the American Revolution, and the French Revolution, the fundamental principle that guided our democracies was established. Indeed the whole cornerstone of our democratic edifice was the principle that from the people and the people alone flows the authority of government.

It is one of our war aims, as expressed in the Atlantic Charter, that the conquered populations of today - shall again become the masters of their destiny. There must be no doubt anywhere that it is the unalterable purpose of the United Nations to restore to conquered peoples their sacred rights...

Today is the anniversary of the birth of a great, plain American. The living memory of Abraham Lincoln is now honored and cherished by all of our people, wherever they may be, and by men and women and children throughout the British Commonwealth, and the Soviet Union, and the Republic of China, and all of our sister American Republics, and indeed in every land on earth where people love freedom and will give their lives for freedom.

President Lincoln said in 1862, "Fellow citizens, we cannot escape history. We of this Congress and this administration will be remembered in spite of ourselves. No personal significance or insignificance can spare one or another of us. The fiery trial through which we pass will light us...in honor or dishonor, to the latest generation."

Today, eighty years after Lincoln delivered that message, the fires of war are blazing across the whole horizon of mankind from Kharkov to Kunming - from the Mediterranean to the Coral Sea - from Berlin to Tokyo.

Again - we cannot escape history. We have supreme confidence that, with the help of God, honor will prevail. We have faith that future generations will know that here, in the middle of the twentieth century, there came a time when men of good will found a way to unite, and produce, and fight to destroy the forces of ignorance, and intolerance, and slavery, and war.

LETTER OF ENCOURAGEMENT TO A VICTIM OF INFANTILE PARALYSIS, TO MISS LAWRENCE FEBRUARY 14, 1943

YOUR COURAGE AND faith and determination in overcoming the after-effects of infantile paralysis and thereby restoring to the public the opportunity of enjoying your beautiful art - all result in a victory - your victory - which is an inspiration to everyone at any time.

But today when all we love and cherish is jeopardized by those who take their rules of life from the brutality of barbarism and preach and practice that all but the physically perfect should be summarily liquidated, your victory exposes with the light of truth the godlessness of the lie they teach.

In the days ahead, while we fight for life itself, those whose trials and sorrows may be many and heavy will courageously carry on in the spirit you have so nobly exhibited.

PRESS CONFERENCE
FEBRUARY 16, 1943

Q: IT WOULD TAKE 45 minutes a day for every legislative day for an entire year to pass those one out of a hundred. I would like to ask whether you think the Senate in wartime could be better employed? (Laughter)

THE PRESIDENT: I think there's a little line in the Bible that says, "Thou hast said it."

PRESS CONFERENCE WITH MADAME CHIANG KAI-SHEK AND PRESIDENT & MRS. ROOSEVELT
FEBRUARY 19, 1943

MADAME CHIANG: We are using as much manpower as there are munitions to be used. We can't fight with bare hands. We have fought with no overhead protection throughout five and a half years. But we can't go there and fight with our bare hands, although we have fought with nothing but swords in hand-to-hand combat...

MADAME CHIANG: Yes. I can't pay sufficiently high tribute to the American Volunteer Group - when they first came out to us. We were being terrifically bombed in Chungking, because our Chinese Air Force had only a few hundred planes in the beginning of the war; and as time went on those planes dwindled...Then the American Volunteer Group came, and they not only helped us materially, because they made it possible for our people to feel that America is really heart and soul with us in our common cause to fight against aggression, but the planes actually kept the enemy planes from bombing indiscriminately certain civilian centers, such as Chungking.

THE PRESIDENT: I don't suppose that there is any one task that is being studied more by transportation people - the military people - than the problem of getting the wherewithal with the planes to go into China...

And...that is our objective, to cut the Japanese line...and we are going to do it more and more by using China as a base of operations...

And it is not only cutting the line, but it means hitting Japan in the Japanese islands themselves...

If I were a member of the Chinese Government, I would say, "But when?...How soon?...and I say that as a member of the American Government too. Just as fast as the Lord will let us, with the best brains that we can bring to bear on it...

Q. Mr. President, could you permit direct quotes of the phrase, "Just as fast as the Lord will let us?"

THE PRESIDENT: No, I wouldn't. A lot of people wouldn't like to have the name of the Lord taken in vain...

MADAME CHIANG: The President just said that "as fast as the Lord will let us." Well, I might add on to that, "The Lord helps those who help themselves."

RADIO ADDRESS ON WASHINGTON'S BIRTHDAY
FEBRUARY 22, 1943

TODAY THIS NATION, which George Washington helped so greatly to create, is fighting all over this earth in order to maintain for ourselves and for our children the freedom which George Washington helped so greatly to achieve. As we celebrate his birthday, let us remember how he conducted himself in the midst of great adversities. We are inclined, because of the total sum of his accomplishments, to forget his days of trial.

Throughout the Revolution, Washington commanded an army whose very existence as an army was never a certainty from one week to another. Some of his soldiers, and even whole regiments, could not or would not move outside the borders of their own States. Sometimes, at critical moments, they would decide to re. turn to their individual homes to get the plowing done, or the crops harvested. Large numbers of the people of the colonies were either against independence or at least unwilling to make great personal sacrifice toward its attainment.

And there were many in every colony who were willing to cooperate with Washington only if the cooperation were based on their own terms.

Some Americans during the War of the Revolution sneered at the very principles of the Declaration of Independence. It was impractical, they said - it was "idealistic" - to claim that "all men are created equal, that they are endowed by their Creator with certain inalienable Rights."

The skeptics and the cynics of Washington's day did not believe that ordinary men and women have the capacity for freedom and self-government. They said that liberty and equality were idle dreams that could not come true - just as today there are many Americans who sneer at the determination to attain freedom from want and freedom from fear, on the ground that these are ideals which can never be realized. They say it is ordained that we must always have poverty, and that we must always have war.

You know; they are like the people who carp at the Ten Commandments because some people are in the habit of breaking one or more of them.

We Americans of today know that there would have been no successful outcome to the Revolution, even after eight long years - the Revolution that gave us liberty - had it not been for George Washington's faith, and the fact that that faith overcame the bickerings and confusion and the doubts which the skeptics and cynics provoked.

When kind history books tell us of Benedict Arnold, they omit dozens of other Americans who, beyond peradventure of a doubt, were also guilty of treason...

It was Washington's faith - and, with it, his hope and his charity - which was responsible for the stamina of Valley Forge - and responsible for the prayer at Valley Forge.

The Americans of Washington's day were at war. We Americans of today are at war.

The Americans of Washington's day faced defeat on many occasions. We faced, and still face, reverses and misfortunes.

In 1777, the victory over General Burgoyne's army at Saratoga led thousands of Americans to throw their hats in the air, proclaiming that the war was practically won and that they should go back to their peacetime occupations - and, shall I say, their peacetime "normalcies."

Today, the great successes on the Russian front have led thousands of Americans to throw their hats in the air and proclaim that victory is just around the corner.

Others among us still believe in the age of miracles. They forget that there is no Joshua in our midst. We cannot count on great walls crumbling and falling down when the trumpets blow and the people shout.

It is not enough that we have faith and that we have hope. Washington himself was the exemplification of the other great need.

Would that all of us could live our lives and direct our thoughts and control our tongues as did the Father of our Country in seeking day by day to follow those great verses:

"Charity suffereth long, and is kind; charity envieth not; charity vaunteth not itself, is not puffed up,

"Doth not behave itself unseemly, seeketh not her own, is not easily provoked, thinketh no evil:

"Rejoiceth not in iniquity but rejoiceth in the truth."

I think that most of us Americans seek to live up to those precepts. But there are some among us who have forgotten them. There are Americans whose words and writings are trumpeted by our enemies to persuade the disintegrating people of Germany and Italy and their captives that America is disunited - that America will be guilty of faithlessness in this war, and will thus enable the Axis powers to control the earth.

It is perhaps fitting that on this day I should read a few more words spoken many years ago - words which helped to shape the character and the career of George Washington, words that lay behind the prayer at Valley Forge.

"Blessed are the poor in spirit: for theirs is the kingdom of heaven.

"Blessed are they that mourn: for they shall be comforted.

"Blessed are the meek: for they shall inherit the earth.

"Blessed are they which do hunger and thirst after righteousness: for they shall be filled.

"Blessed are the merciful: for they shall obtain mercy.

"Blessed are the pure in heart: for they shall see God.

"Blessed are the peacemakers: for they shall be called the children of God.

"Blessed are they which are persecuted for righteousness' sake: for theirs is the kingdom of heaven.

"Blessed are ye, when men shall revile you, and persecute you, and shall say all manner of evil against you falsely, for my sake.

"Rejoice, and be exceeding glad: for great is your reward in heaven: for so persecuted they the prophets which were before you."

Those are the truths which are the eternal heritage of our civilization. I repeat them, to give heart and comfort to all men and women everywhere who fight for freedom.

Those truths inspired Washington, and the men and women of the thirteen colonies.

Today, through all the darkness that has descended upon our Nation and our world, those truths are a guiding light to all.

We shall follow that light, as our forefathers did, to the fulfillment of our hopes for victory, for freedom, and for peace.

ADDRESS AT THE DEDICATION OF THE THOMAS JEFFERSON MEMORIAL, WASHINGTON, D.C. APRIL 13, 1943

TODAY, IN THE midst of a great war for freedom, we dedicate a shrine to freedom.

To Thomas Jefferson, Apostle of Freedom, we are paying a debt long overdue.

Yet, there are reasons for gratitude that this occasion falls within our time; for our generation of Americans can understand much in Jefferson's life which intervening generations could not see as well as we.

He faced the fact that men who will not fight for liberty can lose it. We, too, have faced that fact.

He lived in a world in which freedom of conscience and freedom of mind were battles still to be fought through

- not principles already accepted of all men. We, too, have lived in such a world.

He loved peace and loved liberty - yet on more than one occasion he was forced to choose between them. We, too, have been compelled to make that choice.

Generations which understand each other across the distances of history are the generations united by a common experience and a common cause. Jefferson, across a hundred and fifty years of time, is closer by much to living men than many of our leaders of the years between. His cause was a cause to which we also are committed, not by our words alone but by our sacrifice.

For faith and ideals imply renunciations. Spiritual advancement throughout all our history has called for temporal sacrifices.

The Declaration of Independence and the very purposes of the American Revolution itself, while seeking freedoms, called for the abandonment of privileges...

The words which we have chosen for this Memorial speak Jefferson's noblest and most urgent meaning; and we are proud indeed to understand it and share it:

"I have sworn upon the altar of God, eternal hostility against every form of tyranny over the mind of man."

REMARKS AT DINNER FOR
PRESIDENT OF PARAGUAY
JUNE 9, 1943

I HOPE THAT in the years to come Paraguay and the United States will become closer personal friends than we have ever been before. Toward that end this Government - the Government and President - are going hand in hand; and may this association be carried out more greatly, more usefully - spiritually, economically, materially, in every way.

MESSAGE TO POPE PIUS XII
ON THE INVASION OF ITALY
JULY 10, 1943

BY THE TIME this message reaches Your Holiness a landing in force by American and British troops will have taken place on Italian soil. Our soldiers have come to rid Italy of Fascism and all its unhappy symbols, and to drive out the Nazi oppressors who are infesting her soil.

There is no need for me to reaffirm that respect for religious beliefs and for the free exercise of religious worship is fundamental to our ideas. Churches and religious institutions will, to the extent that it is within our power, be spared the devastations of war during the struggle ahead. Throughout the period of operations the neutral status of Vatican City as well as of the Papal domains throughout Italy will be respected.

I look forward, as does Your Holiness, to that bright day when the peace of God returns to the world. We are convinced that this will occur only when the forces of evil which now hold vast areas of Europe and Asia enslaved have been utterly destroyed. On that day we will joyfully turn our energies from the grim duties of war to the fruitful tasks of reconstruction. In common with all other Nations and forces imbued with the spirit of good will toward men, and with the help of Almighty God, we will turn our hearts and our minds to the exacting task of building a just and enduring peace on earth.

PRESS CONFERENCE
JULY 23, 1943

THE GERMANS HAD destroyed something like four thousand churches - the majority of the four thousand were churches, hospitals, and libraries - in Britain.

ADDRESS TO THE PEOPLE OF THE PHILIPPINES ON POST-WAR INDEPENDENCE
AUGUST 12, 1943

ON DECEMBER 28, 1941, three weeks after the armies of the Japanese launched their attack on Philippine soil, I sent a proclamation to you, the gallant people of the Philippines. I said then:

"I give to the people of the Philippines my solemn pledge that their freedom will be redeemed and their independence established and protected. The entire resources, in men and in material, of the United States stand behind that pledge."

We shall keep this promise, just as we have kept every promise which America has made to the Filipino people.

The story of the fighting on Bataan and Corregidor - and, indeed, everywhere in the Philippines - will be remembered so long as men continue to respect bravery, and devotion, and determination. When the Filipino people resisted the Japanese invaders with their very lives, they gave final proof that here was a Nation fit to be respected as the equal to any on earth, not in size Or wealth, but in the stout heart and national dignity which are the true measures of a people...

I call upon you, the heroic people of the Philippines to stand firm in your faith - to stand firm against the false promises of the Japanese, just as your fighting men and our fighting men stood firm together against their barbaric attacks.

The great day of your liberation will come, as surely as there is a God in Heaven.

The United States and the Philippines have learned the principles of honest cooperation, of mutual respect, in peace and in war.

For those principles we have fought - and by those principles we shall live.

ADDRESS AT OTTAWA, CANADA
AUGUST 25, 1943

THE EVIL CHARACTERISTIC that makes a Nazi a Nazi is his utter inability to understand and therefore to respect the qualities or the rights of his fellow men. His only method of dealing with his neighbor is first to delude him with lies, then to attack him treacherously, then beat him down and step on him, and then either kill him or enslave him. And the same thing is true of the fanatical militarists of Japan.

Because their own instincts and impulses are essentially inhuman, our enemies simply cannot comprehend how it is that decent, sensible individual human beings manage to get along together and live together as good neighbors...

I am everlastingly angry only at those who assert vociferously that the four freedoms and the Atlantic Charter are nonsense because they are unattainable. If those people had lived a century and a half ago they would have sneered and said that the Declaration of Independence was utter piffle.

If they had lived nearly a thousand years ago they would have laughed uproariously at the ideals of Magna Charta. And if they had lived several thousand years ago they would have derided Moses when he came from the Mountain with the Ten Commandments.

We concede that these great teachings are not perfectly lived up to today, but I would rather be a builder than a wrecker, hoping always that the structure of life is growing - not dying.

May the destroyers who still persist in our midst decrease. They, like some of our enemies, have a long road to travel before they accept the ethics of humanity.

Some day, in the distant future perhaps - but some day, it is certain - all of them will remember with the Master, "Thou shalt love thy neighbor as thyself."

FIRESIDE CHAT
SEPTEMBER 8, 1943

ONCE UPON A time, a few years ago, there was a city in our Middle West which was threatened by a destructive flood in the great river. The waters had risen to the top of the banks. Every man, woman, and child in that city was called upon to fill sandbags in order to defend their homes against the rising waters. For many days and nights, destruction and death stared them in the face.

As a result of the grim, determined community effort, that city still stands. Those people kept the levees above the peak of the flood. All of them joined together in the desperate job that had to be done - businessmen, workers, farmers, doctors preachers - people of all races.

To me, that town is a living symbol of what community cooperation can accomplish.

Today, in the same kind of community effort, only very much larger, the United Nations and their peoples have kept the levees of civilization high enough to prevent the floods of aggression and barbarism and wholesale murder from engulfing us all. The flood has been raging for four years.

At last we are beginning to gain on it; but the waters have not yet receded enough for us to relax our sweating work with the sandbags. In this war bond campaign we are filling bags and placing them against the flood-bags which are essential if we are to stand off the ugly torrent which is trying to sweep us all away...

The American people will never stop to reckon the cost of redeeming civilization. They know there never can be any economic justification for failing to save freedom...

I cannot tell you how much to invest in war bonds during this Third War Loan Drive. No one can tell you. It is for you to decide under the guidance of your own conscience...

Every dollar that you invest in the Third War Loan is your personal message of defiance to our common enemies - to the ruthless savages of Germany and Japan - and it is your personal message of faith and good cheer to our allies and to all the men at the front. God bless them!

MESSAGE TO CONGRESS ON PROGRESS OF WAR
SEPTEMBER 17, 1943

ON THE THIRD day of September they landed on the toe of the Italian peninsula. These were the first Allied troops to invade the continent of Europe in order to liberate the conquered and oppressed countries. History will always remember this day as the beginning of the answer to the prayer of the millions of liberty-loving human beings not only in these conquered lands but all over the world.

TOAST TO THE KING OF ARABIA AT A DINNER FOR THE MINISTER OF FOREIGN AFFAIRS SEPTEMBER 30, 1943

YOUR ROYAL HIGHNESS, I think that all of us here realize that tonight is a very historic occasion. In the long history of our country, and in the much longer history of Arabia, there have been no dinners like this. We have come to know each other, and I think our great hosts in both Nations are agreed that in the future we should seek to know each other better.

There are very few Americans in all Arabia, and there are very few Arabians in all America. And so the more we see of each other in the days to come, the more it will mean not merely a diplomatic friendship, but it will mean a personal friendship.

We have much in common. We both love liberty - both Nations. And there is no reason why both Nations should not maintain liberty.

We have much to learn from each other. And so I hope that in the days to come we will be able to discuss things, as friends.

I was telling His Royal Highness, at supper, that I knew that one of their problems in Arabia was an insufficiency of water in many places, and also of not enough trees. And I was telling him of what we in our younger years used to call the Great American Desert, a strip running from the North in our own country to the South, where there was very little water, and where there were very few trees...

I think we all know that the King is a very wonderful person. I was reading this afternoon a little magazine, and it was all about the King; and there was one little paragraph at the end that I liked a lot - all of it goes along with my own philosophy.

"Ibn Saud's most engaging quality is a kingly belief in eventual rightness. It did not surprise him greatly when Allah, who sent Arabia its ancient rains, provided also its new oil. Nor will it surprise him greatly if God presently provides also not merely victory but even the bright and honest world that should go with it."

I think with that kind of philosophy, which is an Arabian philosophy and also an American philosophy, that working together we can contribute something toward a brighter world, and a more honest world, in the years to come.

STATEMENT CONDEMNING SUSPENSION OF JEWISH NEWSPAPERS IN ARGENTINA OCTOBER 15, 1943

I HAVE BEEN informed that the Argentine Government has suspended the publication of Jewish newspapers, some of which have been in existence for many years.

While this matter is, of course, one which concerns primarily the Argentine Government and people, I cannot forbear to give expression to my own feeling of apprehension at the taking in this hemisphere of action obviously anti-Semitic in nature and of a character so closely identified with the most repugnant features of Nazi doctrine. I believe that this feeling is shared by the people of the United States and by the people of the other American Republics.

In this connection I recall that one of the resolutions adopted at the Eighth International Conference of American States at Lima in 1938 set forth that "any persecution on account of racial or religious motives which makes it impossible for a group of human beings to live decently is contrary to the political and juridical system of America."

ADDRESS ON THE SIGNING OF THE AGREEMENT ESTABLISHING THE UNITED NATIONS RELIEF AND REHABILITATION ADMINISTRATION NOVEMBER 9, 1943

THE GERMAN AND the Japanese have carried on their campaigns of plunder and destruction with one purpose in mind: that in the lands they occupy there shall be left only a generation of half-men - undernourished, crushed in body and spirit, without strength or incentive to hope - ready, in fact, to be enslaved and used as beasts of burden by the self-styled master races.

FIRESIDE CHAT DECEMBER 24, 1943

ON THIS CHRISTMAS Eve there are over 10,000,000 men in the armed forces of the United States alone. One year ago 1,700,000 were serving overseas. Today, this figure has been more than doubled to 3,800,000 on duty overseas. By next July 1 that number overseas will rise to over 5,000,000 men and women...

In the Southwest Pacific, in Australia, in China and Burma and India, it is already Christmas Day. So we can correctly say that at this moment, in those Far Eastern parts where Americans are fighting, today is tomorrow.

But everywhere throughout the world - throughout this war that covers the world - there is a special spirit that has warmed our hearts since our earliest childhood - a spirit that brings us close to our homes, our families, our friends and neighbors the Christmas spirit of "peace on earth, good will toward men." It is an unquenchable spirit.

During the past years of international gangsterism and brutal aggression in Europe and in Asia, our Christmas celebrations have been darkened with apprehension for the future. We have said, "Merry Christmas - Happy New Year," but we have known in our hearts that the clouds which have hung over our world have prevented us from saying it with full sincerity and conviction.

And even this year, we still have much to face in the way of further suffering, and sacrifice, and personal tragedy. Our men, who have been through the fierce battles in the Solomons, the Gilberts, Tunisia, and Italy know, from their own experience and knowledge of modern war, that many bigger and costlier battles are still to be fought.

But - on Christmas Eve this year - I can say to you that at last we may look forward into the future with real, substantial confidence that, however great the cost, "peace on earth, good will toward men" can be and will be realized and insured. This year I can say that. Last year I could not do more than express a hope. Today I express a certainty - though the cost may be high and the time may be long.

Within the past year - within the past few weeks - history has been made, and it is far better history for the whole human race than any that we have known, or even dared to hope for, in these tragic times through which we pass...

Indeed, Mr. Churchill has become known and beloved by many millions of Americans, and the heartfelt prayers of all of us have been with this great citizen of the world in his recent serious illness...

At Cairo, Prime Minister Churchill and I spent four days with the Generalissimo, Chiang Kai-shek. It was the first time that we had an opportunity to go over the complex situation in the Far East with him personally. We were able not only to settle upon definite military strategy, but also to discuss certain long-range principles which we believe can assure peace in the Far East for many generations to come...

On the mainland of Asia, under the Generalissimo's leadership, the Chinese ground and air forces augmented by American air forces are playing a vital part in starting the drive which will push the invaders into the sea...

I met in the Generalissimo a man of great vision, great courage, and a remarkably keen understanding of the problems of today and tomorrow. We discussed all the manifold military plans for striking at Japan with decisive force from many directions, and I believe I can say that he returned to Chungking with the positive assurance of total victory over our common enemy. Today we and the Republic of China are closer together than ever before in deep friendship and in unity of purpose...

The United Nations have no intention to enslave the German people. We wish them to have a normal chance to develop, in peace, as useful and respectable members of the European family. But we most certainly emphasize that word "respectable" for we intend to rid them once and for all of Nazism and Prussian militarism and the fantastic and disastrous notion that they constitute the "master race."...

There have always been cheerful idiots in this country who believed that there would be no more war for us if everybody in America would only return into their homes and lock their front doors behind them. Assuming that their motives were of the highest, events have shown how unwilling they were to face the facts...

If we are willing to fight for peace now, is it not good logic that we should use force if necessary, in the future, to keep the peace?...

Less than a month ago I flew in a big Army transport plane over the little town of Bethlehem, in Palestine.

Tonight, on Christmas Eve, all men and women everywhere who love Christmas are thinking of that ancient town and of the star of faith that shone there more than nineteen centuries ago.

American boys are fighting today in snow-covered mountains, in malarial jungles, on blazing deserts; they are fighting on the far stretches of the sea and above the clouds, and fighting for the thing for which they struggle. I think it is best symbolized by the message that came out of Bethlehem.

On behalf of the American people - your own people - I send this Christmas message to you who are in our armed forces:

In our hearts are prayers for you and for all your comrades in arms who fight to rid the world of evil.

We ask God's blessing upon you - upon your fathers, mothers, wives and children - all your loved ones at home.

We ask that the comfort of God's grace shall be granted to those who are sick and wounded, and to those who are prisoners of war in the hands of the enemy, waiting for the day when they will again be free.

And we ask that God receive and cherish those who have given their lives, and that He keep them in honor and in the grateful memory of their countrymen forever.

God bless all of you who fight our battles on this Christmas Eve.

God bless us all. Keep us strong in our faith that we fight for a better day for humankind - here and everywhere.

STATEMENT ON NEW YEAR'S DAY
JANUARY 1, 1944

MANY OF US in the United States are observing this first day of the New Year as a day of prayer and reflection and are considering the deeper issues which affect us as part of the family of Nations at a crucial moment in history.

STATE OF THE UNION ADDRESS
JANUARY 11, 1944

WE ARE UNITED in determination that this war shall not be followed by another interim which leads to new disaster - that we shall not repeat the tragic errors of ostrich isolationism - that we shall not repeat the excesses of the wild twenties when this Nation went for a joy ride on a roller coaster which ended in a tragic crash...

The foreign policy that we have been following - the policy that guided us at Moscow, Cairo, and Teheran - is based on the common sense principle which was best expressed by Benjamin Franklin on July 4, 1776: "We must all hang together, or assuredly we shall all hang separately."

I have often said that there are no two fronts for America in this war. There is only one front. There is one line of unity which extends from the hearts of the people at home to the men of our attacking forces in our farthest outposts. When we speak of our total effort, we speak of the factory and the field, and the mine as well as of the battleground - we speak of the soldier and the civilian, the citizen and his Government.

Each and every one of us has a solemn obligation under God to serve this Nation in its most critical hour - to keep this Nation great - to make this Nation greater in a better world.

RADIO APPEAL FOR THE NATIONAL FOUNDATION FOR INFANTILE PARALYSIS JANUARY 29, 1944

HOW DIFFERENT IT is in the lands of our enemies! In Germany and Japan, those who are handicapped in body or mind are regarded as unnecessary burdens to the state. There, an individual's usefulness is measured solely by the direct contribution that he can make to the war machine - not by his service to a society at peace.

The dread disease that we battle at home, like the enemy we oppose abroad, shows no concern, no pity for the young. It strikes - with its most frequent and devastating force - against children. And that is why much of the future strength of America depends upon the success that we achieve in combating this disease...

The tireless men and women working night and day over test tubes and microscopes - searching for drugs and serums, for methods that will prevent and cure - these are the workers on the production line in this war against disease. The gallant chapter workers, the doctors and nurses in our hospitals, the public health officials, the volunteers who go into epidemic areas to help the physician - these are the front-line fighters.

And just as in war - there is that subtle weapon that, more than anything else, spells victory or defeat. That weapon is morale - the morale of a people who know that they are fighting "the good fight" -that they are keeping the faith - the only faith through which civilization can survive - the faith that man must live to help and not to destroy his fellowmen...

We may thank God that here in our country we are keeping alive the spirit of good will toward one another - that spirit which is the very essence of the cause for which we fight. Godspeed the spirit of good will.

PRESS CONFERENCE FOR THE NEGRO NEWSPAPER PUBLISHERS ASSOCIATION FEBRUARY 5, 1944

THEY HAD NO religion except the old forms of voodooism, which were tribal and came down through the centuries. The one religion that is gaining today in Gambia and contiguous colonies is Mohammedanism. Now people don't know about that here. Those people, of course, are completely incapable of self-government. You have got to give them some education first.

STATEMENT ON THE NAZIS' USING ROME MARCH 14, 1944

EVERYONE KNOWS the Nazi record on religion. Both at home and abroad, Hitler and his followers have waged a ruthless war against the churches of all faiths.

Now the German army has used the Holy City of Rome as a military center. No one could have been surprised by this - it is only the latest of Hitler's many affronts to religion. It is a logical step in the Nazi policy of total war - a policy which treats nothing as sacred.

We on our side have made freedom of religion one of the principles for which we are fighting this war. We have tried scrupulously - often at considerable sacrifice to spare religious and cultural monuments, and we shall continue to do so.

STATEMENT ON OPENING FRONTIERS TO WAR VICTIMS AND JUSTICE FOR WAR CRIMES
MARCH 24, 1944

THE UNITED NATIONS are fighting to make a world in which tyranny and aggression cannot exist; a world based upon freedom, equality, and justice; a world in which all persons regardless of race, color, or creed may live in peace, honor, and dignity.

In the meantime in most of Europe and in parts of Asia the systematic torture and murder of civilians - men, women, and children - by the Nazis and the Japanese continue unabated...

In one of the blackest crimes of all history - begun by the Nazis in the day of peace and multiplied by them a hundred times in time of war - the wholesale systematic murder of the Jews of Europe goes on unabated every hour.

As a result of the events of the last few days hundreds of thousands of Jews, who while living under persecution have at least found a haven from death in Hungary and the Balkans, are now threatened with annihilation as Hitler's forces descend more heavily upon these lands.

That these innocent people, who have already survived a decade of Hitler's fury, should perish on the very eve of triumph over' the barbarism which their persecution symbolizes, would be a major tragedy.

It is therefore fitting that we should again proclaim our determination that none who participate in these acts of savagery shall go unpunished. The United Nations have made it clear that they will pursue the guilty and deliver them up in order that Justice be done. That warning applies not only to the leaders but also to their functionaries and subordinates in Germany and in the satellite countries.

All who knowingly take part in the deportation of Jews to their death in Poland or Norwegians and French to their death in Germany are equally guilty with the executioner. All who share the guilt shall share the punishment.

Hitler is committing these crimes against humanity in the name of the German people.

I ask every German and every man everywhere under Nazi domination to show the world by his action that in his heart he does not share these insane criminal desires. Let him hide these pursued victims, help them to get over their borders, and do what he can to save them from the Nazi hangman. I ask him also to keep watch, and to record the evidence that will one day be used to convict the guilty.

In the meantime, and until the victory that is now assured is won, the United States will persevere in its efforts to rescue the victims of brutality of the Nazis and the Japs. Insofar as the necessity of military operations permit, this Government will use all means at its command to aid the escape of all intended victims of the Nazi and Jap executioner - regardless of race or religion or color.

We call upon the free peoples of Europe and Asia temporarily to open their frontiers to all victims of oppression. We shall find havens of refuge for them, and we shall find the means for their maintenance and support until the tyrant is driven from their homelands and they may return.

In the name of justice and humanity let all freedom-loving people rally to this righteous undertaking.

ADDRESS TO AN INTERNATIONAL LABOR CONFERENCE
MAY 17, 1944

YOU HAVE BEEN meeting in Philadelphia where, one hundred and sixty-eight years ago, the Fathers of this Republic affirmed certain truths to be self-evident. They declared among other things that all men are endowed by their Creator with certain inalienable rights, among them Life, Liberty, and the Pursuit of Happiness. In these words are expressed the abiding purpose of all peoples imbued with the ideals of freedom and democracy. Let us never forget those words...

You have affirmed the right of all human beings to material well-being and spiritual development under conditions of freedom and dignity and under conditions of economic security and opportunity.

FIRESIDE CHAT
JUNE 5, 1944

IN ADDITION TO the monuments of the older times, we also see in Rome the great symbol of Christianity, which has reached into almost every part of the world. There are other shrines and other churches in many places, but the churches and shrines of Rome are visible symbols of the faith and determination of the early saints and martyrs that Christianity should live and become universal. And tonight it will be a source of deep satisfaction that the freedom of the Pope and the Vatican City is assured by the armies of the United Nations.

It is also significant that Rome has been liberated by the armed forces of many Nations. The American and

British armies - who bore the chief burdens of battle - found at their sides our own North American neighbors, the gallant Canadians. The fighting New Zealanders from the far South Pacific, the courageous French and the French Moroccans, the South Africans, the Poles, and the East Indians - all of them fought with us on the bloody approaches to the city of Rome...

But Rome is of course more than a military objective.

Ever since before the days of the Caesars, Rome has stood as a symbol of authority. Rome was the Republic. Rome was the Empire. Rome was and is in a sense the Catholic Church, and Rome was the capital of a United Italy. Later, unfortunately, a quarter of a century ago, Rome became the seat of Fascism - one of the three capitals of the Axis.

For this quarter century the Italian people were enslaved. They were degraded by the rule of Mussolini from Rome. They will mark its liberation with deep emotion. In the north of Italy, the people are still dominated and threatened by the Nazi overlords and their Fascist puppets...

In the past, Italians have come by the millions into the United States. They have been welcomed, they have prospered, they have become good citizens, community and Governmental leaders. They are not Italian-Americans. They are Americans Americans of Italian descent...

And so I extend the congratulations and thanks tonight of the American people to General Alexander, who has been in command of the whole Italian operation; to our General Clark and General Leese of the Fifth and the Eighth Armies; to General Wilson, the Supreme Allied Commander of the Mediterranean theater, to General Devers, his American Deputy; to General Eaker; to Admirals Cunningham and Hewitt; and to all their brave officers and men.

May God bless them and watch over them and over all of our gallant, fighting men.

PRAYER ON D-DAY
JUNE 6, 1944

MY FELLOW AMERICANS: Last night, when I spoke with you about the fall of Rome, I knew at that moment that troops of the United States and our allies were crossing the Channel in another and greater operation. It has come to pass with success thus far.

And so, in this poignant hour, I ask you to join with me in prayer:

Almighty God: Our sons, pride of our Nation, this day have set upon a mighty endeavor, a struggle to preserve our Republic, our religion, and our civilization, and to set free a suffering humanity.

Lead them straight and true; give strength to their arms, stoutness to their hearts, steadfastness in their faith.

They will need Thy blessings. Their road will be long and hard. For the enemy is strong. He may hurl back our forces. Success may not come with rushing speed, but we shall return again and again; and we know that by Thy grace, and by the righteousness of our cause, our sons will triumph.

They will be sore tried, by night and by day, without rest - until the victory is won. The darkness will be rent by noise and flame. Men's souls will be shaken with the violences of war.

For these men are lately drawn from the ways of peace. They fight not for the lust of conquest. They fight to end conquest. They fight to liberate. They fight to let justice arise, and tolerance and good will among all Thy people.

They yearn but for the end of battle, for their return to the haven of home.

Some will never return. Embrace these, Father, and receive them, Thy heroic servants, into Thy kingdom.

And for us at home - fathers, mothers, children, wives, sisters, and brothers of brave men overseas - whose thoughts and prayers are ever with them - help us, Almighty God, to rededicate ourselves in renewed faith in Thee in this hour of great sacrifice.

Many people have urged that I call the Nation into a single day of special prayer. But because the road is long and the desire is great, I ask that our people devote themselves in a continuance of prayer. As we rise to each new day, and again when each day is spent, let words of prayer be on our lips, invoking Thy help to our efforts.

Give us strength, too - strength in our daily tasks, to redouble the contributions we make in the physical and the material support of our armed forces.

And let our hearts be stout, to wait out the long travail, to bear sorrows that may come, to impart our courage unto our sons wheresoever they may be.

And, O Lord, give us Faith. Give us Faith in Thee; Faith in our sons; Faith in each other; Faith in our united crusade. Let not the keenness of our spirit ever be dulled. Let not the impacts of temporary events, of temporal matters of but fleeting moment let not these deter us in our unconquerable purpose.

With Thy blessing, we shall prevail over the unholy forces of our enemy. Help us to conquer the apostles of greed and racial arrogancies. Lead us to the saving of our country, and with our sister Nations into a world unity that will spell a sure peace a peace invulnerable to the schemings of unworthy men. And a peace that will let all of men live in freedom, reaping the just rewards of their honest toil.

Thy will be done, Almighty God.
Amen.

MESSAGE TO CONGRESS ON REFUGEES
JUNE 12, 1944

CONGRESS HAS REPEATEDLY manifested its deep concern with the pitiful plight of the persecuted minorities in Europe whose lives are each day being offered in sacrifice on the altar of Nazi tyranny.

This Nation is appalled by the systematic persecution of helpless minority groups by the Nazis. To us the unprovoked murder of innocent people simply because of race, religion, or political creed is the blackest of all possible crimes. Since the Nazis began this campaign many of our citizens in all walks of life and of all political and religious persuasions have expressed our feeling of repulsion and our anger. It is a matter with respect to which there is and can be no division of opinion amongst us.

As the hour of the final defeat of the Hitlerite forces draws closer, the fury of their insane desire to wipe out the Jewish race in Europe continues undiminished. This is but one example:

Many Christian. groups also are being murdered. Knowing that they have lost the war, the Nazis are determined to complete their program of mass extermination. This program is but one manifestation of Hitler's aim to salvage from military defeat victory for Nazi principles - the very principles which this war must destroy unless we shall have fought in vain.

This Government has not only made clear its abhorrence of this inhuman and barbarous activity of the Nazis, but, in cooperation with other Governments, has endeavored to alleviate the condition of the persecuted peoples...

Operating quietly, as is appropriate, the Board, through its representatives in various parts of the world, has actually succeeded in saving the lives of innocent people. Not only have refugees been evacuated from enemy territory, but many measures have been taken to protect the lives of those who have not been able to escape..

To the Hitlerites, their subordinates and functionaries and satellites, to the German people, and to all other peoples under the Nazi yoke, we have made clear our determination to punish all participants in these acts of savagery. In the name of humanity we have called upon them to spare the lives of these innocent people.

Notwithstanding this Government's unremitting efforts, which are continuing, the numbers actually rescued from the jaws of death have been small compared with the numbers still facing extinction in German territory. This is due principally to the fact that our enemies, despite all our appeals and our willingness to find havens of refuge for the oppressed peoples, persist in their fiendish extermination campaign and actively prevent the intended victims from escaping to safety.

In the face of this attitude of our enemies we must not fail to take full advantage of any opportunity, however limited, for the rescue of Hitler's victims. We are confronted with a most urgent situation.

Therefore, I wish to report to you today concerning a step which I have just taken in an effort to save additional lives and which I am certain will meet with your approval. You will, I am sure, appreciate that this measure is not only consistent with the successful prosecution of the war, but that it was essential to take action without delay...

FIRESIDE CHAT
JUNE 12, 1944

SOME OF OUR landings were desperate adventures; but from advices received so far, the losses were lower than our commanders had estimated would occur. We have established a firm foothold. We are now prepared to meet the inevitable counterattacks of the Germans - with power and with confidence. And we all pray that we will have far more, soon, than a firm foothold.

ADDRESS TO THE DEMOCRATIC NATIONAL
CONVENTION IN CHICAGO
JULY 20, 1944

WE ALL KNOW how truly the world has become one - that if Germany and Japan, for example, were to come through this war with their philosophies established and their armies intact, our own grandchildren would again have to be fighting in their day for their liberties and their lives.

Some day soon we shall all be able to fly to any other part of the world within twenty-four hours. Oceans will no longer figure as greatly in our physical defense as they have in the past. For our own safety and for our own economic good, therefore - if for no other reason - we must take a leading part in the maintenance of peace and in the increase of trade among all the Nations of the world...

The greatest wartime President in our history, after a wartime election which he called the "most reliable indication of public purpose in this country," set the goal for the United States, a goal in terms as applicable today as they were in 1865 - terms which the human mind cannot improve:

"...with firmness in the right, as God gives us to see the right, let us strive on to finish the work we are in; to bind up the Nation's wounds; to care for him who shall have borne the battle, and for his widow, and his orphan - to do all which may achieve and cherish a just and lasting peace among ourselves, and with all Nations."

REMARKS AT SCHOFIELD BARRACKS, PEARL HARBOR
JULY 27, 1944

I AM AWFULLY glad to come back here and see it with my own eyes ten years to the day later. I wish we could stay here - see more. It is being felt all through this area - all the way down to General MacArthur's area, which thank the Lord is coming a little closer toward us, and automatically closer toward the enemy than it was two years ago.

PRESS CONFERENCE
AUGUST 29, 1944

STEVE EARLY almost had a fit that I would make another nonpolitical speech. (laughter) And I thought of making a speech on a subject that is very close to my heart, because I will make a little money on it - you see how close to my heart it is - this is a dissertation to the public on the planting and the raising and the selling of Christmas trees. I really thought of making a radio speech on that, and then having somebody say that it was on a political subject and demanding equal time on the air.

That would create another controversy, and probably people would want to see my books to prove that I do make money raising Christmas trees; there would be an investigation to prove that I do take a lot of time.

I have some very, very carefully kept books on the subject of Christmas trees - a thing called a check-book. And I pay for the labor of planting these little trees at the age of four years and about six inches high, and I pay a man about once every two years to go through and keep the briars out of them; and then I pay several people - some of them schoolboys - to go in and cut them off.

And then the next entry is on the other side of the checkbook. Along comes a department store or chain store with a truck, and they themselves load these little trees - this is ten years after the planting - into the truck. They take them down to New York, and sell the trees - at a profit. They get a good profit. And then they send me a check for the little trees, which is recorded in the stub of the checkbook on the other side.

I think there probably should be an investigating committee. I will be glad to show them my check-book. No particular secret in it. I thought trees a very good topic for a political talk.

JOINT PRESS CONFERENCE WITH CHURCHILL AND MACKENZIE KING IN QUEBEC, CANADA SEPTEMBER 16, 1944

THANK GOD, we have been blessed with so much good fortune, far more than we deserve; but the fact remains we have conducted successful war, beginning from small beginnings and at great disadvantage, against the most powerful embattled forces...

Do not fear about the future. The same processes that have led us from the dark days of Dunkirk, and the Americans from the dark days of Pearl Harbor, to our present situation when the skies are clearing...

ADDRESS AT UNION DINNER, WASHINGTON, D.C. SEPTEMBER 23, 1944

AND SO, MY friends, we have had affirmation of the vitality of democratic government behind us, that demonstration of its resilience and its capacity for decision and for action - we have that knowledge of our own strength and power - we move forward with God's help to the greatest epoch of free achievement by free men that the world has ever known.

RADIO ADDRESS FROM THE WHITE HOUSE OCTOBER 5, 1944

"THE LAND OF opportunity" - that's what our forefathers called this country. By God's grace, it must always be the land of opportunity for the individual citizen - ever broader opportunity...

What is now being won in battle must not be lost by lack of vision, or lack of knowledge, or by lack of faith, or by division among ourselves and our allies...

We owe it to our posterity, we owe it to our heritage of freedom, we owe it to our God, to devote the rest of our lives and all of our capabilities to the building of a solid, durable structure of world peace..

ADDRESS ACCEPTING FOUR FREEDOMS AWARD FROM ITALIAN-AMERICAN LABOR COUNCIL OCTOBER 12, 1944

OUR OBJECTIVE IS to restore all avenues of trade and commerce and industry, and the free exercise of religion, at the earliest possible moment...

To the people of Italy we have pledged our help - and we will keep the faith!

ADDRESS ON NATIONAL WAR FUND DRIVE OCTOBER 17, 1944

ONCE AGAIN I come to you on behalf of your community war fund, united with the National War Fund in a common federated appeal for us and for our allies...

The great warmhearted good will that you have expressed through these funds has helped immeasurably to revive the spirit of faith and hope in many lands across the seas - and in many homes back here - where there has been bitterness and hatred after years of war and oppression.

CONGRATULATIONS TO GENERAL MACARTHUR OCTOBER 20, 1944

THE WHOLE AMERICAN Nation today exults at the news that the gallant men under your command have landed on Philippine soil. I know well what this means to you. I know what it cost you to obey my order that you leave Corregidor in February, 1942, and proceed to Australia.

Since then you have planned and worked and fought with whole-souled devotion for the day when you would return with powerful forces to the Philippine Islands. That day has come.

You have the Nation's gratitude and the Nation's prayers for success as you and your men fight your way back to Bataan.

MESSAGE FROM THE PRESIDENT TO PRESIDENT OSMENA FOR THE PHILIPPINE PEOPLE OCTOBER 20, 1944

ON THIS OCCASION of the return of General MacArthur to Philippine soil with our airmen, our soldiers, and our sailors, we renew our pledge. We and our Philippine brothers in arms - with the help of Almighty God - will drive out the invader; we will destroy his power to wage war again, and we will restore a world of dignity and freedom - a world of confidence and honesty and peace.

RADIO ADDRESS AT A DINNER OF THE FOREIGN POLICY ASSOCIATION. NEW YORK CITY OCTOBER 21, 1944

TODAY, HITLER AND the Nazis continue the fight - desperately, inch by inch, and may continue to do so all the way to Berlin.

And we have another important engagement in Tokyo. No matter how hard, how long the road we must travel, our forces will fight their way there under the leadership of MacArthur and Nimitz.

All of our thinking about foreign policy in this war must be conditioned by the fact that millions of our American boys are today fighting, many thousands of miles from home, for the first objective: defense of our country; and the second objective, the perpetuation of our American ideals. And there are still many hard and bitter battles to be fought...

Let us always remember that this very war might have been averted if Henry Stimson's views had prevailed when, in 1931, the Japanese ruthlessly attacked and raped Manchuria...

You know, I happen to believe - I'm sort of old-fashioned, I guess I'm old - that, even in a political campaign, we ought to obey that ancient injunction - Thou shalt not bear false witness against thy neighbor...

We have debated our principles, and our determination to aid those fighting for freedom.

Obviously, we could have come to terms with Hitler, and we could have accepted a minor role in his totalitarian world. We rejected that!

We could have compromised with Japan, and bargained for a place in the Japanese-dominated Asia, by selling out the heart's blood of the Chinese people. And we rejected that!...

Peace, like war, can succeed only where there is a will to enforce it, and where there is available power to enforce it...

But, and I should be false to the very foundations of my religious and political convictions if I should ever relinquish the hope - or even the faith - that in all peoples, without exception, there live some instinct for truth, some attraction toward justice, some passion for peace - buried as they may be in the German case under a brutal regime.

We bring no charge against the German race, as such, for we cannot believe that God has eternally condemned any race of humanity. We know in our own land, in these United States of America, how many good men and women of German ancestry have proved loyal, freedom-loving, and peace-loving citizens...

For this generation must act not only for itself, but as a trustee for all those who fell in the last war - a part of their mission unfulfilled.

It must act also for all those who have paid the supreme price in this war - lest their mission, too, be betrayed.

And finally it must act for the generations to come - that must be granted a heritage of peace...

So, in embarking on the building of a world fellowship, we have set ourselves a long and arduous task, which will challenge our patience, our intelligence, our imagination, as well as our faith...

We shall bear our full responsibility, exercise our full influence, and bring our full help and encouragement to all who aspire to peace and freedom.

We now are, and we shall continue to be, strong brothers in the family of mankind - the family of the children of God.

REMARKS AT WILMINGTON, DELAWARE
OCTOBER 27, 1944

IN THE PACIFIC and eastern seas, and the European seas, we have had to send our troops thousands of miles, across both oceans, to land on beaches held by the enemy.

We had to have entirely new kinds of vessels to do the final and the toughest job of all - Sicily, Salerno, and Normandy, the Marshalls, the Gilberts, the Marianas, and now, thank God, the Philippines - all of those historic operations have been made possible by the brilliant work of our Navy and our Army in developing new methods of amphibious attack.

ADDRESS AT SHIBE PARK, PHILADELPHIA, PA.
OCTOBER 27, 1944

IN MY FIRST war message to the Congress, less than a month after Pearl Harbor, I said this:

"We cannot wage this war in a defensive spirit. As our power and our resources are fully mobilized, we shall carry the attack against the enemy - we shall hit him and hit him again wherever and whenever we can reach him. We must keep him far from our shores, for we intend to bring this battle to him on his own home grounds."

And that, my friends, is the policy that we have successfully followed...

The quality of our American fighting men is not all a matter of training or equipment, or organization. It is essentially a matter of spirit. That spirit is expressive of their faith in America.

The most important fact in our national life today is the essential fact of eleven million young Americans in our armed forces - more than half of them overseas.

When you multiply that eleven million by their families and their friends, you have the whole American people personally involved in this war - a war that was forced upon us, a war which we did our utmost to avoid, a war that came upon us as inevitably as an earthquake.

I think particularly of the mothers and wives and sisters and sweethearts of the men in service. There are great numbers of these gallant women who do not have the satisfaction or the distraction of jobs in war plants. But they have the quiet, essential job of keeping the homes going, caring for the children or the old folks...

I have chosen Navy Day, today, to talk about the eleven million Americans in uniform, who with all their strength are engaged in giving us a chance to achieve peace through victory in war.

These men could not have been armed, and they could not be equipped as they are, had it not been for the miracle of our production here back home...

May this country never forget that its power in this war has come from the efforts of its citizens, living in freedom and equality.

May this country hold in piety and steadfast faith those who have battled and died to give it new opportunities for service and growth.

May it reserve its contempt for those who see in it only an . instrument for their own selfish interests.

May it marshal its righteous wrath against those who would divide it by racial struggles. May it lavish its scorn upon the faint-hearted.

Finally, may this country always give its support to those who have engaged with us in the war against oppression and who will continue with us in the struggle for a vital, creative peace.

God Bless the United States of America.

ADDRESS AT SOLDIERS' FIELD, CHICAGO, IL. OCTOBER 28, 1944

WE ARE FIGHTING this war and we are holding this election both for the same essential reason: because we have faith in democracy.

And there is no force and there is no combination of forces powerful enough to shake that faith...

Yes, the American people are prepared to meet the problems of peace in the same bold way that they have met the problems of war.

For the American people are resolved that when our men and women return home from this war, they shall come back to the best possible place on the face of the earth - they shall come back to a place where all persons, regardless of race, and color, or creed or place of birth, can live in peace and honor and human dignity - free to speak, free to pray as they wish - free from want - and free from fear...

Our Economic Bill of Rights - like the sacred Bill of Rights of our Constitution itself - must be applied to all our citizens, irrespective of race, or creed or color...

We must continue this Administration's policy of conserving the enormous gifts with which an abundant Providence has blessed our country - our soil, our forests, and our water...

The creed of our democracy is that liberty is acquired, liberty is kept by men and women who are strong, self-reliant, and possessed of such wisdom as God gives to mankind - men and women who are just, men and women who are understanding, and generous to others - men and women who are capable of disciplining themselves.

For they are the rulers, and they must rule themselves.

I believe in our democratic faith. I believe in the future of our country which has given eternal strength and vitality to that faith.

Here in Chicago you know a lot about that vitality.

And as I say good night to you, I say it in a spirit of faith - a spirit of hope - a spirit of confidence.

REMARKS AT CLARKSBURG, WEST VIRGINIA
OCTOBER 29, 1944

THIS BEING SUNDAY, the Governor, cooperating with me in keeping politics out of it, says that he is not even going to introduce me.

I have been here before, and it is a great comfort to come on a Sunday in a campaign year, because on Sundays my life is made much more comfortable by not having to think about politics. Unfortunately, I do have to think about the war, because every day, including Sundays, dispatches come to me, on the train even, to tell me of the progress of our boys in Europe and in the Pacific and in the Philippines. I cannot get rid of that.

Coming up through the State today, I have been looking out of the window, and I think there is a subject that is a good subject for Sunday, because I remember the line in the poem, "Only God can make a tree."

And one of the things that people have to realize all over the United States, and I think especially in West Virginia - I don't see the trees I ought to see. That is something that we in this country have fallen down on. We have been using up natural resources that we ought to have replaced. I know we can't replace coal - it will be a long time before all the coal is gone - but trees constitute something that we can replace...

I remember a story, and it is taken out of Germany. There was a town there - I don't know what has happened in the last twenty years - but this is back when I used to be in grade school in Germany - and I used to bicycle. And we came to a town, and outside of it there was a great forest. And the interesting thing to me, as a boy even, was that the people in that town didn't have to pay taxes. They were supported by their own forest.

Way back in the time of Louis something of France - the French king was approaching this town with a large army. And the prince of the time asked the townspeople to come out to defend their principality, and he promised them that if they would keep the invader out of the town, out of the principality, he would give them the forest.

The burghers turned out. They repulsed the French king. And very soon the prince made good. He gave the forest to the town. And for over two hundred years that town in Germany had to pay no taxes.

Everybody made money, because they had no taxes. In other words, it was a forest on an annual-yield basis. They cut down perhaps seventy percent of what they could get out of that year's mature crop. And every year they planted new trees. And every year the proceeds from that forest paid the equivalent of taxes.

Now that is true more and more in this country. There are more and more municipalities that are reforesting their watersheds, putting trees on the top of their hills, preventing the erosion of soil. They are not on a self-sustaining basis because it has only been started within the last ten or fifteen years. And yet while only God can make a tree, we have to do a little bit to help ourselves...

When the last war came on, the old woods had some perfectly splendid trees, because I had cleaned them out, cleaned out the poor stuff.

And during that war, I made four thousand dollars, just by cutting out the mature trees. And I kept on every year. And in the winter time, when the men weren't doing much, they cleaned them out. And the trees grew.

And a quarter of a century later, there came this war. I think I cooperated with the Almighty, because I think trees were made to grow. Oh yes, they are useful as mine timbers. I know that. But there are a lot of places in this State where there isn't any mine timber being cut out.

And in this war, back home, I cut last year - and this is not very Christian - over four thousand dollars' worth net of oak trees, to make into submarine chasers and landing craft and other implements of war. And I am doing it again this year...

And so I think my Sunday sermon is just about over.

REMARKS AT SPRINGFIELD, MASSACHUSETTS NOVEMBER 4, 1944

WE FOUGHT BACK - as our forefathers had fought. We took the offensive - and we held it. The kind of America we inherited from our fathers is the kind of America we want to pass on to our children - but, an America more prosperous, more secure - free from want and free from fear.

ADDRESS AT FENWAY PARK, BOSTON, MA NOVEMBER 4, 1944

WHEN I TALKED here in Boston in 1928, I talked about racial and religious intolerance, which was then - as unfortunately it still is, to some extent - "a menace to the liberties of America."...

Religious intolerance, social intolerance, and political intolerance have no place in our American life...

It is our duty to them to make sure that, big as this country is, there is no room in it for racial or religious intolerance - and that there is no room for snobbery.

Our young men and our young women are fighting not only for their existence, their homes, and their families. They also are fighting for a country and a world where men and women of all races, colors, and creeds can live, and work, and speak and worship - in peace, and freedom and security...

On the day of Pearl Harbor they rose up as one man with a mighty shout - a shout heard 'round the world - the shout of "Let's go!"...

I thank God that it cannot be charged that at any time, under any circumstances, have we made the mistake of forgetting our sacred obligation to the American people...

Speaking here in Boston, a Republican candidate said - and pardon me if I quote him correctly - that happens to be an old habit of mine - he said that, quote, "the Communists are seizing control of the New Deal, through which they aim to control the Government of the United States." Unquote.

However, on that very same day, that very same candidate had spoken in Worcester, and he said that with Republican victory in November, quote, "we can end one-man government, and we can forever remove the threat of monarchy in the United States."

Now, really - which is it - Communism or monarchy?...

We face the enormous, the complex problems of building with our allies a strong world structure of peace.

In doing that historic job, we shall be standing before a mighty bar of judgment - the judgment of all of those who have fought and died in this war - the judgment of generations yet unborn - the very judgment of God...

That, my friends, is the conception I have of the meaning of total victory.

And that conception is founded on faith - faith in the unlimited destiny - the unconquerable spirit of the United States of America.

REMARKS AT BRIDGEPORT, CONNECTICUT
NOVEMBER 4, 1944

IN THIS CAMPAIGN, of course, all things taken together, I can't talk about my opponent the way I would like to sometimes, because I try to think that I am a Christian.

I try to think that some day I will go to Heaven, and I don't believe there is anything to be gained in saying dreadful things about other people in any campaign.

RADIO ADDRESS AT HYDE PARK, NEW YORK NOVEMBER 6, 1944

BUT - IN THE midst of fighting - in the presence of our brutal enemies - our soldiers and sailors and airmen will not forget election day back home.

Millions of these men have already cast their own ballots, and they will be wondering about the outcome of the election, and what it will mean to them in their future lives...

And it is for us to make certain that we win for them - the living and the dead - a lasting peace.

There is nothing adequate which anyone in any place can say to those who are entitled to display the gold star in their windows. But each night as the people of the United States rest in their homes which have been safe from violence during all these years of the most violent war in all history - I am sure all of them silently give thought to their feelings of deepest gratitude to the brave departed and to their families for the immeasurable sacrifice that they have made for the cause of decency and freedom and civilization...

Tomorrow, you the people of the United States again vote as free men and women, with full freedom of choice - with no secret police watching over your shoulders. And for generations to come Americans will continue to prove their faith in free elections...

But not for one single moment can you now or later forget the all-important goals for which we are aiming - to win the war and unite our fighting men with their families at the earliest moment, to see that all have honorable jobs; and to create a world peace organization which will prevent this disaster - or one like it - from ever coming upon us again.

To achieve these goals we need strength and wisdom which is greater than is bequeathed to mere mortals. We need Divine help and guidance. We people of America have ever had a deep well of religious strength, far back to the days of the Pilgrim Fathers.

And so, on this thoughtful evening, I believe that you will find it fitting that I read a prayer sent to me not long ago:

"Almighty God, of Whose righteous will all things are and were created, Thou hast gathered our people out of many lands and races into a great Nation. We commend to Thy overruling providence the men and women of our forces by sea, by land, and in the air; beseeching Thee to take into Thine own hands both them and the cause they serve. Be Thou their strength when they are set in the midst of so many and great dangers. And grant that, whether by life or by death, they may win for the whole world the fruits of their sacrifice and a just peace.

"Guide, we beseech Thee, the Nations of the world, into the way of justice and truth, and establish among them that peace which is the reward of righteousness. Make the whole people of this land equal to our high trust, reverent in the use of freedom, just in the exercise of power, generous in the protection of weakness. Enable us to guard for the least among us the freedom we covet for ourselves; make us ill-content with the inequalities of opportunity which still prevail among us. Preserve our union against all the divisions of race and class which threaten it.

"And now, may the blessing of God Almighty rest upon this whole land; may He give us light to guide us, courage to support us, charity to unite us, now and forevermore. Amen."

PRESS CONFERENCE
DECEMBER 22, 1944

THE ATLANTIC CHARTER stands as an objective. A great many of the previous pronouncements that go back many centuries have not been attained yet, and yet the objective is still just as good as it was when it was announced several thousand years ago...

There are a lot of people who say you can't attain an objective or improvement in human life or in humanity, therefore why talk about it. Well, those people who come out for the Ten Commandments will say we don't all live up to the Ten Commandments, which is perfectly true, but on the whole they are pretty good. It's something pretty good to shoot for. The Christian religion most of us in the room happen to belong to, we think it is pretty good. We certainly haven't attained it.

Well, the Atlantic Charter is going to take its place, not comparing it with the Christian religion or the Ten Commandments, but as a definite step, just the same way as Wilson's Fourteen Points constituted a major contribution to something we would all like to see happen in the world. Well, those Fourteen Points weren't all attained, but it was a step towards a better life for the population of the world.

ADDRESS TO THE NATION
DECEMBER 24, 1944

IT IS NOT easy to say "Merry Christmas" to you, my fellow Americans, in this time of destructive war. Nor can

I say "Merry Christmas" lightly tonight to our armed forces at their battle stations all over the world - or to our allies who fight by their side.

Here, at home, we will celebrate this Christmas Day in our traditional American way - because of its deep spiritual meaning to us; because the teachings of Christ are fundamental in our lives; and because we want our youngest generation to grow up knowing the significance of this tradition and the story of the coming of the immortal Prince of Peace and Good Will.

But, in perhaps every home in the United States, sad and anxious thoughts will be continually with the millions of our loved ones who are suffering hardships and misery, and who are risking their very lives to preserve for us and for all mankind the fruits of His teachings and the foundations of civilization itself.

The Christmas spirit lives tonight in the bitter cold of the front lines in Europe and in the heat of the jungles and swamps of Burma and the Pacific islands. Even the roar of our bombers and fighters in the air and the guns of our ships at sea will not drown out the messages of Christmas which come to the hearts of our fighting men.

The thoughts of these men tonight will turn to us here at home around our Christmas trees, surrounded by our children and grandchildren and their Christmas stockings and gifts - just as our own thoughts go out to them, tonight and every night, in their distant places.

We all know how anxious they are to be home with us, and they know how anxious we are to have them - and how determined every one of us is to make their day of home - coming as early as possible. And - above all - they know the determination of all right-thinking people and Nations, that Christmases such as those that we have known in these years of world tragedy shall not come again to beset the souls of the children of God.

This generation has passed through many recent years of deep darkness, watching the spread of the poison of Hitlerism and Fascism in Europe - the growth of imperialism and militarism in Japan - and the final clash of war all over the world. Then came the dark days of the fall of France, and the ruthless bombing of England, and the desperate battle of the Atlantic, and of Pearl Harbor and Corregidor and Singapore.

Since then the prayers of good men and women and children the world over have been answered. The tide of battle has turned, slowly but inexorably, against those who sought to destroy civilization.

On this Christmas day, we cannot yet say when our victory will come. Our enemies still fight fanatically. They still have reserves of men and military power. But, they themselves know that they and their evil works are doomed. We may hasten the day of their doom if we here at home continue to do our full share.

And we pray that that day may come soon. We pray that until then, God will protect our gallant men and women in the uniforms of the United Nations - that He will receive into His infinite grace those who make their supreme sacrifice in the cause of righteousness, in the cause of love of Him and His teachings.

We pray that with victory will come a new day of peace on earth in which all the Nations of the earth will join together for all time. That is the spirit of Christmas, the holy day. May that spirit live and grow throughout the world in all the years to come.

STATE OF THE UNION ADDRESS
JANUARY 6, 1945

WE AND THE other United Nations are going forward, with vigor and resolution, in our efforts to create such a system by providing for it strong and flexible institutions of joint and cooperative action.

The aroused conscience of humanity will not permit failure in this supreme endeavor...

In the State of the Union message last year I set forth what I considered to be an American economic bill of rights.

I said then, and I say now, that these economic truths represent a second bill of rights under which a new basis of security and prosperity can be established for all - regardless of station, race, or creed.

RADIO ADDRESS SUMMARIZING THE STATE OF THE UNION MESSAGE
JANUARY 6, 1945

OUR MEN HAVE fought with indescribable and unforgettable gallantry under most difficult conditions.

The high tide of this German attack was reached two days after Christmas. Since then we have reassumed the offensive, rescued the isolated garrison at Bastogne, and forced a German withdrawal along the whole line of the salient.

The speed with which we recovered from this savage attack was possible primarily because we have one Supreme Commander in complete control of all the Allied armies in France. General Eisenhower has faced this period of trial with admirable calm and resolution and with steadily increasing success. He has my complete confidence...

There is an old and true saying that the Lord hates a quitter. And this Nation must pay for all those who leave their essential jobs - for all those who lay down on their essential jobs for nonessential reasons. And that payment must be made with the life's blood of our sons...

In these days, our thoughts and our hopes and our prayers are with our sons and brothers, our loved ones who are far from home...

I quote from an editorial in the Stars and Stripes, our soldiers' own newspaper in Europe:

"For the holy love of God let's listen to the dead. Let's learn from the living. Let's join ranks against the foe. The bugles of battle are heard again above the bickering."

That is the demand of our fighting men. We cannot fail to heed it...

Most important of all, 1945 can, and must, see the substantial beginning of the organization of world peace - for we all know what such an organization means in terms of security, and human rights, and religious freedom...

We pray that we may be worthy of the unlimited opportunities that God has given us.

THE FAITH OF FDR

FOURTH TERM
JANUARY 20, 1945 - APRIL 12, 1945

FOURTH INAUGURAL ADDRESS
JANUARY 20, 1945

WE AMERICANS OF today, together with our allies, are passing through a period of supreme test. It is a test of our courage - of our resolve - of our wisdom - of our essential democracy.

If we meet that test - successfully and honorably - we shall perform a service of historic importance which men and women and children will honor throughout all time.

As I stand here today, having taken the solemn oath of office in the presence of my fellow countrymen - in the presence of our God - I know that it is America's purpose that we shall not fail.

In the days and the years that are to come, we shall work for a just and honorable peace, a durable peace, as today we work and fight for total victory in war...

We shall strive for perfection. We shall not achieve it immediately - but we still shall strive. We may make mistakes - but they must never be mistakes which result from faintness of heart or abandonment of moral principle.

I remember that my old schoolmaster, Dr. Peabody, said - in days that seemed to us then to be secure and untroubled, "Things in life will not always run smoothly. Sometimes we will be rising toward the heights - then all will seem to reverse itself and start downward. The great fact to remember is that the trend of civilization itself is forever upward; that a line drawn through the middle of the peaks and the valleys of the centuries always has an upward trend."

Our Constitution of 1787 was not a perfect instrument; it is not perfect yet. But it provided a firm base upon which all manner of men, of all races and colors and creeds, could build our solid structure of democracy...

The Almighty God has blessed our land in many ways. He has given our people stout hearts and strong arms with which to strike mighty blows for freedom and truth. He has given to our country a faith which has become the hope of all peoples in an anguished world.

So we pray to Him now for the vision to see our way clearly to see the way that leads to a better life for ourselves and for all our fellow men - and to the achievement of His will to peace on earth.

MESSAGE TO PRESIDENT OSMEHA ON THE LIBERATION OF MANILA FEBRUARY 4, 1945

WE ARE PROUD of the mighty blows struck by General MacArthur, our sailors, soldiers, and airmen; and in their comradeship-in-arms with your loyal and valiant people who in the darkest days have not ceased to fight for their independence...

We will join you in that effort - with our armed forces, as rapidly and fully as our efforts against our enemies and our responsibilities to other liberated peoples permit.

With God's help we will complete the fulfillment of the pledge we renewed when our men returned to Leyte.

PRESS CONFERENCE ABOARD THE U.S.S. QUINCY EN ROUTE FROM YALTA FEBRUARY 23, 1945

Q. DO YOU CONSCIENTIOUSLY believe that the Conference can be the foundation of world peace for more than the generation of the men who are building that peace?

THE PRESIDENT: I can answer that question if you can tell me who your descendants will be in the year 2057.

Q. Can we look forward?

THE PRESIDENT: We can look as far ahead as humanity believes in this sort of thing. The United Nations will evolve into the best method ever devised for stopping war, and it will also be the beginning of something else to go with it.

Last year I flew to Teheran - across Persia. Persia probably is the poorest country in the world. In the early days, Persia was a pretty well-wooded country. The Turks cut down all the woods. It has been a woodless country since. Ninety seven percent of the people of Persia are tenants. Only one or two percent of the whole Nation owns land or property. The only part where they live in Persia is in river bottoms.

Really, the people of Persia have no money. They can barely get enough to eat. The soil is all eroded - boulders where there should be fields. There's no rainfall, because it has absolutely no moisture; the sun can't draw any out of the land, and the moisture in the land runs off in a few hours' time. Persia has no purchasing power in the world except for certain things God gave it, like oil. It is neither sustaining nor has it any money to buy things...

The same thing is true about Iraq, Arabia, Lebanon, Syria, Palestine, and Turkey. They've got no purchasing power to do anything with. Their only purchasing instrument is oil. Their people are not educated, do not get enough to eat, cannot cope with health problems...

ADDRESS TO CONGRESS ON YALTA CONFERENCE MARCH 1, 1945

NEVER BEFORE HAVE the major Allies been more closely united - not only in their war aims but also in their peace aims. And they are determined to continue to be united with each other - and with all peace-loving Nations - so that the ideal of lasting peace will become a reality...

By compelling reparations in kind - in plants, in machinery, in rolling stock, and in raw materials - we shall avoid the mistake that we and other Nations made after the last war, the demanding of reparations in the form of money which Germany could never pay.

We do not want the German people to starve, or to become a burden on the rest of the world...

During my stay in Yalta, I saw the kind of reckless, senseless fury, the terrible destruction that comes out of German militarism. Yalta, on the Black Sea, had no military significance of any kind. It had no defenses.

Before the last war, it had been a resort for people like the Czars and princes and for the aristocracy of Russia - and the hangers-on. However, after the Red Revolution, and until the attack on the Soviet Union by Hitler, the palaces and the villas of Yalta had been used as a rest and recreation center by the Russian people.

The Nazi officers took these former palaces and villas - took them over for their own use...all of these villas were looted by the Nazis, and then nearly all of them were destroyed by bombs placed on the inside. And even the humblest of the homes of Yalta were not spared.

There was little left of it except blank walls - ruins - destruction and desolation...

I had read about Warsaw and Lidice and Rotterdam and Coventry - but I saw Sevastopol and Yalta! And I know that there is not room enough on earth for both German militarism and Christian decency...

The structure of world peace cannot be the work of one man, or one party, or one Nation. It cannot be just an American peace, or a British peace, or a Russian, a French, or a Chinese peace. It cannot be a peace of large Nations - or of small Nations. It must be a peace which rests on the cooperative effort of the whole world.

It cannot be a structure of complete perfection at first. But it can be a peace - and it will be a peace - based on the sound and just principles of the Atlantic Charter - on the concept of the dignity of the human being - and on the guarantees of tolerance and freedom of religious worship...

For instance, on the problem of Arabia, I learned more about that whole problem - the Moslem problem, the Jewish problem - by talking with Ibn Saud for five minutes, than I could have learned in the exchange of two or three dozen letters...

I am confident that the Congress and the American people will accept the results of this Conference as the beginnings of a permanent structure of peace upon which we can begin to build, under God, that better world in which our children and grandchildren - yours and mine, the children and grandchildren of the whole world - must live, and can live.

PRESIDENT FRANKLIN D. ROOSEVELT DIED, APRIL 12, 1945, IN WARM SPRINGS, GEORGIA.

VICE-PRESIDENT Harry S Truman took the oath of office that same day at 7:09p.m. in the Cabinet Room of the White House, administered by Chief Justice Harlan F. Stone.

PRESIDENT HARRY S TRUMAN'S ADDRESS TO A JOINT SESSION OF CONGRESS UPON THE DEATH OF PRESIDENT FRANKLIN D. ROOSEVELT APRIL 16, 1945

IT IS WITH a heavy heart that I stand before you, my friends and colleagues, in the Congress of the United States.

Only yesterday, we laid to rest the mortal remains of our beloved President, Franklin Delano Roosevelt. At a time like this, words are inadequate. The most eloquent tribute would be a reverent silence.

Yet, in this decisive hour, when world events are moving so rapidly, our silence might be misunderstood and might give comfort to our enemies.

In His infinite wisdom, Almighty God has seen fit to take from us a great man who loved, and was beloved by, all humanity...

So much blood has already been shed for the ideals which we cherish, and for which Franklin Delano Roosevelt lived and died, that we dare not permit even a momentary pause in the hard fight for victory...

With great humility I call upon all Americans to help me keep our nation united in defense of those ideals which have been so eloquently proclaimed by Franklin Roosevelt...

Having to pay such a heavy price to make complete victory certain, America will never become a party to any plan for partial victory!...

But the laws of God and of man have been violated and the guilty must not go unpunished. Nothing shall shake our determination to punish the war criminals even though we must pursue them to the ends of the earth...

In the difficult days ahead, unquestionably we shall face problems of staggering proportions. However, with the faith of our fathers in our hearts, we do not fear the future...

All of us are praying for a speedy victory. Every day peace is delayed costs a terrible toll.

The armies of liberation today are bringing to an end Hitler's ghastly threat to dominate the world. Tokyo rocks under the weight of our bombs...

Our forefathers came to our rugged shores in search of religious tolerance, political freedom and economic opportunity. For those fundamental rights, they risked their lives. We well know today that such rights can be preserved only by constant vigilance, the eternal price of liberty!...

In the memory of those who have made the supreme sacrifice - in the memory of our fallen President - we shall not fail!...

Aggressors could not dominate the human mind. As long as hope remains, the spirit of man will never be crushed.

But hope alone was not and is not sufficient to avert war. We must not only have hope but we must have faith enough to work with other peace-loving nations to maintain the peace. Hope was not enough to beat back the aggressors as long as the peace-loving nations were unwilling to come to each other's defense. The aggressors were beaten back only when the peace-loving nations united to defend themselves...

You, the Members of the Congress, surely know how I feel. Only with your help can I hope to complete one of the greatest tasks ever assigned to a public servant. With Divine guidance, and your help, we will find the new passage to a far better world, a kindly and friendly world, with just and lasting peace...

America must assist suffering humanity back along the path of peaceful progress. This will require time and tolerance. We shall need also an abiding faith in the people, the kind of faith and courage which Franklin Delano Roosevelt always had!...

At this moment, I have in my heart a prayer. As I have assumed my heavy duties, I humbly pray Almighty God, in the words of King Solomon:

"Give therefore thy servant an understanding heart to judge thy people, that I may discern between good and bad; for who is able to judge this thy so great a people?"

I ask only to be a good and faithful servant of my Lord and my people.

INDEX

Color 106, 160, 237, 274, 320, 362, 363, 380, 383, 394

Commandment 40, 76, 335, 337, 343, 351, 387

Communist 165, 203, 204, 233, 234, 235, 272, 273, 384

Confidence 51, 58, 63, 68, 109, 128, 137, 139, 157, 189, 191, 199, 230, 235, 265, 289, 290, 322, 334, 340, 356, 370, 375, 380, 391

Conscience 33, 34, 47, 63, 64, 71, 73, 84, 93, 110, 124, 125, 134, 156, 176, 237, 246, 280, 302, 303, 346, 352, 390

Creed 38, 65, 76, 78, 79, 80, 106, 160, 171, 183, 202, 216, 231, 274, 318, 331, 362, 368, 380, 383, 390, 394

D

Deception 298
Denial 126, 272
Devotion 65, 70, 108, 112, 124, 128, 130, 150, 152, 167, 168, 198, 208, 225, 226, 228, 229, 238, 257, 273, 278, 306, 331, 349, 375
Disciples of Christ 206

Divine 32, 56, 70, 74, 92, 113, 120, 139, 153, 185, 191, 215, 216, 273, 279, 285, 310, 324, 336, 386, 400

Dutch Reform 26, 27

E

Easter 81, 147
Ecclesiastic 35
Editor 11, 57, 125, 146, 159, 265, 318, 391
Episcopal 11, 14, 16, 17, 25, 26, 27, 29, 101
Ethic 36, 39, 51, 66, 67, 203, 235, 245, 264, 265, 268, 294, 351

F

Faith 9, 26, 29, 30, 31, 32, 34, 47, 48, 49, 51, 58, 65, 69, 73, 77, 79, 80, 85, 90, 91, 102, 105, 106, 109, 110, 112, 113, 114, 115, 116, 119, 124, 126, 139, 140, 142, 143, 144, 145, 149, 150, 156, 157, 169, 170, 171, 173, 177, 181, 184, 189, 190, 191, 197, 198, 199, 202, 206, 208, 210, 211, 214, 215, 225, 226, 228, 229, 230, 231, 232, 234, 235,

238, 245, 246, 248, 256, 257, 258, 261, 262, 263, 271, 273, 277, 284, 285, 305, 306, 310, 311, 319, 320, 321, 323, 324, 325, 326, 327, 329, 333, 337, 338, 340, 344, 345, 347, 349, 352, 358, 359, 360, 361, 364, 366, 367, 373, 374, 376, 377, 378, 379, 380, 384, 385, 394, 399, 400

Family 11, 23, 24, 41, 42, 56, 57, 80, 81, 115, 126, 148, 153, 167, 180, 182, 184, 187, 189, 199, 200, 202, 216, 224, 236, 271, 287, 308, 330, 339, 357, 359, 377

Fifth Column 211, 212, 272, 326
Fireside 14, 23, 50, 58, 80, 99, 121, 147, 174, 179, 180, 211, 248, 278, 290, 312, 314, 326, 351, 355, 364, 370
Forefather 21, 218, 224, 303, 346, 373, 383, 399
Freedom 33, 37, 49, 59, 63, 64, 71, 72, 73, 76, 83, 90, 91, 92, 93, 94, 95, 96, 101, 103, 107, 108, 110, 115, 121,

THE FAITH OF FDR

Printed in the United States
48163LVS00005B/79-87

9 780977 808502